Macromedia Dreamweaver® UltraDev™ 4

fast&easy®
web development

Check the Web for Updates

To check for updates or corrections relevant to this book and/or CD-ROM visit our updates page on the Web at **http://www.prima-tech.com/updates**.

Send Us Your Comments

To comment on this book or any other PRIMA TECH title, visit our reader response page on the Web at **www.prima-tech.com/comments**.

How to Order

For information on quantity discounts, contact the publisher: Prima Publishing, P.O. Box 1260BK, Rocklin, CA 95677-1260; (916) 787-7000. On your letterhead, include information concerning the intended use of the books and the number of books you want to purchase.

Macromedia® Dreamweaver® UltraDev™ 4

fast&easy® *web development*

Aneesha Bakharia

PRIMA TECH

A DIVISION OF PRIMA PUBLISHING

A Division of Prima Publishing

Prima Publishing and colophon are registered trademarks of Prima Communications, Inc. PRIMA TECH and *Fast & Easy Web Development* are registered trademarks of Prima Communications, Inc., Roseville, California 95661.

Publisher: Stacy L. Hiquet

Associate Marketing Manager: Heather Buzzingham

Managing Editor: Sandy Doell

Acquisitions Editor: Emi Smith

Project Editor: Heather Talbot

Technical Reviewer: Dan Ransom

Copy Editor: Randy Clark

Interior Layout: Marian Hartsough

Cover Design: Prima Design Team

Indexer: Sharon Shock

Proofreader: Kelly Marshall

Dreamweaver, Fireworks, and Flash are registered trademarks of Macromedia. UltraDev is a trademark of Macromedia. HomeSite, ColdFusion, JRun, and Kawa are registered trademarks of Allaire.

Important: Prima Publishing cannot provide software support. Please contact the appropriate software manufacturer's technical support line or Web site for assistance.

Prima Publishing and the author have attempted throughout this book to distinguish proprietary trademarks from descriptive terms by following the capitalization style used by the manufacturer.

ISBN: 0-7615-3517-9

Library of Congress Catalog Card Number: 2001-086175

Printed in the United States of America

00 01 02 03 04 DD 10 9 8 7 6 5 4 3 2 1

This book is dedicated to my grandmother,
Rada Bakharia.

Acknowledgments

I would like to thank the following people:

My Grandmother who took care of me before I started school. **My Mum** for taking care of me even though I'm all grown up now. **My Dad** for forcing me to attend a computer course 11 years ago. That is where my career began.

Emi Smith (acquisitions editor) for being understanding, patient, supportive, and encouraging throughout the project.

Heather Talbot (project editor) for her expert editing and project guidance.

Dan Ransom (technical editor) and **Randy Clark** (copy editor) for providing useful reviews and suggestions.

The entire **Prima team** for a job well done. **Jason Haines** (CD producer), **Marian Hartsough** (layout technician), **Sharon Shock** (indexer) and **Kelly Marshall** (proofreader).

Everybody who helped produce the first edition of this book. **Lori Swan** (project editor), **Karen Oliver** (technical editor), **Judy Drummond** (copy editor), **Johnna VanHoose Dinse** (indexer), **Arlie Hartman** (CD producer), **Michael Woodward** (proofreader), and **Argosy** and **Marian Hartsough** (graphics and layout).

My family (**Kulsum**, **Hajira**, **Shaida**, **Julie**, **Celine**, **Zaeem**, **Ebrahem**, **Rashid**, **Cassim**, **Anne** & **Judy**) for their encouragement and support.

Tracy Williams for giving me the opportunity to write professionally.

Madonna for making excellent *MUSIC*.

Macromedia for making a great product.

Finally, **you** for purchasing this book.

About the Author

ANEESHA BAKHARIA is a freelance Web developer and author. She is fluent in C++, Java, JavaScript, ASP, JSP, HTML, XML, and Visual Basic. Aneesha specializes in creating dynamic database-driven Web sites. She has a bachelor of engineering in Microelectronic Engineering and has various postgraduate qualifications in multimedia, online course development, and Web design. In her spare time, she is a keen Madonna fan. She can be reached via e-mail at **bakharia@squirrel.com.au**.

Contents at a Glance

Contents

Introduction

Introducing Dreamweaver UltraDev 4

While the Web is still in its infancy, the technologies used to deliver it are always changing. I remember a time when I had to hand-code every page in a Web site. At that time, a Web site was just a couple of static pages. Still, dealing with raw HTML tags was not very pleasant. A few WYSIWYG (What You See Is What You Get) tools began to appear, but nothing really impressed me. Most tools did not produce clean HTML that looked identical in popular Web browsers like Microsoft Internet Explorer and Netscape Navigator. Static content seemed to rule. The size of Web sites that I was developing grew beyond the point where I could hand-code every page.

I dreamed of a tool that could answer all my prayers, a tool that would allow me to create Web sites visually and still allow me to tweak the code. In 1997, Macromedia made my dream come true when it released Dreamweaver. It certainly answered the prayers of Web developers from all over the world. Dreamweaver is currently one of the most popular Web site design tools, used by more than 700,000 developers worldwide.

Today, static pages no longer rule the Web. The trend has once again shifted, and database-driven Web sites are now the norm. Once again, you have to acquire new skills—this time in database design and server-side scripting.

All this required knowledge can be overwhelming unless you have a sound programming background or the time to leverage your existing skills to create dynamic database-driven applications. Until recently, you had a steep learning curve ahead.

Enter Dreamweaver UltraDev, an amazing upgrade to Dreamweaver. UltraDev makes creating a Web-enabled database a breeze. You can simply design your database without having to worry about writing code to perform standard tasks such as displaying, inserting, updating, and deleting records. So even if you're an expert at hand-coding dynamic Web sites, UltraDev can vastly improve your productivity. Probably the best feature is that UltraDev supports three of the most popular application servers available: ASP (Active Server Pages), JSP (JavaServer Pages), and ColdFusion. Using a single tool to develop for multiple application servers is now a reality. As a Web developer who is comfortable with using UltraDev, you can now develop applications that will run just about anywhere.

UltraDev still incorporates all those features that made Dreamweaver great in the first place:

- **WYSIWYG Web page design.** UltraDev has an array of visual tools to help you build flawless HTML. Tables, image maps, links, frames, and layers can all be created by clicking a few buttons.

- **Round-trip HTML.** You can configure UltraDev to generate HTML exactly the way you want. All code can be edited without any interference from UltraDev.

- **Web site management.** The Site window provides a central location from which you can manage your entire Web site in terms of structure and links.

- A **built-in FTP (File Transfer Protocol)** client that allows you to transfer files to a remote Web server. You don't need to use another application just to upload and download files to a remote server.

- **Templates.** You can easily create templates for your Web site. Templates allow you to concentrate on content rather than layout.

- **Collaboration tools.** Design Notes and File Check in/Check out make it a pleasure to work in a team environment. You don't need to worry about overwriting files and communicating with other team members.

- **Automation.** Almost everything that you do in UltraDev is recorded in the History palette. Your actions can be edited and stored for later use. There is no reason why you should have to do repetitive tasks over and over.

- **Behaviors.** Behaviors allow you to create image rollovers, play sounds, open browser windows, and animate layers. Behaviors do all the hard work and insert the required client-side JavaScript into your Web page.

- **Extensibility.** You have full access to the Dreamweaver UltraDev JavaScript API (Application Programming Interface) and DOM. With a working knowledge of JavaScript you can create new extensions (objects, commands, and behaviors). You can also download extensions from Dreamweaver Exchange (**http://www.macromedia.com/exchange**).

Dreamweaver Versus Dreamweaver UltraDev

The following additions make creating dynamic database-driven Web sites possible in UltraDev:

- The Data Bindings palette simplifies the process normally used to retrieve and display data from a database. You can now query your database and bind the returned data to a Web page in a totally visual manner. You can also retrieve and display posted form data, cookies, and session variables.

- Server behaviors are the key to UltraDev's success. Server behaviors generate server-side code to provide the database functionality you require. They can be used to create multi-paged search results with intuitive navigation. Server behaviors also allow you to create a Web-based interface for your database. Web site visitors can insert, update, and delete records in a database. All of this functionality can be implemented on any of the three application servers that UltraDev supports.

- UltraDev is the first Web development tool to allow server-side data (including data retrieved from a database) to be viewed and edited in the same environment. There is no need to switch repeatedly between your Web browser and UltraDev. You can bind data to a Web page, instantly view the results, and apply formatting in this Live Data View.

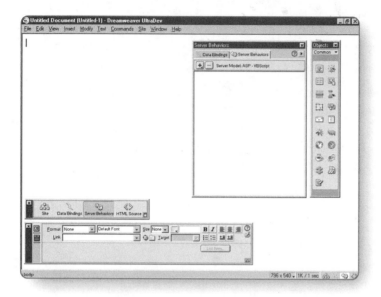

Upgrading from UltraDev 1

Macromedia has certainly done an excellent job with UltraDev 4. It incorporates the entire core Dreamweaver 4 functionality and has a few pleasant surprises of its own. The following new features will definitely boost your productivity without a steep learning curve:

- **Live Data Objects.** These objects facilitate the creation of common features found in database-driven Web sites. A wizard-driven interface will guide you though the process creating customized master/detail page sets, inserting new records, updating existing records, displaying recordset statistics, and navigating search results that span multiple pages. The resulting Web pages are completely editable in UltraDev.

- **Authentication Server Behaviors.** Password protection is now easier then ever to implement with the introduction of Authentication Server Behaviors. You can now build login pages, validate users against a database, and restrict access to pages in your Web site. It is also possible to allow Web site visitors to register before they are allowed to access your Web site.

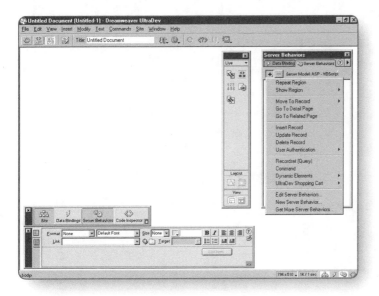

- **Server Behavior Builder.** The Server Behavior Builder has tremendously simplified the creation of server behaviors. You don't need to spend any time learning about the UltraDev API or reading through the lengthy extending UltraDev reference manual. The Server Behavior Builder transforms your server-side code into a reusable server behavior. This leaves you with more time to concentrate on building dynamic Web applications.

Upgrading from Dreamweaver 3/4

Even if you only have limited experience with Dreamweaver, you will have no trouble adjusting to UltraDev. Dreamweaver UltraDev still contains the entire core Dreamweaver functionality that you know and love. UltraDev has the same user interface, so you should feel at home from the moment you open it.

There are, however, two new palettes to master: The Data Bindings palette and the Server Behaviors palette. You'll use both of these extensively in the creation of dynamic database-driven Web sites. Think of UltraDev as an upgrade to Dreamweaver, not as an entirely different product. Taking this approach will make it very easy to master all of UltraDev's powerful features immediately.

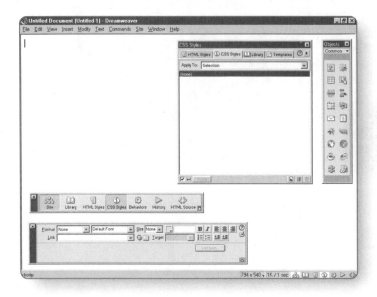

Upgrading from Drumbeat 2000

UltraDev includes the best features from Dreamweaver and Drumbeat 2000. Drumbeat allowed you to create database-enabled Web sites. Its built-in functionality was very similar to that of UltraDev. In fact, UltraDev is essentially a replacement for Drumbeat. While Drumbeat was an excellent product, it had some major shortcomings. In particular, you could not edit the server-side code that it generated. You also had to purchase separate versions to build ASP and JSP applications. Drumbeat's interface was also very cluttered, which made layout and design a real chore.

The main reason for Drumbeat's demise was its considerable overlap with Dreamweaver in terms of functionality. Rather than continue to support and improve both products, Macromedia decided to combine the best features of both. The result was Dreamweaver UltraDev.

UltraDev addresses all the flaws that were evident in Drumbeat. UltraDev allows you to:

- Build ASP, JSP, and ColdFusion applications in one environment.
- Edit the generated source code.
- Design Web sites in a clean and intuitive interface.

With a working knowledge of dialog boxes, menus, and palettes you will have no trouble becoming accustomed to UltraDev. You should, however, be aware that UltraDev does not resemble Drumbeat at all. It looks exactly like Dreamweaver.

The hardest part of upgrading to UltraDev is coming to terms with new terminology and finding everything. The following table will help you do just that.

Drumbeat Feature	Learn to Use the UltraDev Equivalent by ReadingSmart
	Element toolbar & Attributes tab
	Chapter 1, "UltraDev HTML Basics"
Data Form Wizard	Chapter 9, "Using Live Data Objects"
Interactions Center	Chapter 4, "An Overview of Server Behaviors"
	Chapter 11, "Searching a Database"
	Chapter 12, "Creating Dynamic Form Objects"
	Chapter 13, "Inserting, Updating, and Deleting Records"
	Chapter 14, "Password-Protecting Your Web Site"
Managing Assets	Chapter 2, "Managing Web Sites with UltraDev"
Query Manager	Chapter 8, "Retrieving Data from a Database"
	Chapter 10, "Advanced Database Queries"

Conventions Used in This Book

Many Dreamweaver UltraDev commands can be selected with either a mouse or the keyboard, so menu commands in this book are written in a way that enables you to choose the method you prefer. For example, if the instruction says "Choose File, Open," click on the File menu to open the menu, and then click on the Open option. Alternatively, you can press the Alt key and the letter F to open the File menu, and then press the letter O to select Open.

When you need to hold down the first key while you press a second key, a plus sign (+) is used to show this combination (such as Alt+f or Ctrl+z). When two keys are pressed in sequence, they are separated with a comma. For example, the hot-key sequence for opening a file would be written as "Alt+f, o."

Bold text indicates text you should type, typically in the console.

You will also find several special elements that will make using this book easier as you read each chapter.

   Tips tell you about new and faster ways to accomplish a goal.

   Notes delve into background information regarding a given topic.

1

UltraDev HTML Basics

Before you can master creating dynamic, database-driven Web sites, you will need to be comfortable with using Dreamweaver UltraDev as an HTML editor. UltraDev is an excellent WYSIWYG (What You See Is What You Get) editor that will allow you to build complex HTML layouts in a matter of minutes. The flexibility that UltraDev brings to HTML editing is unmatched. In this chapter, you'll learn to:

- Open UltraDev
- Create, save, open, and close pages in UltraDev
- Format text
- Create hyperlinks
- Incorporate images in your Web pages
- Create and modify tables

Working with Web Pages

The most basic tasks you will have to do are opening, saving, and closing files in UltraDev. You will always be performing these tasks, no matter what you are doing in UltraDev. They are simple to master and after a while will no doubt become second nature.

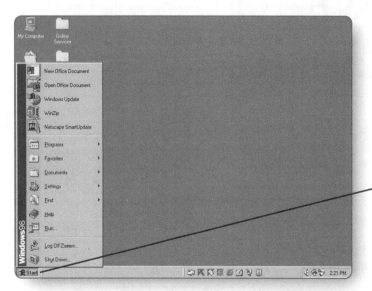

Opening UltraDev

After UltraDev has been installed, you can launch UltraDev from the Start menu. Appendix A contains a step-by-step guide to installing UltraDev.

1. Click on the Start button. The Start menu will appear.

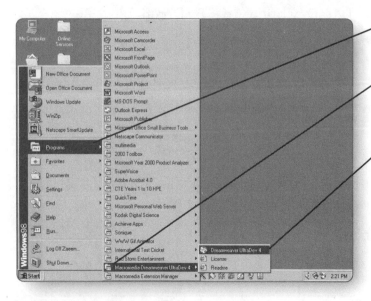

2. Click on Programs. A submenu will appear.

3. Click on Macromedia Dreamweaver UltraDev. The Programs menu will appear.

4. Click on Dreamweaver UltraDev. UltraDev will open and display a blank Web page in the Document window.

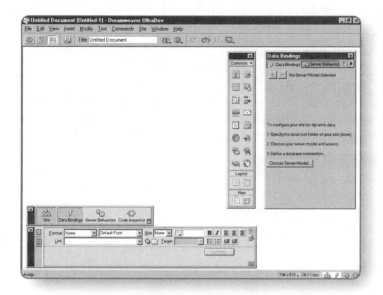

> **NOTE**
> The Launcher, Data Bindings palette, Properties Inspector, and Object palette will all be open by default when you start UltraDev the first time.

Creating a New Web Page

Before you can start work on your award-winning Web site, you may first need to create a blank page. This is easily done in UltraDev.

1. Click on File. The File menu will appear.

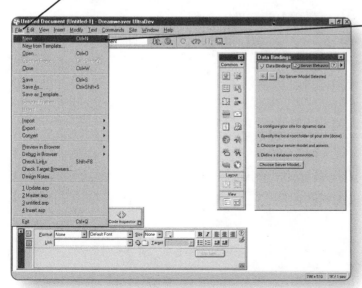

2. Click on New. A blank Web page will appear in the Document window.

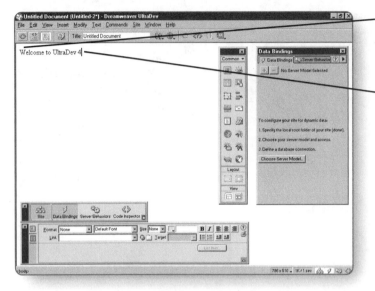

3. Click inside the Document window. The cursor will appear where you click.

4. Type some text. The text will appear in the Document window.

Saving a Web Page

You've just created the world's best Web page ever, but nobody will see it if you don't remember to save it. Luckily this is a simple task in UltraDev.

1. Click on File. The File menu will appear.

2. Click on Save. The Save As dialog box will open.

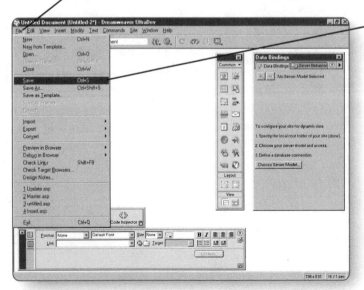

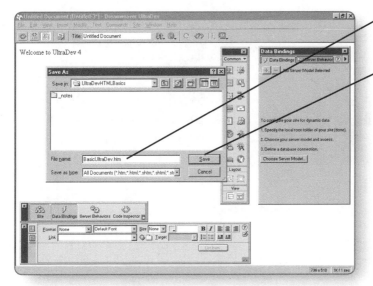

3. Type the name of the file in the File name field.

4. Click on Save. The Save As dialog box will close and the file will be saved.

Closing a Web Page

It is a good idea to close files that are not currently in use. This prevents you from accidentally editing the Web pages and conserves precious memory.

1. Click on File. The File menu will appear.

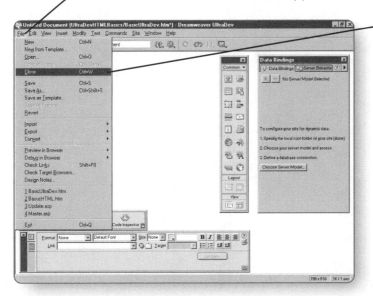

2. Click on Close. If your file has changed since the last time it was saved, you will be prompted to save the file.

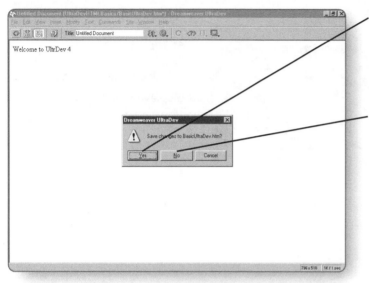

3a. Click on Yes. The Web page will be saved and then closed.

OR

3b. Click on No. The Web page will close without saving new content.

Opening a Web Page

Most Web developers will spend half their time creating Web pages and the other half editing existing pages. But before pages can be edited, they must first be opened.

1. Click on File. The File menu will appear.

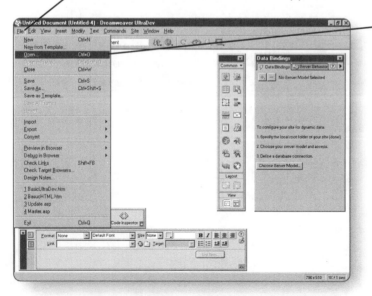

2. Click on Open. The Open dialog box will open.

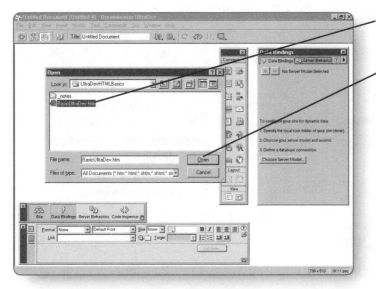

3. Click on a file. The file name will be highlighted

4. Click on Open. The file will be displayed in the Document window.

Previewing a Web Page in a Browser

UltraDev is a great WYSIWYG editor, but you can't always trust that "what you see" in UltraDev "is what you'll get" in a Web browser. It is always wise to test your Web pages in popular browsers such as Netscape and Internet Explorer.

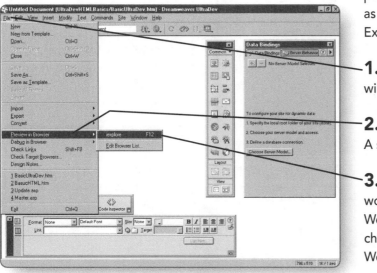

1. Click on File. The File menu will appear.

2. Click on Preview in Browser. A submenu will appear.

3. Click on the browser you would like use to preview the Web page. The browser of your choice will open and the current Web page will be displayed.

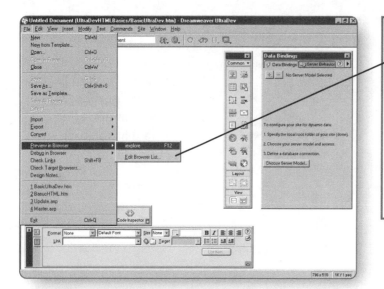

NOTE

If your preferred browser does not appear in the list, you can manually add it in the Preferences dialog box. Press Ctrl+u to open the Preferences dialog box, or choose Edit Browser List from the submenu shown here.

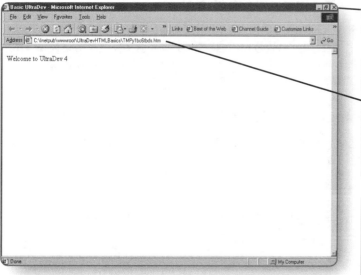

4. Click on the Close icon. The Web browser will close.

NOTE

The Web page is assigned a temporary file name when it is previewed in a browser.

TIP

You can also press F12 to load the current page in a browser.

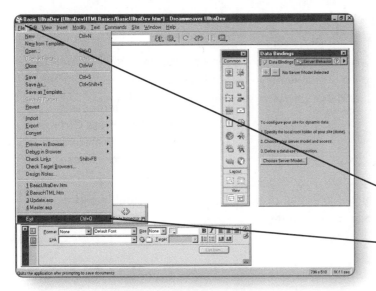

Quitting UltraDev

When you have completed your Web site, you will want to quit UltraDev. This is not a lengthy process, but UltraDev first makes sure that you have saved all your files before it exits.

1. Click on File. The File menu will appear.

2. Click on Exit. UltraDev will close.

NOTE

If you have not saved your files, you will be prompted to do so before you exit UltraDev.

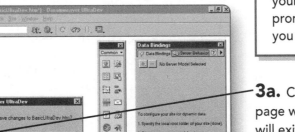

3a. Click on Yes. The Web page will be saved and UltraDev will exit.

OR

3b. Click on No. UltraDev will exit without saving the Web page.

Working with Text

Creating, editing, and formatting text is no longer a chore. UltraDev incorporates functionality that used to be available only in word processing software. Master these simple techniques, and working with text will always be a breeze.

Selecting Text

Text can be selected by using the mouse. You must select text before you can apply formatting or move text to a new location within the Document window.

> **TIP**
> You can double-click on a word to select it.

1. Click and hold the mouse button within the Document window. The cursor will appear where you click.

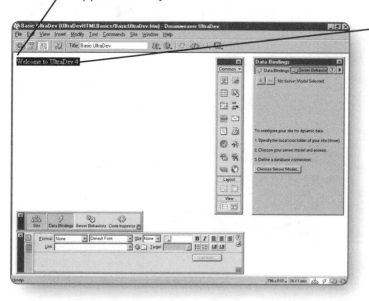

2. Drag the pointer across a line of text. The text will be highlighted as you move the mouse. Release the mouse button. The selected text will be highlighted on the screen.

> **NOTE**
> To deselect the high-lighted text, simply click anywhere in the Document window.

Deleting Text

The Delete key is used to remove selected text from the Web page.

1. Select the text you wish to delete. The text will be highlighted.

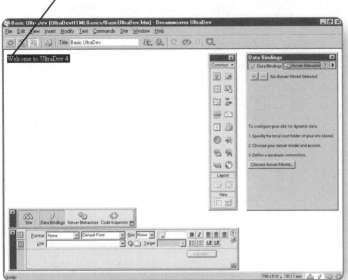

2. Press the Delete key. The text will be removed from the Web page.

TIP

If you accidentally delete text, you can use Undo from the Edit menu to reverse your actions, or click the Undo icon on the Menu bar. You can also press Ctrl+z to undo your last action.

Formatting Text

UltraDev allows you to format text in an extremely intuitive manner. You can easily change the font, size, and color of the currently selected text. All the changes to formatting are immediately reflected in the Document window, because UltraDev is a WYSIWYG editor.

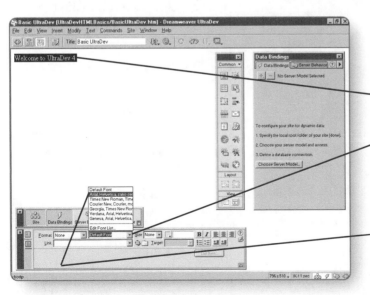

1. Select some text. The text will be highlighted.

2. Click on the down arrow next to the Font Name list on the on the Properties palette. A list of available fonts will appear.

3. Click on a font name. The font style in your selected text will change accordingly.

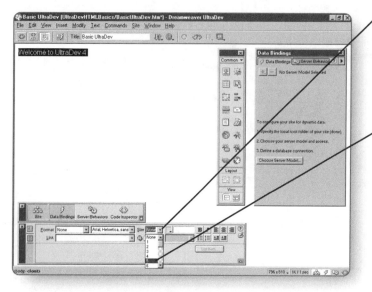

4. With the text still selected, click on the down arrow next to the Font Size on the Properties palette. A list of available font sizes will appear.

5. Click on an appropriate size. The size of the selected text will change.

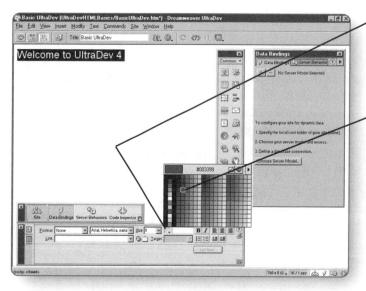

6. With the text still selected, click on the Text Color button on the Properties palette. The Colors palette will appear.

7. Click on a color with the eyedropper cursor to select it. The color of the text will change.

NOTE

You can also use the Properties Inspector to format the selected text with:

- Bold
- Italic
- Left-aligned
- Centered
- Right-aligned

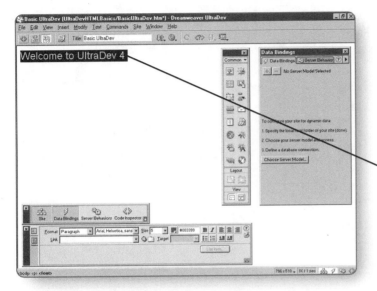

Moving Text

You can easily cut text from a page, move it to another location, or remove the text from the current Web page entirely.

1. Select the text you would like to move. The text will be highlighted.

2. Press Ctrl+x. The selected text will be removed from the document, but still stored on the clipboard for easy retrieval.

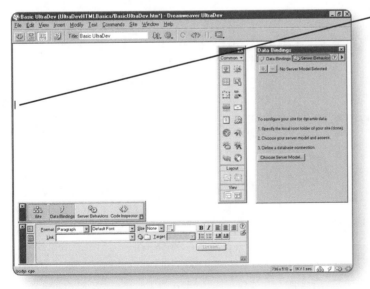

3. Click inside the Document window where you would like to insert the text. The cursor will appear where you click.

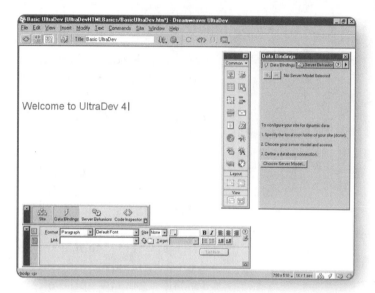

4. Press Ctrl+v. The text will appear at the new location. All the formatting that has been applied to the text is retained.

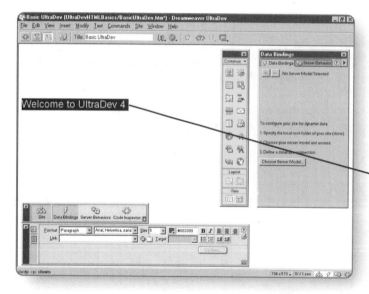

Copying and Pasting Text

You can copy text to a new location in the current Web page or to another page using keyboard shortcuts.

1. Select the text you would like to copy to a new location. The text will be highlighted.

2. Press Ctrl+c. The selected text will be copied to the Clipboard.

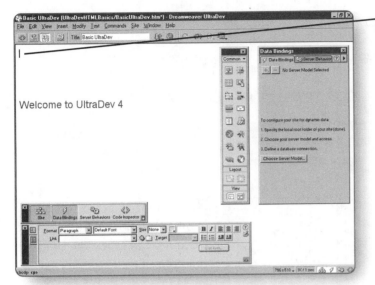

3. Click the mouse pointer at the new location where you would like to insert the text. The cursor will appear where you clicked.

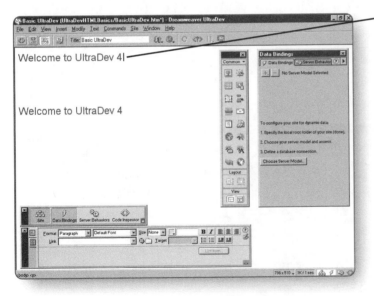

4. Press Ctrl+v. The copied text will appear at the new location.

Drag-and-Drop Text Editing

In UltraDev, you can drag text around your Web page using the mouse.

1. Select the text you want to move. The text will be highlighted.

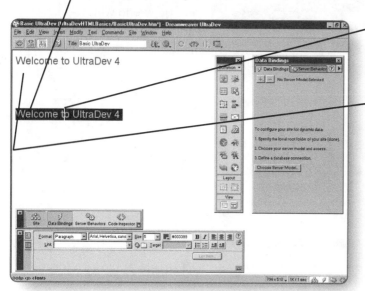

2. Click on the selected text. The mouse pointer will change to the drag pointer.

3. Drag the selected text to another location in the Document window. The drag pointer will move to the new location.

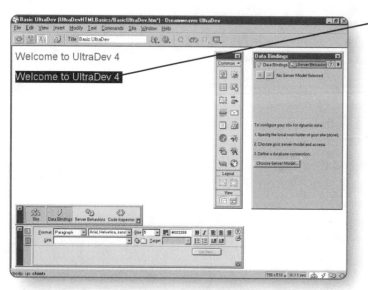

4. Release the mouse button. The selected text will appear at the new location in the Document window.

Creating Links

The World Wide Web is really just a series of documents held together by hyperlinks. Links may seem mysterious and complex if you have never created one before. Fear not, because you can't go wrong with UltraDev leading the way. Both text and images can be hyperlinked.

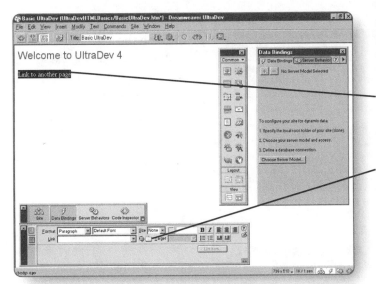

1. Select the text you want to link to another Web page. The text will be highlighted.

2. Click on the Folder icon in the Properties palette. The Select File dialog box will open.

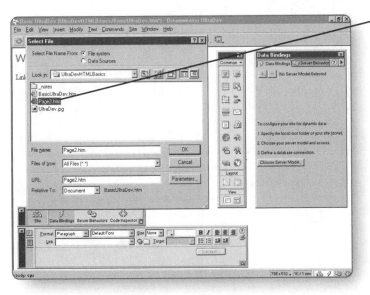

3. Click on the file to be linked. The file name will be highlighted.

NOTE

The file that you are linking to may not always be another Web page. You can also link to Word documents, Excel spreadsheets, PowerPoint presentations, Adobe Acrobat files and more.

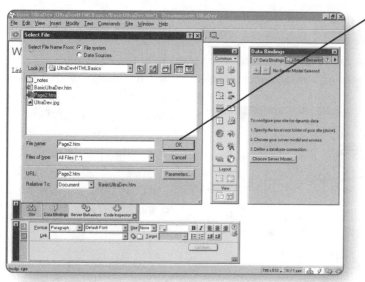

4. Click on OK. The Select File dialog box will close, and the linked text will appear underlined on-screen.

TIP

Assuming you know the complete URL, you can skip the preceding steps and type the Web page address directly in the Link field.

NOTE

The linked text will now be underlined and appear in a different color. You will need to view the page in a browser to test the link.

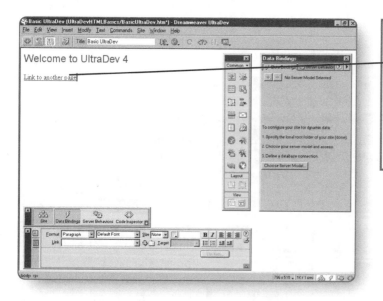

Working with Images

Web sites that only contain text can be pretty dull and boring. Images help to make Web sites visually appealing. Inserting and positioning images in a Web page has never been easier.

Inserting Images

The two most common image file formats are GIF (Graphics Interchange Format) and JPEG (Joint Photographic Experts Group). You may need to use an image editor (such as Adobe Photoshop or JASC Paint Shop Pro) to convert your graphics to either of these formats before you can insert them into a Web page.

1. Click in the document window where you would like the image to appear. The cursor will appear where you click.

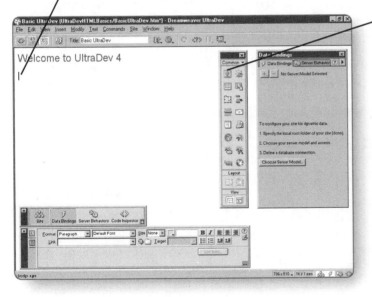

2. Click on the Insert Image button in the Objects palette. The Select Image Source dialog box will open.

> **TIP**
>
> As a general rule, convert all line art graphics to the GIF format and all photographs to the JPEG format.

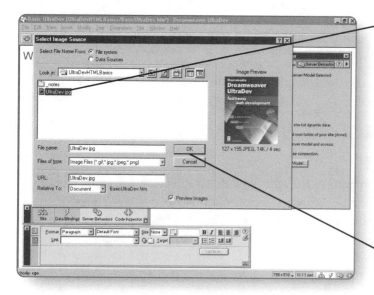

3. Click on the image file to be opened. The file name will be highlighted.

4. If desired, click in the check box named Preview Images. A check will appear in the check box, and a thumbnail of the image will be displayed in the Image Preview area of the dialog box.

5. Click on OK. The image will be inserted into the Web page.

Aligning Images

By default, an inserted image is aligned with the left margin of a Web page. Use the Properties Inspector to change the alignment of an image.

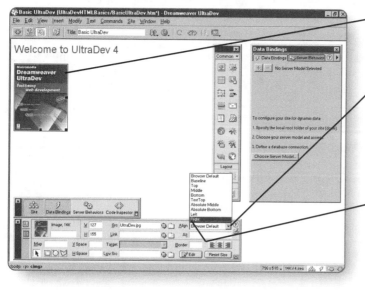

1. Select the image by clicking on it. The image will be highlighted.

2. Click on the down arrow of the Align drop-down box in the Properties palette. A list of alignment options will be displayed.

3. Click on an alignment option. The image will be repositioned accordingly.

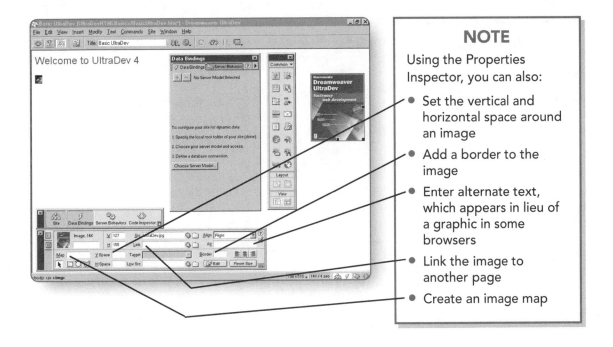

Working with Tables

With the help of tables, you can easily create and modify complex HTML layouts. Without tables, it is difficult to align text and images on a Web page. Editing complex tables has never been easier than it is with UltraDev. Tables are also particularly important in building database-driven Web sites, where they are used to format and display search results.

Inserting a Table

When you create a table, you need to specify the number of rows and columns your table requires. This is the first step to creating interesting layouts.

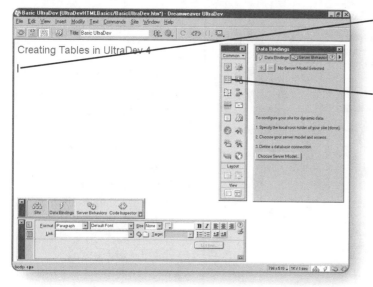

1. Click within your Document window. The cursor will appear where you click.

2. Click on Insert Table in the Objects palette. The Insert Table dialog box will open.

3. Type the number of rows required in the table row field.

4. Type the number of columns required in the table column field.

5. Type the number of pixels required between the contents of a cell and the cell border. This is known as cell padding.

6. Type the number of pixels required between the cells in a table. This is known as cell spacing.

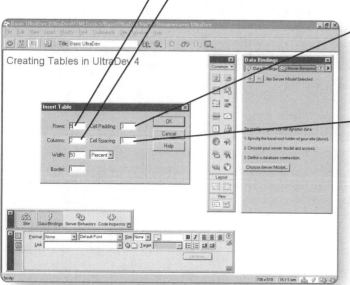

7. Type the width of the table in the Width field.

8. Click on the down arrow of the width list box. A list of options for specifying the width of a table is displayed.

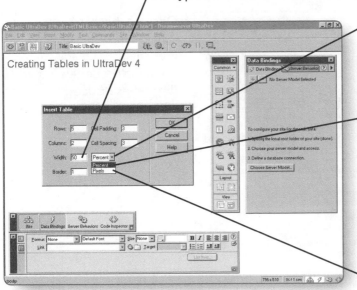

9a. Click on Percent. The percentage option will be selected. This will make the width of the table vary according to the size of the Browser window.

OR

9b. Click on Pixels. The absolute pixel option will be selected. This will make the width of the table a fixed size.

10. Type the size of the table border in pixels. A zero (0) value means that the table will have no border.

11. Click OK. The table will be created.

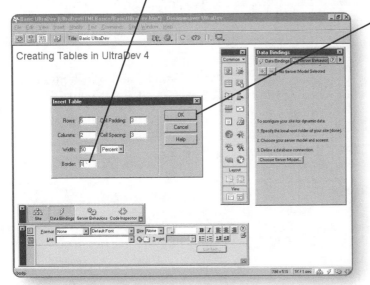

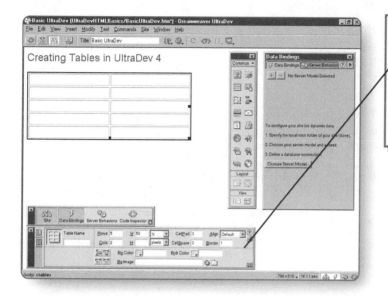

NOTE

Once a table has been inserted, you can modify it at any time by adjusting the table properties in the Properties Inspector.

Adding Text to a Table Cell

Tables are used to display and organize tabular data. Each cell in a table can hold text.

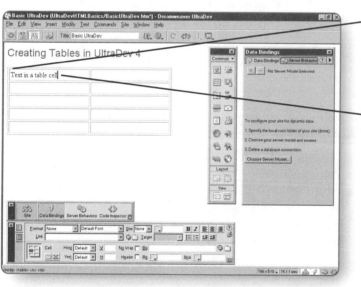

1. Click in a cell where you would like to insert text. The cursor will appear where you click.

2. Type some text. The text will appear within the cell.

Adding Images to a Table Cell

Tables provide a practical way to display complex layouts involving both text and images. Inserting an image into a cell is as easy as inserting text into a cell.

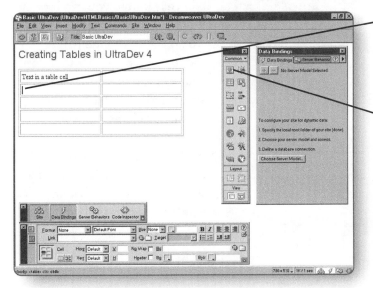

1. Click in a cell where you would like to insert an image. The cursor will appear where you click.

2. Click on the Insert Image button in the Objects palette. The Select Image Source dialog box will open.

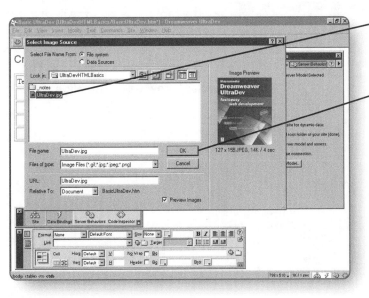

3. Select the image to be inserted. The file name will be highlighted.

4. Click on OK. The image will be inserted in the table cell.

Selecting Table Elements

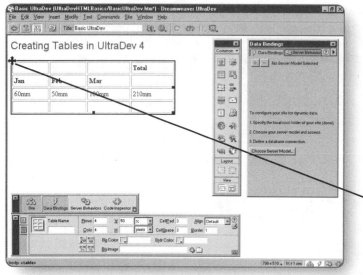

You will need to select table elements such as rows, columns, and cells before you can format them. Select a table if you would like to change its background color or width, for example. UltraDev allows you to select and format individual rows and columns as well.

1. Click the top left corner of the table. The cursor will change to a four-pointed arrow and Selection handles will appear around the selected table.

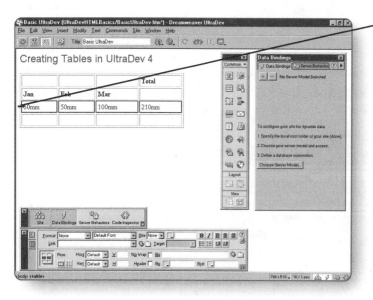

2. To select a row, place the cursor next to the left margin of the table. The cursor will change to an arrow.

3. Click to select the row. The table row will be highlighted.

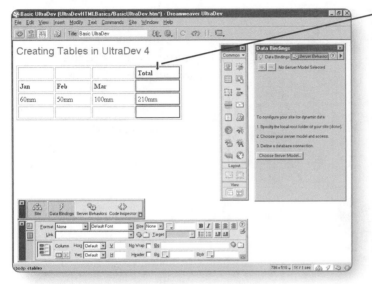

4. To select a column, place the cursor above the top table margin. The cursor will change to an arrow.

5. Click to select the column. The table column will be highlighted.

NOTE

To select individual cells, hold down the Shift key and then click on the cell.

Adding Color to a Table

You can change the background color of a table, cell, row, or column. Color can make your table easier to read. You can also use it to draw attention to certain values.

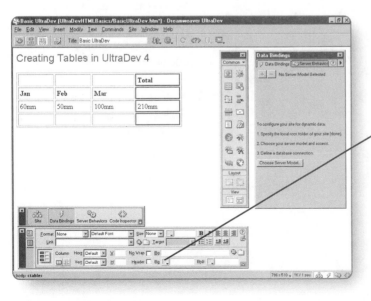

1. Select the table, row, or column where you would like to change the background color. The selected item will be highlighted.

2. Click on the Color button in the Properties palette. The Colors palette will appear.

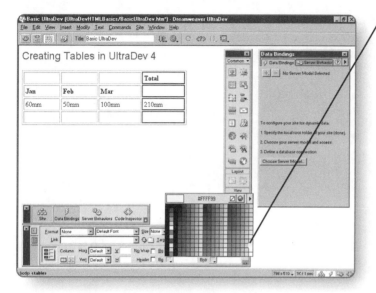

3. Click on a color with the eyedropper cursor. The background color of the selected item will change.

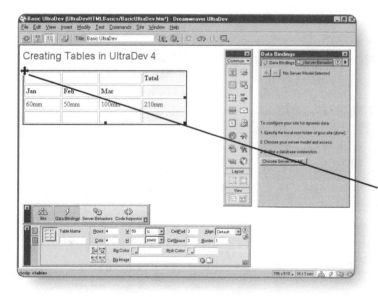

Resizing a Table

It will take you a while to create the perfect layout for your Web page. UltraDev assists in the process by allowing you to resize tables by simply dragging selection handles.

1. Select the table. The table will be highlighted.

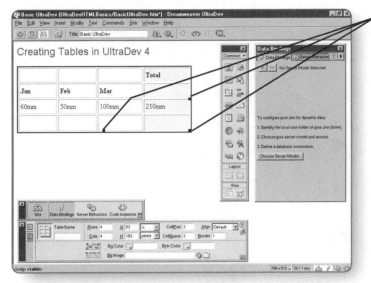

2. Click on and drag the selection handles to resize the table. The size of the table will change.

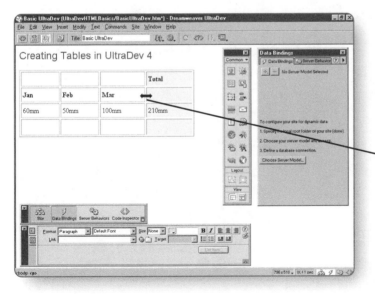

Resizing a Column or Row

The easiest way to adjust row height and column width is to drag the row or column border.

1. Move the mouse pointer over a row or column border. The cursor will change to a double-arrow.

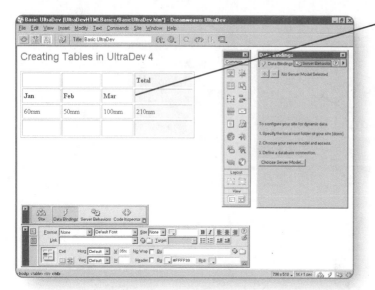

2. Drag the cell border to resize the row or column. The size of the row or column will change.

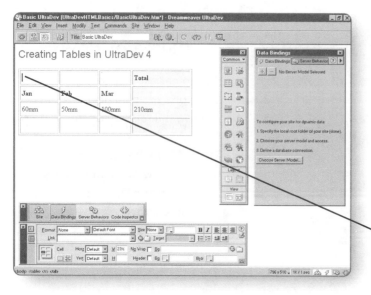

Adding Rows and Columns

When you create a table you need to enter the number of rows and columns that your table should contain. However, as you design your Web page you may decide that you need additional rows and columns.

1. Click in a cell. The cursor will appear where you click.

2. Click on Modify. The Modify menu will appear.

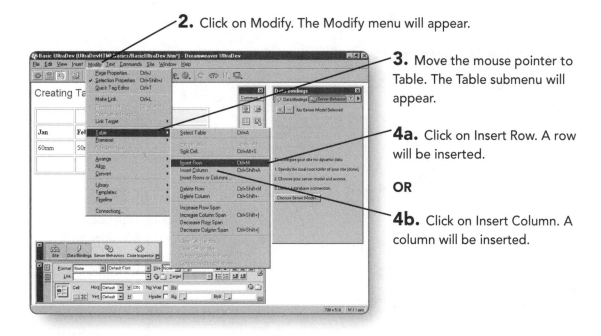

3. Move the mouse pointer to Table. The Table submenu will appear.

4a. Click on Insert Row. A row will be inserted.

OR

4b. Click on Insert Column. A column will be inserted.

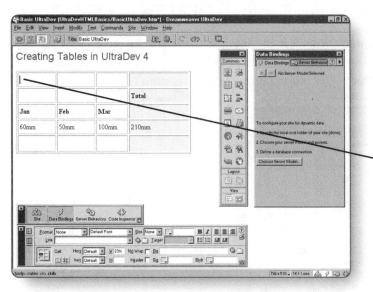

Deleting a Row or Column

You can easily delete rows and columns that you no longer need.

1. Click in any cell within the row or column you want to delete. The cursor will appear where you clicked.

2. Click on Modify. The Modify menu will appear.

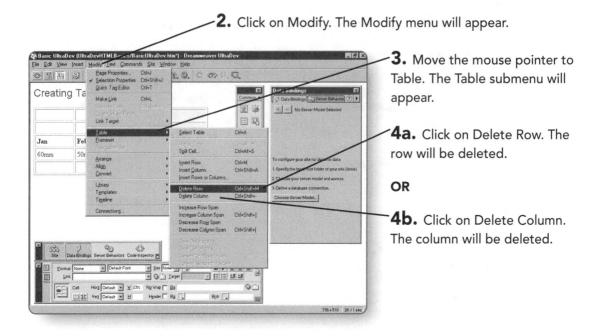

3. Move the mouse pointer to Table. The Table submenu will appear.

4a. Click on Delete Row. The row will be deleted.

OR

4b. Click on Delete Column. The column will be deleted.

Inserting Tables within Tables

It may not always be possible to create the layout you want using a single table. You can, however, insert tables within tables. This is known as nesting. Nesting tables may be the only way that you can create a complex layout in HTML.

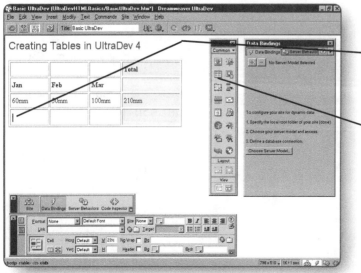

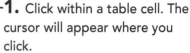

1. Click within a table cell. The cursor will appear where you click.

2. Click the Insert Table button in the Object palette. The Insert Table dialog box will open.

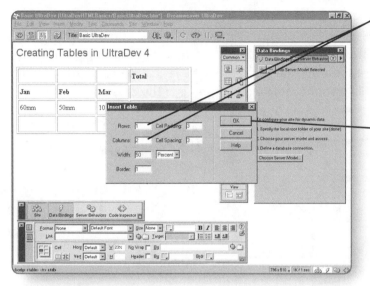

3. Type the number of columns and rows required. You can also specify values for cell padding, cell spacing, table width, and border.

4. Click on OK. A nested table will be created.

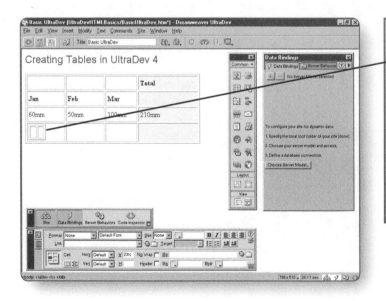

NOTE

Nested tables can each have their own properties. You can specify the size, border width, spacing, color, and background image of each nested table. This allows you great flexibility when laying out a Web page.

Merging Table Cells

Each row in a table has the same number of columns, and all cells in a column are the same size. Sometimes, you will need to create a table that is not a perfect grid. In UltraDev, you can easily create a table in which some of the cells are wider than others. This is known as merging cells.

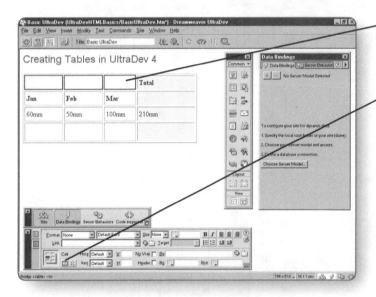

1. Select the cells to be merged. The cells will be highlighted.

2. Click on the Merge Cells button in the Properties Inspector. The cells will be merged.

> ## NOTE
> You can select multiple cells by dragging across the cells you would like to select. Hold down the Shift key while clicking on each cell to add to the selection.

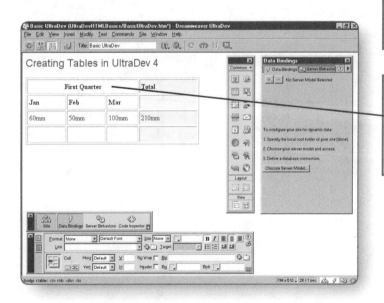

> ## NOTE
> The same technique can be used to merge cells that span multiple rows.

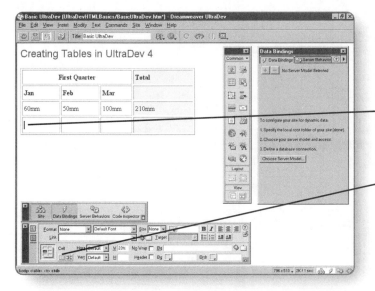

Splitting Table Cells

A cell can also be split into either rows or columns.

1. Click inside the cell to be split. The cursor will appear in the cell.

2. Click on the Split Cell button in the Properties Inspector. The Split Cell dialog box opens.

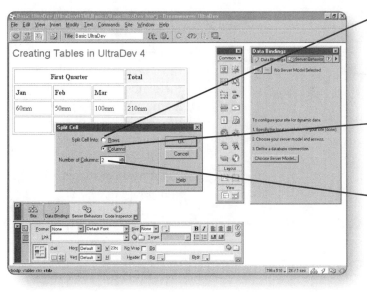

3a. Click on the Split Row option button. The option will be selected.

OR

3b. Click on the Split Column option button. The option will be selected.

4. Enter the number of rows or columns into which the cell should split.

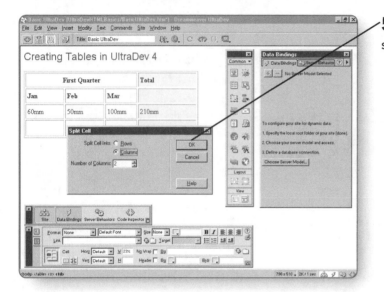

5. Click on OK. The cell will be split.

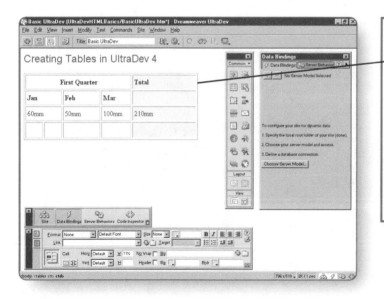

NOTE

You can create complex table layouts by applying the simple techniques you learned in this chapter. When you are designing, keep in mind that you can add/delete rows and columns, nest tables and merge/split cells.

2

Managing Web Sites with UltraDev

UltraDev has many features that make managing Web sites a breeze. In particular, it can keep track of all your Web site links and publish your Web site to a Web server using FTP (File Transfer Protocol). UltraDev can also synchronize local and remote files. In this chapter, you'll learn to:

- Create a site
- Create files and folders
- Check links
- Change links globally
- Use UltraDev to FTP files to and from a remote server
- Synchronize local and remote files

Working with Sites

A site consists of a set of pages on your local hard disk that make up a Web site. A site helps you manage the files in your Web site by making it easier for you to locate pages, check links, and transfer files to and from a remote server. Within the Site window, you can manage all the files and folders in your Web site.

Creating a Site

It is a good idea to create a site for each Web site that you work on. As your project grows, UltraDev can automatically update links when you move or rename files. Every database-driven Web site that you create must be in a site. A site can be created for a new Web site or an existing one.

1. Click on the Start button. A submenu will appear.

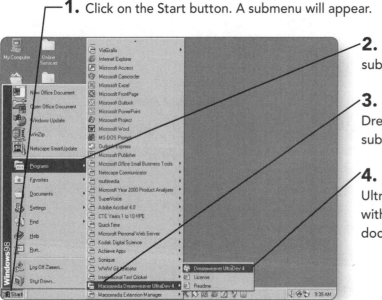

2. Click on Programs. A submenu will appear.

3. Click on Macromedia Dreamweaver UltraDev. A submenu will appear.

4. Click on Dreamweaver UltraDev. UltraDev will open with a blank Web page in the document window.

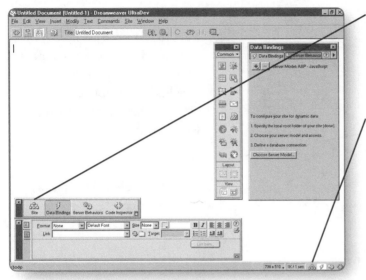

5a. Click the Site button on the Launcher. The Site window will open.

OR

5b. Click the Site icon on the Mini-Launcher at the bottom of the document window. The Site window will open.

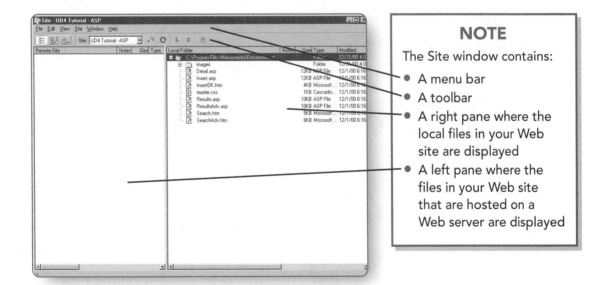

NOTE

The Site window contains:

- A menu bar
- A toolbar
- A right pane where the local files in your Web site are displayed
- A left pane where the files in your Web site that are hosted on a Web server are displayed

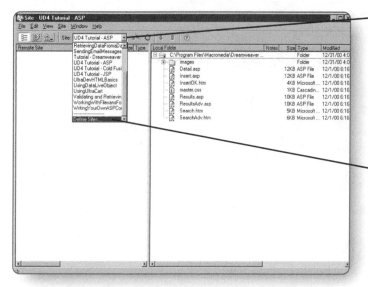

6. Click on the down arrow next to the Sites list box. A list of pre-defined sites will appear. These sites contain all the files required to complete the UltraDev tutorials found in the Help documentation.

7. Click on the Define Sites item. The Define Sites dialog box will open.

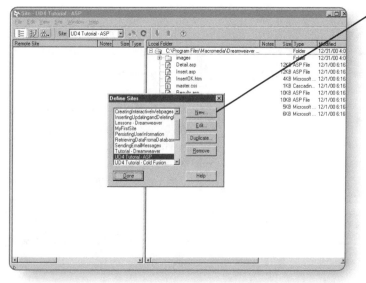

8. Click on New. The Site Definition dialog box will open.

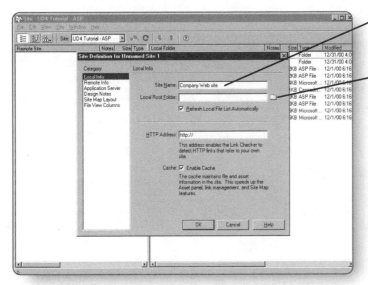

9. Type the name of your site into the Site Name field.

10. Click on the Folder icon next to the Local Root field. The Choose Local Folder dialog box will open.

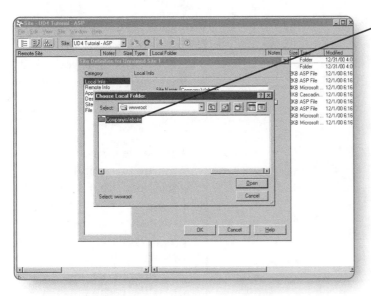

11. Double-click on a directory folder to open the directory. The folders within this subdirectory will be displayed. No files are displayed in the Choose Local Folder, because a folder must be specified before a site can be created.

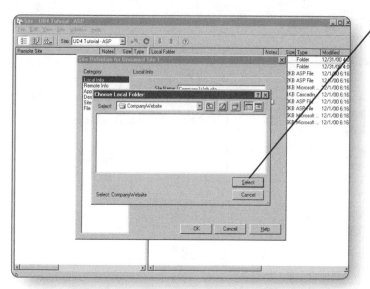

12. Click on Select. The dialog box will close and the path name will appear in the Site Definition dialog box.

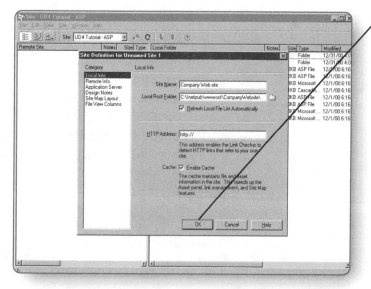

13. Click on OK. The Site Definition dialog box will close, and UltraDev informs you that it is about to create a cache file.

NOTE

A cache file allows UltraDev to monitor links within your site. Basically, a cache file stores information about all the files in your Web site and how they link to each other. UltraDev can readily access the cache file whenever it updates links or generates a site map. The use of a cache file can drastically improve performance.

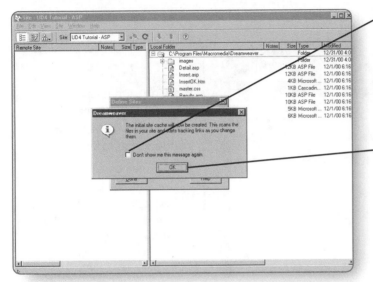

14. Click inside the Don't Show Me This Message Again check box if you don't want to confirm the creation of a cache file every time you define a new site.

15. Click on OK. A cache file will be created.

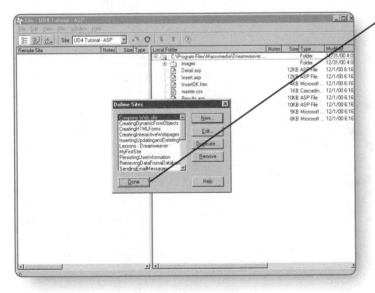

16. Click on Done. The Define Sites dialog box will close.

The contents of your Web site will now appear in the Local Folder pane.

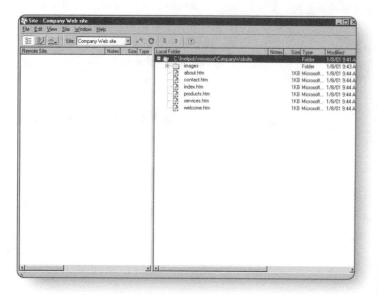

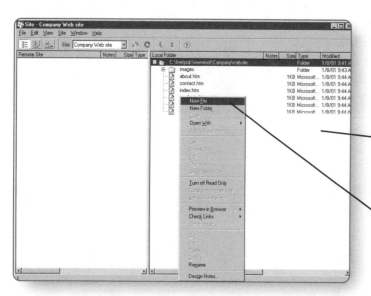

Creating Files

Within the Site window, you can create new files using a few simple steps.

1. Right-click on a blank area of the Local Folder pane. A shortcut menu will appear.

2. Click on New File. A new file called untitled.asp will appear and be highlighted in the Local Folder pane.

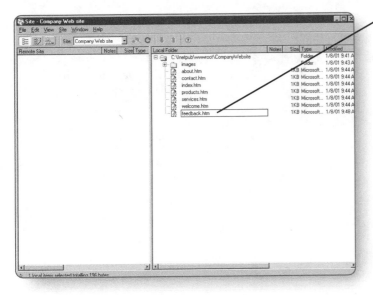

3. Type in the name (with an appropriate extension) for the file that has just been created. The file name will already be selected.

4. Press Enter when finished. The new file will be created.

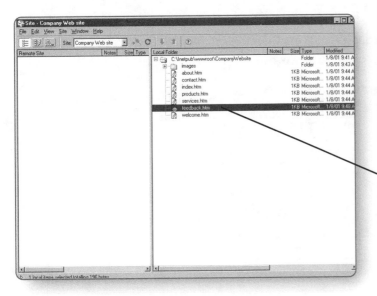

5. Double-click on the file name to open it. The file will open in the document window.

NOTE

The following file extensions can be used:

- .asp if you're creating an ASP (Active Server Pages) file
- .jsp if you're creating a JSP (Java Server Pages) file
- .cfm if you're creating a ColdFusion file
- .htm or .html if you're creating an HTML-only Web page

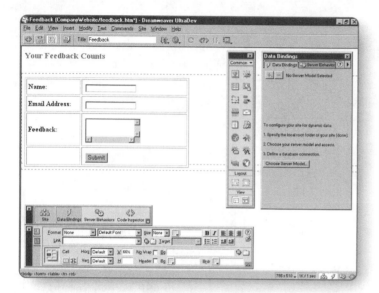

NOTE

You will now be able to use UltraDev to create and format the Web page visually. Please refer to Chapter 1, "UltraDev HTML Basics," if you are not familiar with using UltraDev to create a Web page.

Creating Folders

Folders allow you to organize your files in a logical manner. Creating a new folder in UltraDev is as simple as creating a new file.

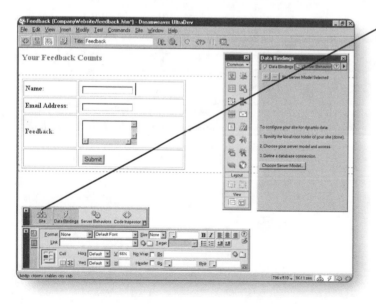

1. Click the Site button on the Launcher. The Site window will open.

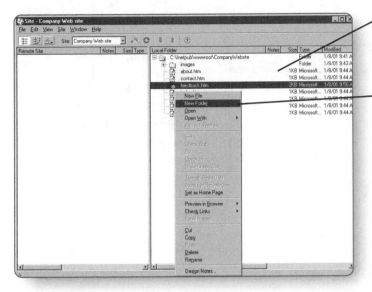

2. Right-click on a blank area of the Local Folder pane. A shortcut menu will appear.

3. Click on New Folder. A new folder called untitled will be created in the Local Folder pane. The folder name is already selected.

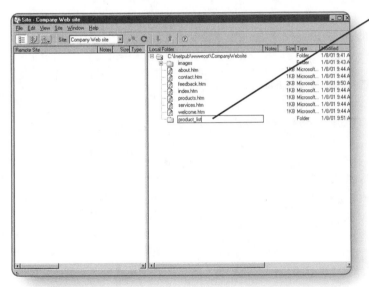

4. Type a name for the folder that has just been created.

5. Press Enter when finished. The new folder will be created.

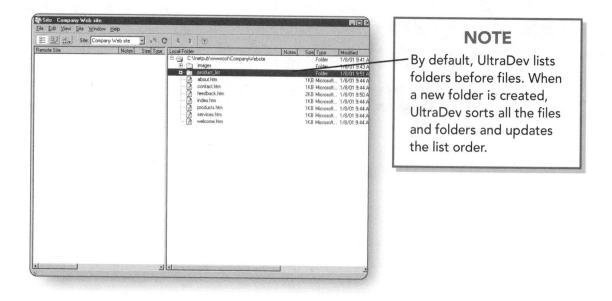

NOTE

By default, UltraDev lists folders before files. When a new folder is created, UltraDev sorts all the files and folders and updates the list order.

Checking Links

Broken links can be really annoying to Web site visitors. A few years ago, it used to be a tedious and time-consuming task to test every link in your Web site. UltraDev makes finding and repairing broken links a snap.

1. Click the Site button on the Launcher. The Site window will open.

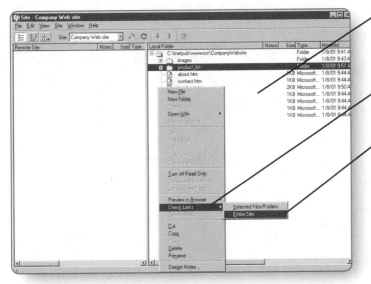

2. Right-click on a blank area of the Local Folder pane. A shortcut menu will appear.

3. Click on Check Links. A submenu will appear.

4. Click on Entire Site. The Link Checker window will open and display a list of broken links.

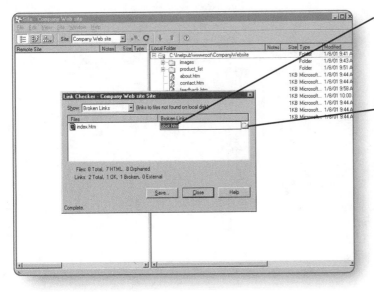

5. Click in the Broken Link column if there are any broken links in the site. A field and folder icon will be displayed.

6. Click on the Folder icon. The Select File dialog box will open.

NOTE

You can also view external links and orphaned files by selecting the corresponding option from the Show drop-down box on the Link Checker window. Orphaned files are files that are not linked to any file in your Web site.

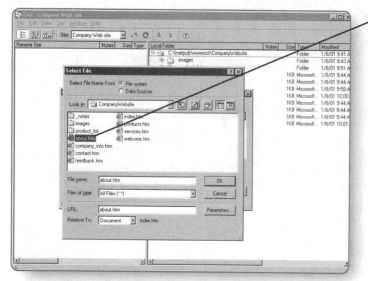

7. Double-click on the file you want to link. The dialog box will close and desired file and path names will be added to the Link field.

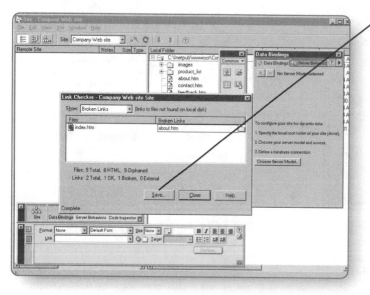

8. Click on Save to close the Link Checker window. The Site window will be displayed.

Changing Links Globally

If the location of a file that you often link to has changed, UltraDev can help you update all occurrences of that link. This will come in handy when you're dealing with large Web sites that multiple people have worked on.

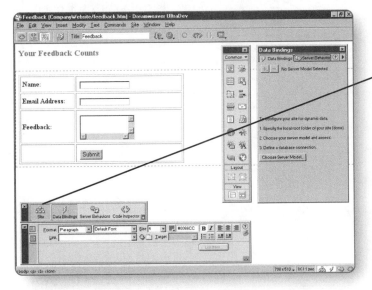

1. Click on Site on the Launcher. The Site window will open.

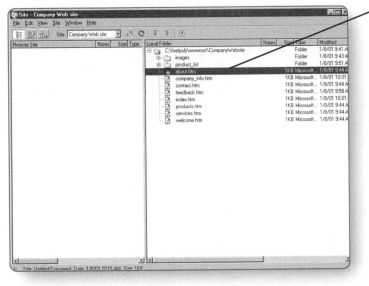

2. Click on the file to which you would like to update all links in the Local Folder pane. The file will be selected.

3. Click on Site. The Site menu appears.

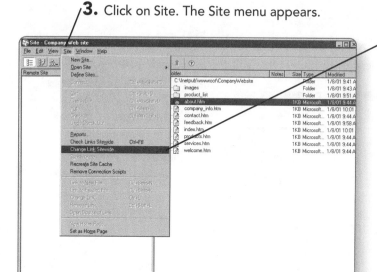

4. Click on Change Link Sitewide. The Change Link Sitewide dialog box will open.

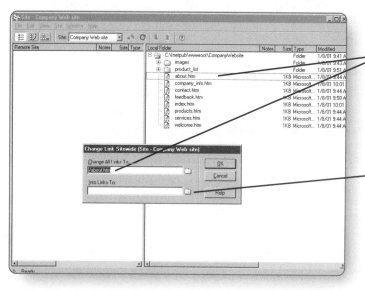

NOTE

By default, the Change All Links To field will automatically display the name and path to the file that was selected.

5. Click on the Folder icon next to the Into Links To field. The Select New Link dialog box opens.

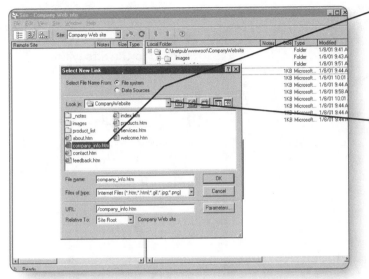

6. Double-click on the desired file. The Change Link Sitewide window will open.

TIP

You may need to use the Look In drop-down list to find your file.

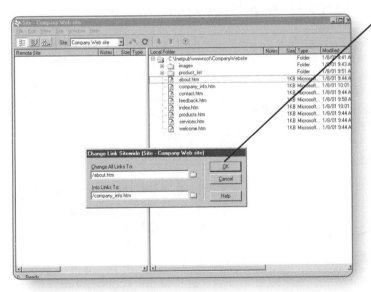

7. Click on OK. The Update Files dialog box will open and display all the pages that contain links to the specified file.

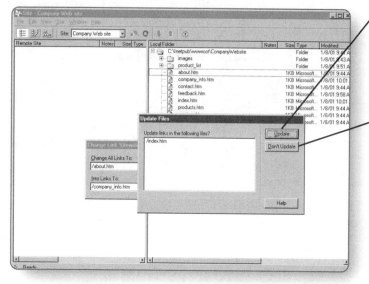

8a. Click on Update. All links will be updated and you will be returned to the Site window.

OR

8b. Click on Don't Update. The Update will be cancelled and you will be returned to the Site window.

Setting Up a Remote FTP Site

The FTP (File Transfer Protocol) is used to publish your Web site to a Web server. There is no need to use a stand-alone FTP client, because the Site window has built-in FTP features. You can upload files from your local folder to a remote Web

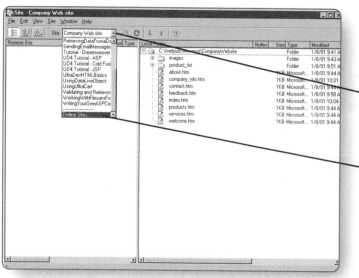

server as well as download files from your remote Web server. The details of the remote server must first be entered.

1. Click on the down arrow of the Sites drop-down box. A list of sites will appear.

2. Click on Define Sites. The Site Definition dialog box will open.

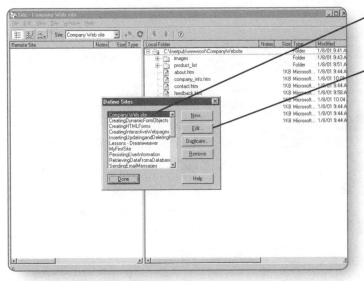

3. Click on a Site name. The Site will be selected.

4. Click on the Edit button. The Site Definition dialog box will open.

5. Click on Remote Info in the Category list. The setting for Web Server Info is displayed.

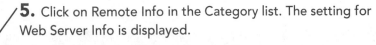

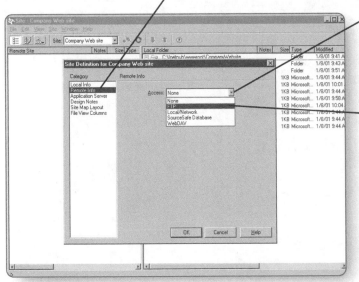

6. Click on the down arrow of the Server Access drop-down box. The drop-down box will open.

7. Click on FTP. Fields for entering FTP details will be displayed.

TIP

Your FTP details, such as host location, user name, and password can all be obtained from your server administrator. Usually, these details are supplied to you when an FTP account is created.

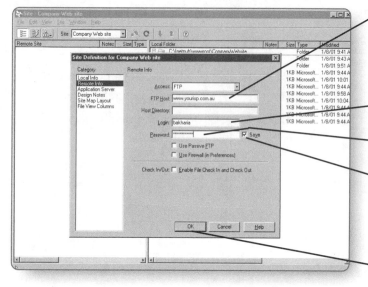

8. Enter the FTP host location. The host location is an alphanumeric address for the Web server.

9. Enter your user name.

10. Enter your password.

11. Click in the Save check box if you want to save your password. A check will appear in the checkbox.

12. Click on OK to save your settings and close the Site Definition dialog box.

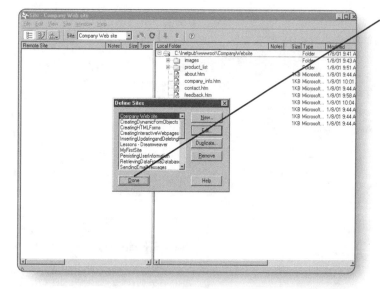

13. Click on Done. The Define Sites dialog box will close.

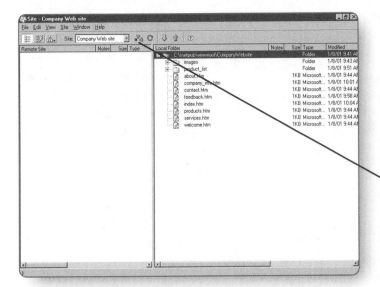

Connecting and Disconnecting to a Remote Server

Within UltraDev you can connect and disconnect from a remote server with a single click.

1. Click on the Connect button. Once clicked, the text on the button will change to Disconnect.

NOTE

The contents of the remote Web server will be displayed in the Remote Site pane.

You can move, rename, and create new files on a remote site using the same techniques you have learned when working with local files.

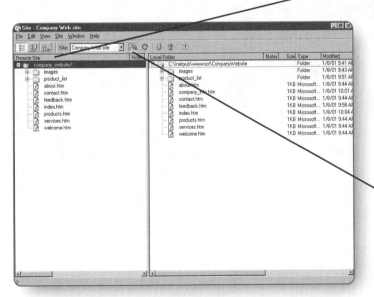

2. Click on Disconnect. The FTP connection will be disconnected. The text on the button will change to Connect.

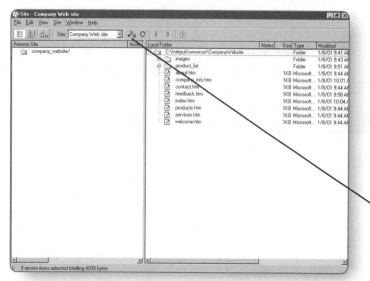

Uploading Files

Uploading files involves transferring files from your local folder to a remote server. The uploading process allows you to publish your Web site or selected pages on the WWW (World Wide Web).

1. Click on Connect. The text on the button will change to Disconnect.

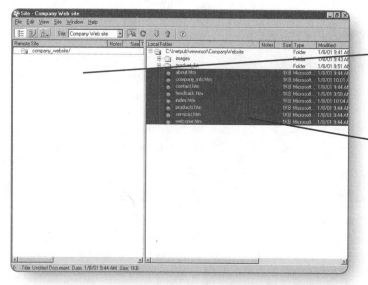

NOTE

The remote Web site will be displayed in the Remote Site pane.

2. Select the files you want to upload from your local folder to the remote site. To select more than one file, hold down the Ctrl key, and then click the files you want to include.

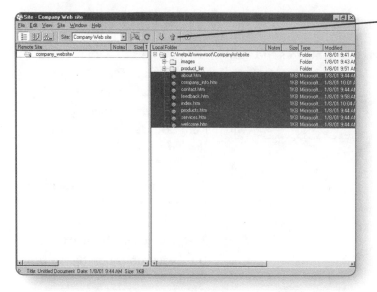

3. Click on Put Files. The selected files will be uploaded.

Downloading Files

Downloading files involves transferring files from a remote Web server to your local folder.

1. Select the files on the remote site that you would like to download to your local folder. To select more than one file, hold down the Ctrl key, and then click the files you want to include.

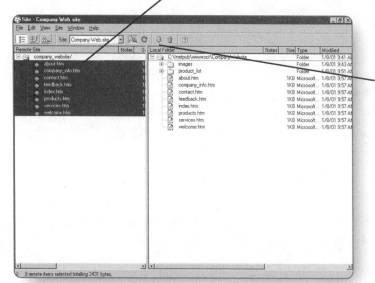

2. Click on Get Files. The selected files will be downloaded.

Synchronizing Files

File synchronization basically compares the files on the remote site with those in your local folder and only keeps the newest versions of the files. File synchronization involves uploading/downloading files from both remote and local sites.

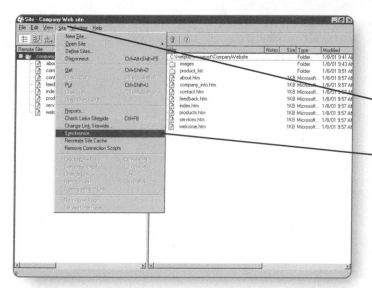

1. Click on Site. The Site menu appears.

2. Click on Synchronization. The Synchronization dialog box opens.

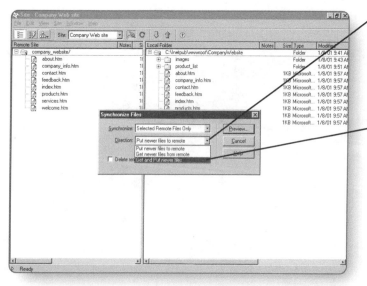

3. Click on the down arrow next to the Direction drop-down list. The types of Synchronization will be displayed.

4. Click on Get and Put newer files. The option will be selected.

5. Click on Preview. The Synchronized Files dialog box will close and the Site dialog box will open.

NOTE

- Put newer files to the remote server. Files on the remote site will be compared with those in the local folder. Newer versions that are found in the local folder will be uploaded to the remote site.
- Get newer files from the remote server. Files on the remote site will be compared with those in the local folder.
- Get & Put newer files. Files on the remote site will be compared with those in the local folder. Only the newest versions of the files found on either the local or remote sites will be kept.

NOTE

The list of files to be synchronized is displayed.

- Files that will be up-loaded to the remote site have a Put action.
- Files that will be down-loaded to the local site have a Get action.

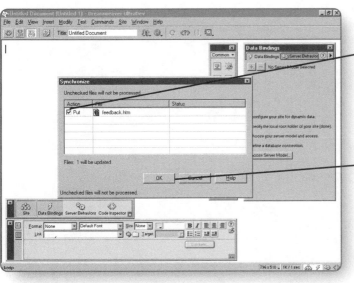

6. Click in the check box next to the action of a file if you do not want the file to be synchronized. The check will be removed from the check box.

7. Click on OK. The synchronization process will begin. The OK button will change to a Save Log button when synchronization is complete.

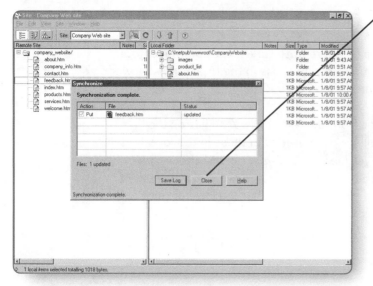

8. Click on Close. The dialog box will close and you will be returned to the Site window.

CAUTION

It is a good idea to back-up files before they are synchronized. You can sometimes accidentally delete files because the file with the latest date may not be the correct version.

3

Planning a Database-Driven Web Site

UltraDev can generate code for three of the most popular
application servers available. These include ASP, JSP, and
ColdFusion. UltraDev has totally revolutionized the way in which
database-driven Web sites are created. Once you're familiar with
UltraDev, you'll be able to use your skills to build dynamic Web
sites for any of the supported application servers. This has
drastically lowered the learning curve for implementing a Web
site in an unfamiliar technology. You will still, however, need to
make an informed decision when selecting an appropriate
application server and backend. In this chapter, you'll learn to:

- Select an application server for your dynamic Web site
- Select a database for your Web site
- Configure UltraDev to handle ASP-driven Web sites

Selecting an Application Server

UltraDev has made it much easier to develop for multiple application servers, but you still need to make a decision on whether you will implement your dynamic site in ASP, JSP, or ColdFusion. There is no definitive answer. You will have to make a decision based upon the functionality required, where the site will be hosted, and your development expertise. Here are some possible scenarios that may dictate what you will have to use.

- **The application server that you choose will depend upon where the site is hosted**
  Sometimes your client may already have its own Web server or one that is externally hosted. If this is the case, you will need to find out whether the server is UNIX- or Windows-based, what Web server is being used, and what server-side scripting languages are available. In a situation like this, the solution you develop will need to be compatible with the current technology and still implement the required functionality. This may be very difficult in some situations, but you will be in luck if at least one of the application servers that UltraDev supports is available. UltraDev will allow you to utilize your existing skills and achieve instant results.

- **The application server must support specific functionality**
  There are times when the required functionality is only available on a particular application server. If this is the case, your decision is obvious. However, if the features that the Web site requires are available on multiple application servers, you'll need to compare the cost and time to implement each solution. You should also make sure that the application server can handle the traffic that the site will attract. There is nothing worse than having a site fall over because heaps of visitors are making requests to the server.

- **You and your development team must have the required expertise**
  It often makes sense to stick to what you know. This will reduce the project duration and maximize your profit. The possibility of encountering technical difficulties is also greatly reduced.

Using ASP

ASP takes a template-based approach to server-side scripting. Code is embedded in a Web page. This allows content and logic to be separated. ASP can be scripted in either VBScript or JScript. Both of these scripting languages are easy to learn, even if you have no programming experience. The template-based approach makes it easier to edit and maintain dynamic content. The script on the Web page is processed, and only HTML is sent to the Web browser.

The Advantages of Using ASP

- It is relatively cheap and easy to find a host for an ASP-driven Web site.

- There is a large ASP community, and it is easy to find resources (books and Web sites).

- ASP is stable and mature in the Windows environment.

- ASP is free. It is bundled with IIS (Internet Information Server) on Windows NT.

- ASP can interface to ODBC-compliant databases (Access & SQL Server) through ADO (ActiveX Data Objects).

- ASP can be extended by third-party components. You can also build your own components so that code can be reused and execution speed is improved.

- ASP has built-in objects that aid Web development, such as the Request object (retrieves posted form data) and the Session object (handles user sessions).

- Microsoft is committed to improving ASP and the supporting scripting languages. Watch for ASP.NET.

The Disadvantages of Using ASP

- ASP is not totally cross-platform. You will need to purchase plug-ins (Chillisoft or InstantASP) to run ASP on a UNIX platform. These plug-ins are not free. Many third-party components will only function on the Windows NT/2000 platform.

- Third-party components can be expensive. If your Web-based application requires many components, you should look to either ColdFusion or JSP.

- Not all Web hosting companies will allow third-party components to be installed.

- VBScript and JScript are only scripting languages.

Recommended Servers

The following servers are recommended for running ASP-driven Web sites:

- Microsoft PWS (Personal Web Server). This can be downloaded from the Microsoft Web site or installed from the Windows 98 CD.

- IIS. This Web server comes with Windows NT/2000.

Using JSP

JSP is modelled after ASP and has many similar objects to aid Web development. JSP is much more powerful, because it allows developers to leverage the power of Java, a cross-platform, object-oriented programming language.

The Advantages of Using JSP

- Although JSP is similar to ASP and ColdFusion, it is much more powerful because Java code is embedded in a Web page.

- JSP is a cross-platform, server-side technology.

- Web applications built with JSP are highly scalable.

- JSP uses JDBC as an interface to databases.

- You can build your own tag libraries to extend JSP.

- JSP is a key component of J2EE (Java 2 Enterprise Edition) and has a bright future.

- Many Web server vendors already support JSP.

- JSP can be extended through Javabeans. Javabeans are very similar to components in ASP. You can purchase them or build your own. It is very easy to build a Javabean with a basic grasp of the Java language.

- JSP is free and can be downloaded from Sun's Web site. Both J2EE and JSWDK (JavaServer Web Development Kit) 1.1 are available.

The Disadvantages of Using JSP

- JSP has a steep learning curve if you don't have a good programming background.

- The backend database must have a JDBC driver.

- Web site hosting may be harder to find and slightly more expensive.

- JSP is not as popular as ASP.

- While the JSP community is substantial, there are a limited number of JSP-specific resources available.

Recommended Servers

The following servers are recommended for running JSP-driven Web applications:

- IBM's WebSphere Server. You'll find a copy in your UltraDev box.

- Allaire's JRun.

- Netscape's iPlanet Enterprise Server.

Using ColdFusion

ColdFusion uses a tag-based scripting language that cleanly interfaces with HTML. The tag-based language is known as CFML (ColdFusion Markup Language) and includes more than 70 tags.

The Advantages of Using ColdFusion

- ColdFusion is simple to learn.

- ColdFusion is very powerful. It has tags to access databases, send e-mail messages, transfer files through FTP (File Transfer Protocol), and programming constructs. These include loops and conditional statements.

- ColdFusion is cross-platform. There are versions for Windows NT, Linux, and Solaris.

- ColdFusion has a large developer community.

- You can build your own tags.

The Disadvantages of Using ColdFusion

- ColdFusion is not free. You will have to purchase a ColdFusion server from Allaire.

- Hosting ColdFusion-based applications can be quite expensive.

- It is sometimes hard to follow and debug nested tags. This should only be a concern if the logic that you're building into a page is complex.

Recommended Servers

The following servers are recommended for running ColdFusion:

- Allaire's ColdFusion Server. UltraDev comes with a single-user version. You will have to purchase the full server to deploy your Web applications.

Selecting a Database

Although UltraDev will allow you to connect to most commercially available databases, the database you select will need to be compatible with the application server. The chosen database needs an ODBC- (Open DataBase Connectivity) compliant driver to interface to ASP, and a JDBC- (Java DataBase Connectivity) compliant driver to interface to JSP. It is also important that the database can handle the amount of data you wish to store and the traffic that your site could receive.

Microsoft Access is a low-end database that can be Web-enabled through ODBC. Access is not a client/server database and will not handle a large number of requests in an efficient manner. It should only be used on small-scale Web sites. If you have no prior experience with relational databases, then I would recommend learning Access. It is very easy to learn and is probably already installed on your computer if you have Microsoft Office. All the concepts you learn will also apply to other databases. It would not take a genius to figure out that you need a database before you can create a database-enabled Web site. UltraDev makes light work of binding the actual data to a Web page, but you're probably wondering how to create a database in the first place. Chapter 7, "Designing a Database," will answer all your questions. It will explain relational database theory in a practical manner and take you step-by-step through creating your first Access database.

If your Web site needs to handle a great number of simultaneous users, you will need to consider using an enterprise database. Enterprise databases are powerful and complicated, but can also be quite expensive. Here are some of the most popular enterprise databases:

- Oracle
- Microsoft SQL Server
- IBM DB2

These are all true client/server databases. Databases that run in a client/server environment can handle gigabytes of data and a large number of users. Client/server databases can also store and run powerful scripts. This removes complex code from your Web page and improves performance. Enterprise databases can usually run on a wide variety of platforms, and offer enhanced security, data locking, scalability, and data replication capabilities.

Developing ASP Applications in UltraDev

UltraDev needs to know where all the pages on your Web server are stored. You need to specify the physical path to your Web site and the URL of your Web server. This will allow you to view and edit the dynamic content generated by your application server within the Live Data window. All Web pages that you preview through your browser will be served from your local Web server.

NOTE

The following steps will guide you through the process of configuring UltraDev so that you can preview and test ASP-driven Web sites locally. You need to have PWS running on your local machine. This is a free Web server that supports ASP and is available for computers running Windows 95/98/2000. Please refer to Appendix B for instructions on installing and using PWS.

If you're not using ASP as your application server, you'll need to consult your application server's documentation on how to publish files to your Web server.

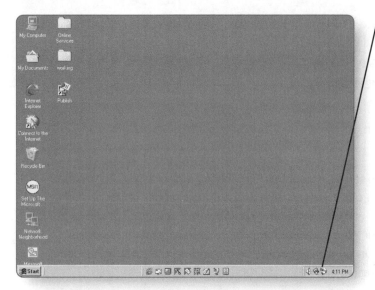

1. Double-click on the PWS icon located in the Quick Launch taskbar. Personal Web Manager will open.

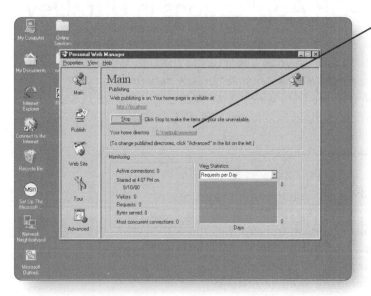

2. Click on the link to your home directory. Windows Explorer will open and display the contents of your home directory. Make a note of the physical path to the home directory and the URL of your Web server. You will need these later.

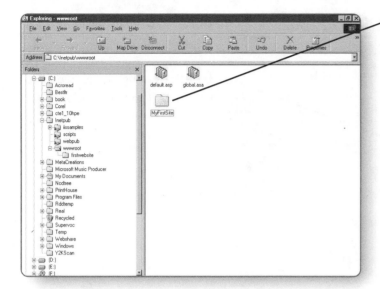

3. Create a new folder within the home directory. This folder will be used to store a Web site on your Web server. You should store each Web site in a separate folder.

TIP

Right-click in the right pane to create a new folder. A shortcut menu will appear. Select New and then Folder.

4. Click on the Close icon. Windows Explorer will close.

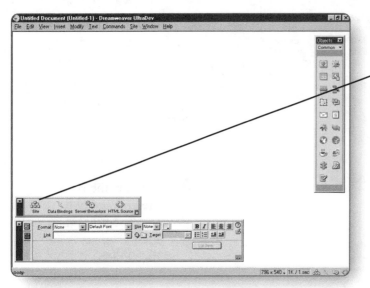

5. Open Dreamweaver UltraDev 4.

6. Click on the Site icon on the Launcher. The Site window will open.

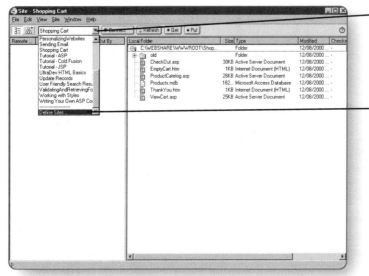

7. Click on the down arrow of the Sites drop-down list. All the sites in UltraDev will be displayed.

8. Click on Define Sites. The Define Sites dialog box will open.

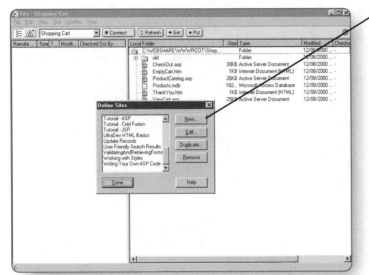

9. Click on New. The Site Definition dialog box will open.

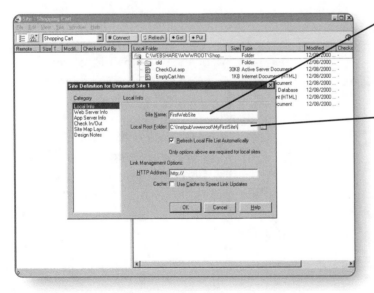

10. Enter a name for the site in the Site Name field. This name will be used to identify your Web site in UltraDev.

11. Enter the physical path to the folder that you created within the home directory of your local Web server.

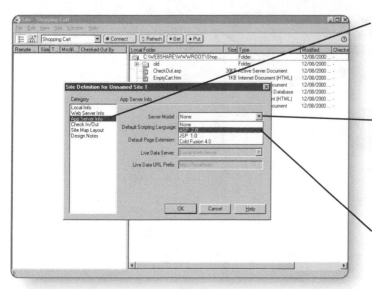

12. Click on Application Server in the Category list. The application server options will be displayed.

13. Click on the down arrow of the Server Model drop-down list. The list of supported application servers will be displayed.

14. Click on ASP 2.0. The option will be selected.

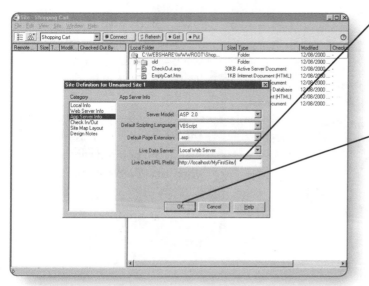

15. Enter the URL prefix for your Web site. The prefix is made up of the URL of your Web server and the folder that will store your Web site.

16. Click on OK. The Site Definition dialog box will close. UltraDev will indicate that a cache file will be created.

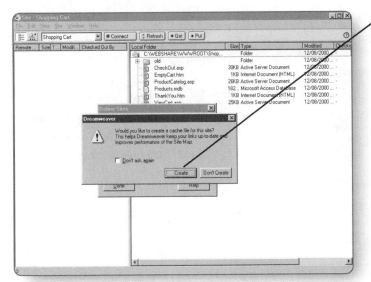

17. Click on Create. A cache file for your site will be created.

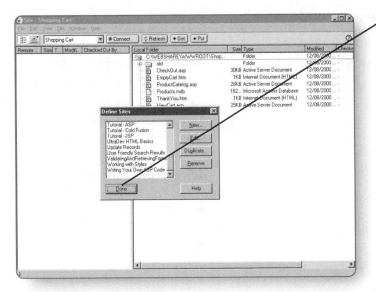

18. Click on Done. The Define Sites dialog box will close.

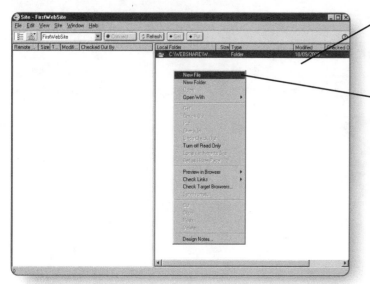

19. Right-click on the Local Folder pane. A shortcut menu will appear.

20. Click on New File. A new file called untitled.asp will be created in the Local Folder pane. The file name will be selected.

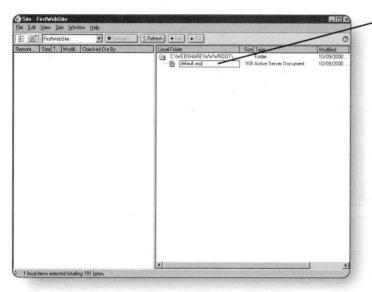

21. Type in the name (with an appropriate extension) for the file that has just been created. The file name will be selected.

22. Press Enter when finished. The new file will be created.

23. Double-click on the file name. The Web page will open in the Document window.

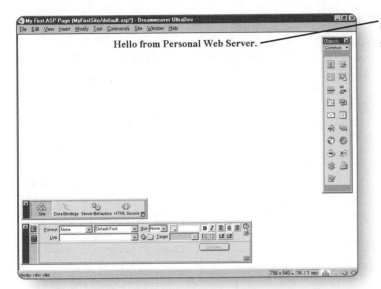

24. Type some text to create a simple Web page.

25. Click on File. The File menu will appear.

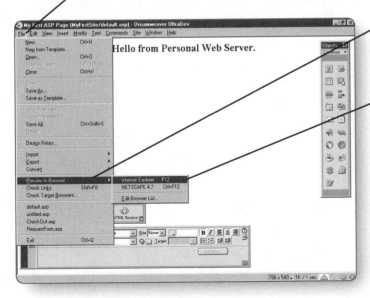

26. Click on Preview in Browser. A list of browsers will be displayed.

27. Click on the browser that you would like to use to preview the Web page. The browser will open and load the Web page.

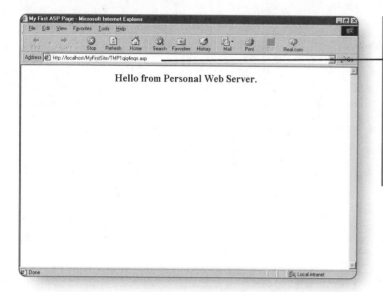

NOTE

The URL indicates that the Web page is being served by PWS. UltraDev assigns a temporary file name to all Web pages that you preview in a browser.

4

An Overview of Server Behaviors

Behaviors allow you to achieve complex tasks without having to write a single line of code. Behaviors make UltraDev the powerful Web site development tool that it is. UltraDev has both client and server behaviors. It is essential that you know the difference between the two and are familiar with the functionality that can be achieved with each. In this chapter you'll learn:

- The difference between client and server behaviors
- About the client-side behaviors in UltraDev
- About the server behaviors in UltraDev

Server-Side Versus Client-Side Behaviors

Client-side behaviors insert JavaScript code into a Web page. The script is only processed when the Web page is displayed in a Web browser. A client-side behavior is interpreted on a user's own computer (i.e., the client). Client-side scripting is very dependent upon the type of browser that the user has installed. This is perhaps the biggest disadvantage in using client-side behaviors. Browsers implement JavaScript differently, so it is very important that the behaviors you insert function without errors in popular browsers such as Microsoft Internet Explorer and Netscape Navigator. Luckily, UltraDev takes care of inserting compatible code once you have decided upon your target browsers. This will make life much easier.

A server-side behavior, on the other hand, inserts JSP, ASP, or ColdFusion script into a Web page. Server-side scripts are interpreted in the server. Once the script is processed, only HTML is sent to the browser. You have total control over the environment in which your script will be executed, and don't have to worry about the capabilities of a Web browser.

Client and server behaviors are by no means competing technologies. There are features that you can use from both to make your Web site more compelling and dynamic. Client-side behaviors will help you create a visually appealing Web site. You can create image rollovers, play sounds, and use layers to create complex timeline animations. Server-side behaviors allow you to create dynamic database-driven Web sites. There are behaviors that will generate code to display, insert, update, and delete records from a database.

The Behaviors Palette

The Behaviors palette contains all the available client-side behaviors. Before you insert a behavior you need to select the browsers you wish to target.

NOTE

It is beyond the scope of this book to explain how to implement all the available behaviors. This section will only highlight the functionality that can be achieved.

1. Click on Window. The Window menu will appear.

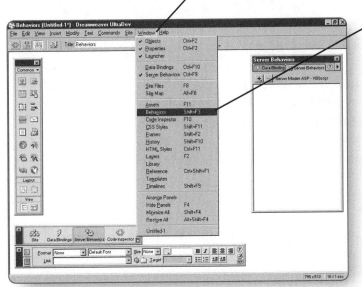

2. Click on Behaviors. The Behaviors palette will be displayed.

TIP

You can also press Shift+F3 to open the Behaviors palette.

NOTE

Before you use a behavior, you need to specify the Web browsers that you will be targeting.

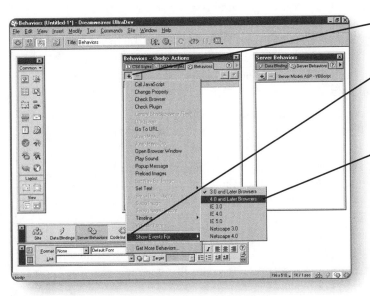

3. Click on the + button. A submenu will appear

4. Click on Show Events For. A list of browsers that you can target is displayed.

5. Click on the Web browser version(s) that you want to support. The option(s) will be selected.

NOTE

You can utilize behaviors to:

- Swap images. This allows you to swap images by moving a mouse over or clicking on an image.

- Preload images. You should preload images that are being swapped. This will reduce the time it takes for an image to be displayed.

- Play sounds. You can play a sound once a button is clicked on or the page loads.

- Display a message on the status bar. The status bar can be used to provide feedback and guidance to your users.

- Open a URL. You can use an event other than a click to open a new Web page.

- Display a pop-up alert message. This can be used to confirm users' actions.

- Open a new browser window. You can display a Web page in a new browser. Both the size and attributes of the new window are configurable.

- Detect whether a user's browser has a plug-in installed. This is important if your Web site is using either Shockwave or Flash. You can redirect a user without the required plug-in to a low bandwidth HTML version of the page.

- Check browser type and function. Sometimes you may implement functionality that will only work in a specific browser and version. If your script is displayed in the incorrect browser, an error message will appear. You need to detect the browser being used and redirect the user to a page that their browser can view.

- Control Shockwave or Flash movies. You can allow users to play, stop, or rewind interactive movies.

- Control layers. Layers allow you to create DHTML (Dynamic HTML) applications. The Behaviors palette contains a set of behaviors that allow you to hide/show layers and create timeline-based animations.

- Validate forms. You can ensure that a user has filled out all of the mandatory fields on an HTML form. You can also check the format (text, numeric, or e-mail address) of the data entered. Using the Validate Form behavior is fully explained in Chapter 6, "Validating and Retrieving Form Data."

Some behaviors are grayed out. This means that they are disabled until your Web page contains the required elements. You need to have layers before you can use the behaviors that control layers. You also need a form before you can use the Validate Form behavior.

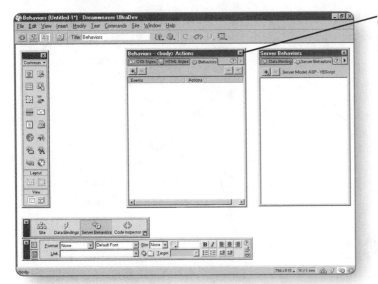

6. Click on the Close icon. The Behaviors palette will close.

The Server Behaviors Palette

Server behaviors are new additions to Dreamweaver UltraDev that allow you to create dynamic database-driven Web sites. Server behaviors do all the hard work by inserting all the required code. Perhaps the greatest feature of server behaviors is that you can target multiple application servers (ASP, JSP, and ColdFusion). Thus, after you are familiar with UltraDev, you can use your skills to build Web applications for all three of the most popular application servers.

While server behaviors are very easy to use, you still need to have a clear understanding of what each server behavior can achieve and where it can be used. As a new user, you may find the names given to server behaviors slightly confusing. Names like Repeat Region and Link to Detail Page certainly don't make any sense if you're not familiar with programming jargon. This makes using a server behavior for the first time quite difficult, but this section will give you a sound overview with helpful examples.

The Server Behaviors palette is used to insert server behaviors. Unlike client-side behaviors, you don't need to specify target browsers. You do, however, need to select an appropriate application server. You learned to do this in Chapter 3, "Planning a Database-Driven Web Site."

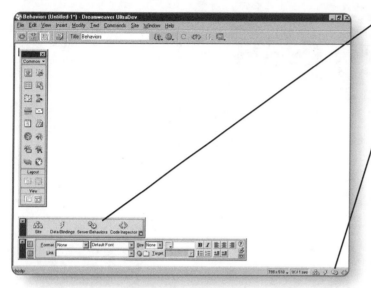

1a. Click on the Server Behaviors icon on the Launcher. The Server Behaviors palette will be displayed.

OR

1b. Click on the Server Behaviors icon on the Mini-Launcher. The Server Behaviors palette will be displayed.

2. Click on the + sign. A submenu will appear.

Use the following server behaviors to display search results on a Web page:

Recordset (Query)	The Recordset (Query) server behavior allows you to query a database and bind the returned data to a Web page.
Repeat Region	The Repeat Region server behavior allows multiple records to be displayed on a Web page. If your database contains many records, you need only display a few records at a time by splitting the results across multiple pages.
Move to Record	The Move to Record server behavior allows you to create a navigation panel for paged search results. You can create links to move to the next and previous pages.
Show Region	The Show Region server behavior makes the navigation panel more intuitive to use. The previous link can be disabled on the first page, while the next link can be disabled when the last page is reached. You can also use the Show Region server behavior to display a message if the search request returned no records.
Go To Detail Page	A search results Web page usually only displays summary data from a record. You need to provide the user with an opportunity to view the entire record. The Go To Detail Page server behavior is used to link to a detail page, a Web page that displays all the important fields in a record. The ID of the chosen record is appended to the URL of the detail page.

Use the following server behaviors to create a detail page:

Recordset (Query)	The Recordset (Query) server behavior retrieves the record that matches the ID appended to the URL of the detail page, and then binds the record to the Web page.
GoTo Related Page	This server behavior can be used to create a link to a page that contains related information.

Use the following server behaviors to maintain a database from a Web interface:

Insert Record	Inserts a new record into a database table. You need to create a form that contains all the fields to populate a record in a database.
Update Record	Updates an existing record in a database table. You need to display the existing record in a form, so that the user can edit the data and then click a button to update the record.
Delete Record	Deletes an existing record in a database. You need to let users preview the record so that they know what will be deleted.

Use the User Authentication server behaviors to password-protect pages in your Web site:

Log In User	Used to check whether the username and password entered by a user is valid and allows them to access password-protected pages in your Web site.
Restrict Access To Pages	Allows you to define the pages in your site that should be password-protected.
Check New Username	Provides a link or button, which the user can click on to log out of the Web site.
Log Out User	This server behavior is used when you allow users to register before they can access restricted areas on your Web site. It checks to see whether a username is already in use.

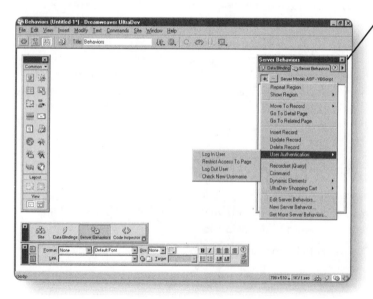

3. Click on the Close icon. The Server Behaviors palette will close.

5

Creating HTML Forms

HTML forms are fundamental to building interactive Web sites. Forms are used to gather information from users that requires processing. They contain standard graphical interface elements such as text fields, check boxes, radio buttons, and drop-down lists. Forms are extremely important in database-driven Web sites where users are required to insert, update, and search data. In this chapter, you'll learn to:

- Add form objects (text fields, password fields, check boxes, radio buttons, and drop-down lists)
- Use a table to format a form
- Use a button to submit a form
- Use an image to submit a form
- Use a button to reset a form

Creating HTML Forms

The Forms panel on the Objects palette allows you to insert form objects into a Web page. This is done in a visual and intuitive manner. The available form objects include text fields, check boxes, radio buttons, drop-down lists, and menus. Form object properties can be edited from the Properties Inspector.

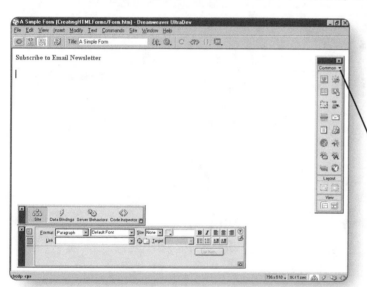

1. Press Ctrl+n. A blank Web page will be displayed in the Document window.

2. Click on the drop-down arrow at the top of the Objects palette. A submenu containing all available panels will be displayed.

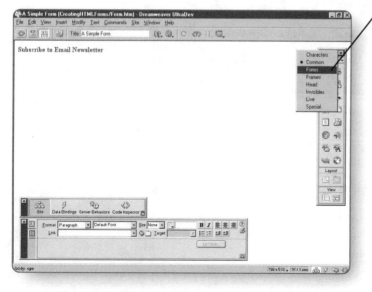

3. Click on Forms. The Forms Object panel will open.

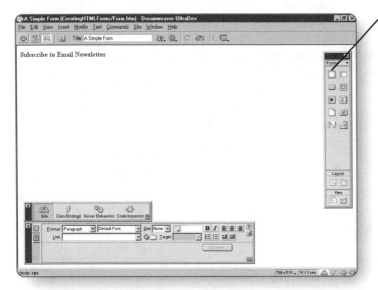

4. Click on the Insert Form button. A form will be inserted when selected.

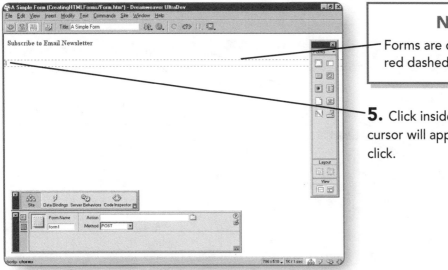

5. Click inside the form. The cursor will appear where you click.

6. Click on Insert. The Insert menu will appear.

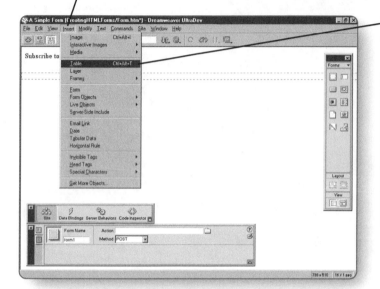

7. Click on Table. The Insert Table dialog box will open.

> ## NOTE
> Forms take up 100% of the page width and can't be resized. Tables must therefore be used to format elements within a form.

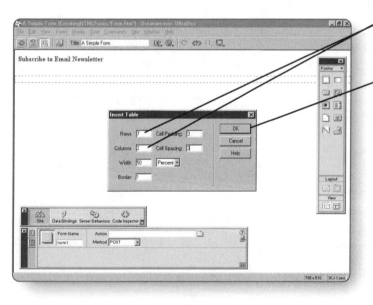

8. Enter the number of rows and columns for your table.

9. Click on OK. The table will be inserted within the form on the Web page.

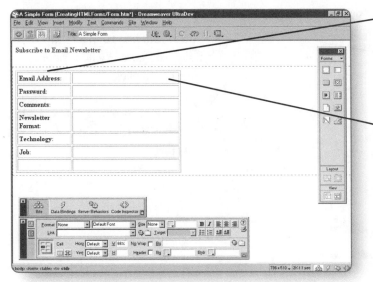

10. Type the titles for all the information you would like to collect in the left column of cells.

NOTE

In the next column, you will determine the appropriate form elements to be used to collect data from your visitors. You can choose from the following element types.

● Text fields
● Password fields
● Multi-line text fields
● Radio buttons
● Check boxes
● Drop-down lists

The following sections will discuss each type of element in more detail.

Inserting Text Fields

Text fields allow free-form data entry. A text field is ideal for users to enter data such as names, addresses, and telephone numbers. Text fields only allow users to enter a single line of text. Use a multiline text field if you would like users to be able to enter lengthy sentences.

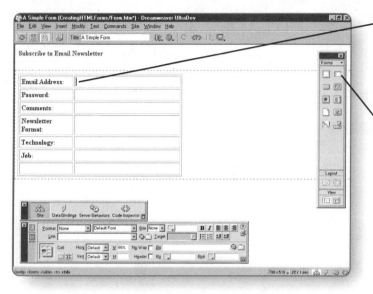

1. Click in the table cell where you would like to insert the text field. The cursor will appear where you click.

2. Click on the Insert Text Field button. The text field will be inserted.

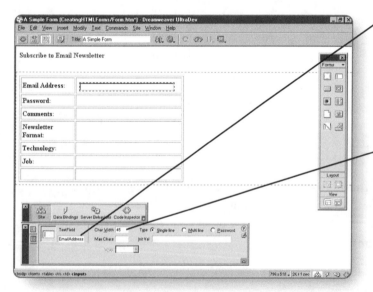

3. Type a name for the text field in the Properties palette. All form objects must be given a unique name. The name of a form object is required when retrieving posted form data.

4. Enter the number of characters the field should hold. This will determine the length of the field when displayed in a Browser. The number of characters that a text field should hold will depend on the data you wish to collect.

Inserting Password Fields

A password field is a text field that uses asterisks to mask the data being entered. Use a password field when the user has to enter sensitive data that should not be viewed by anybody else, such as a password or credit card number.

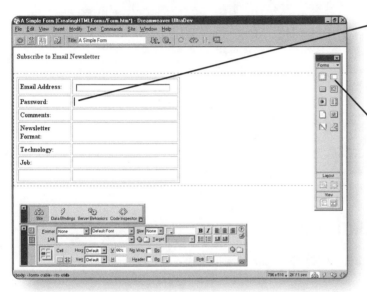

1. Click in the table cell where you would like to insert the text field. The cursor will appear where you click.

2. Click on the Insert Text Field button. The text field will be inserted.

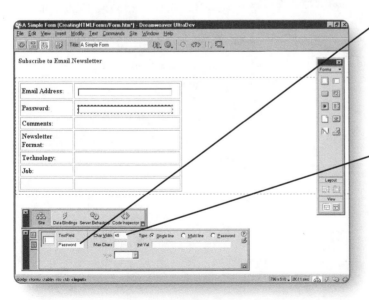

3. Type a name for the text field. All form objects must be given a unique name. The name of a form object is required when retrieving posted form data.

4. Enter the number of characters the field should hold. This will determine the length of the field when displayed in a Browser. The number of characters that a text field should hold will depend on the data you wish to collect.

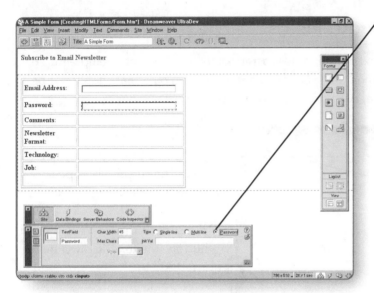

5. Click on the Password option button. The option will be selected.

Inserting Multiline Text Fields

Unlike a text field, a multiline text field can handle large amounts of information that span multiple lines.

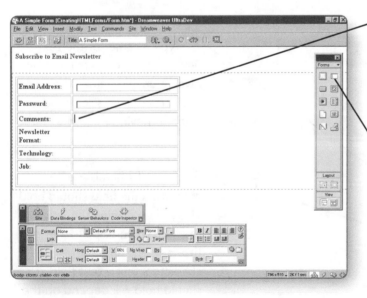

1. Click inside the table cell where you would like to insert the multiline text field. The cursor will appear where you click.

2. Click on the Insert Text Field button. A text field will be inserted.

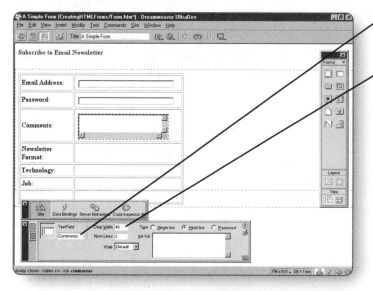

3. Type a name for the multi-line text field.

4. Enter the number of characters the field should hold. This will define the width of the multiline text field when displayed in a Web browser.

5. Click on the Multi line option button to change the text field into a multiline text field. The option will be selected.

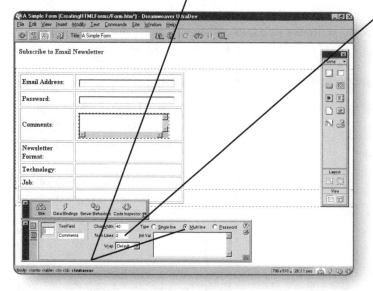

6. Type the number of lines required in the Num Lines field. This will define the number of lines that can be displayed at any one time. The number that you specify will depend on the data you want to collect.

NOTE

A multiline text field allows the user to enter text beyond the constraints that you set. When the user enters more data than the browser can display, scrollbars will be included in the display.

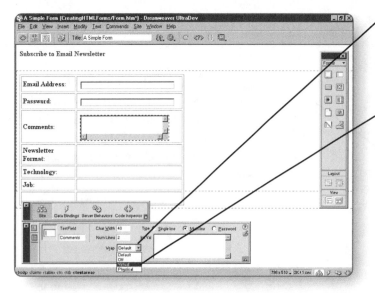

7. Click the down arrow on the Wrap drop-down list. A list of wrapping options will be displayed.

8. Click on Virtual. This will wrap text automatically as the user types. The user will not have to press Enter to go to a new line.

Inserting Radio Buttons

Radio buttons provide the user with a set of options from which only one option can be selected. Radio buttons must be grouped, and only one button in a group can be selected at a time. Selecting another option will deselect the previously selected option. The minimum number of radio buttons that you can place in a group is two.

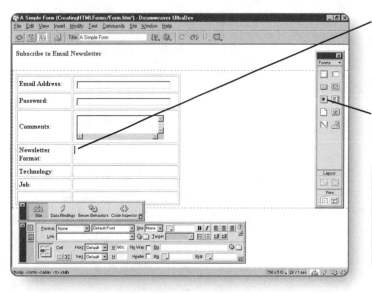

1. Click inside the table cell where you would like to insert the group of options. The cursor will appear where you click.

2. Click on the Radio button. A radio button will be inserted.

NOTE
Radio buttons are also commonly known as option buttons.

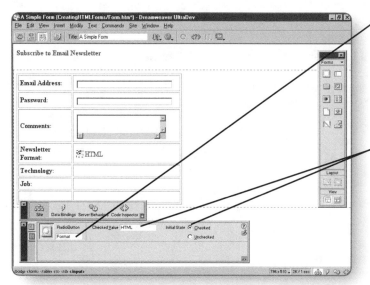

3. Type a name for the button. The name will be used to define a group of radio buttons. All other radio buttons added to the group must have the same name.

4. Click in the Checked Value text box and enter a value for the radio button. The value attribute of a radio button represents that data that will be posted if the user selects this option. Each radio button in a group must have a unique value.

5. Repeat steps 2-4 for each radio button you would like to add to the group. Remember that all radio buttons in the same group must share the same name.

TIP

Click on the Checked option box if you would like an option to be selected by default when the Web page loads.

Inserting Check Boxes

Check boxes allow users to enter True/False or Yes/No answers in a form.

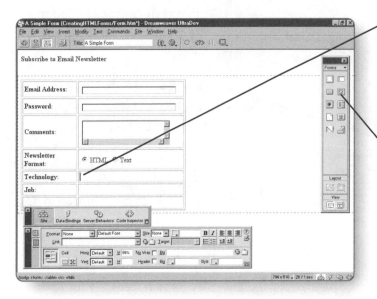

1. Click inside the table cell where you want to insert a group of check boxes. The cursor will appear where you click.

2. Click on the Check Box button. A check box will be inserted.

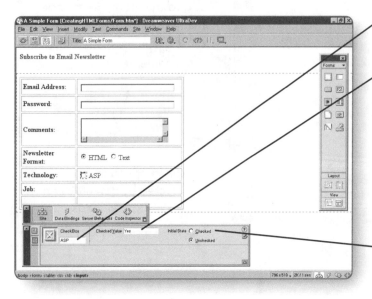

3. Type a name for the check box.

4. Type a value for the check box. The value contains the data that will be posted to the server when the form is submitted if the user has checked the check box.

NOTE

Click on the Checked option box if you want a check box to be selected by default when the Web page loads.

Inserting Drop-Down Lists

Drop-down lists should be used when several options are available but you only want the user to be able to select one of them. Drop-down lists preserve valuable screen space compared to radio button groups.

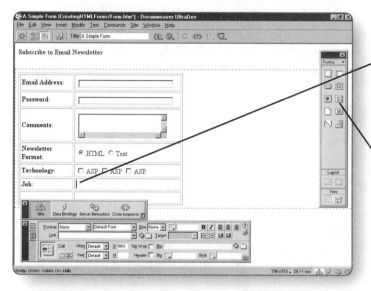

1. Click inside the table cell where you want to insert a drop-down box. The cursor will appear where you click.

2. Click on the List/Menu button. A drop-down list will be inserted.

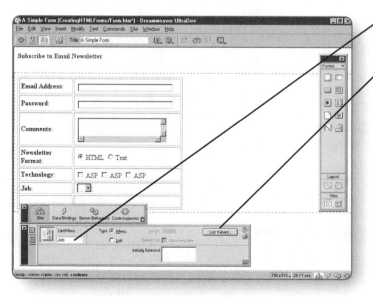

3. Type a name for the drop-down list.

4. Click on the List Values button. The List Values dialog box will open.

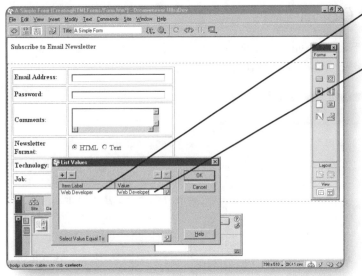

5. Type the name of the option into the Item Label column.

6. Type the value of the option into the Value Column.

7. Click on the + button to add new options to the drop-down list. A new row will be inserted for you to enter the names and values of new options.

8. Repeat this process for each option you add.

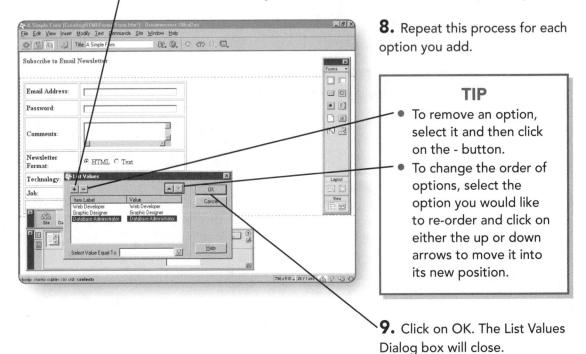

TIP

- To remove an option, select it and then click on the - button.
- To change the order of options, select the option you would like to re-order and click on either the up or down arrows to move it into its new position.

9. Click on OK. The List Values Dialog box will close.

Inserting List Menus

List menus should be used when a large number of options are available to the user and more than one can be selected. Unlike drop-down lists, list menus can be scrolled and can display multiple items at a time.

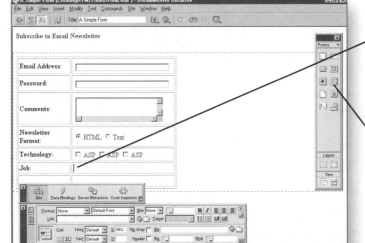

1. Click inside the table cell where you want to insert a list menu. The cursor will appear where you click.

2. Click the List/Menu button. A drop-down list will be inserted.

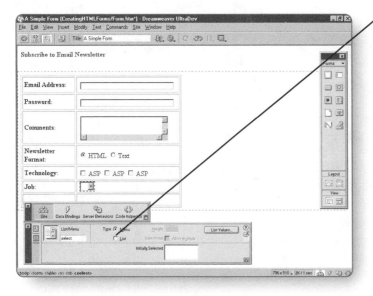

3. Click on List to change the drop-down box to a list. The Height and Selection fields are enabled.

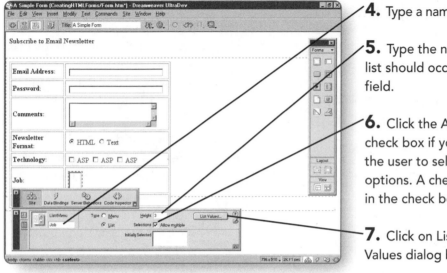

4. Type a name for the list menu.

5. Type the number of lines the list should occupy in the Height field.

6. Click the Allow Multiple check box if you want to allow the user to select multiple options. A check will be placed in the check box.

7. Click on List Values. The List Values dialog box will open.

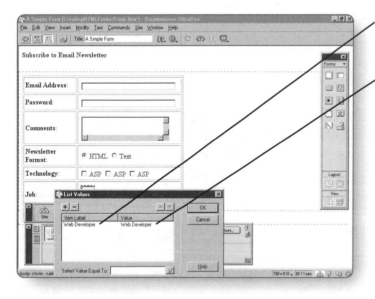

8. Type the name of the option in the Item Label column.

9. Type the value of the option in the Value column.

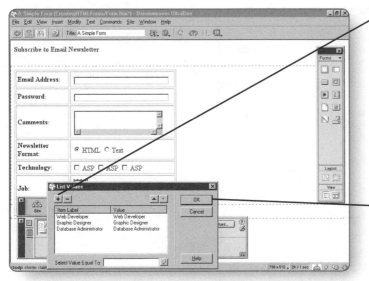

10. Click on the + button to add new options to the list menu. A new row will be inserted for you to enter the names and values of new options.

11. Repeat this process for each option you want to add.

12. Click on OK. The List Values dialog box will close.

Inserting Hidden Form Fields

Hidden fields are used to store data within a form that can't be viewed or edited by a user. They provide a way to send additional information to the server for processing. Hidden fields are not displayed and will not affect the layout of your form.

1. Click anywhere within the Form. The cursor will appear where you click.

2. Click on the Hidden Field button. A Hidden Field icon will be inserted in the document.

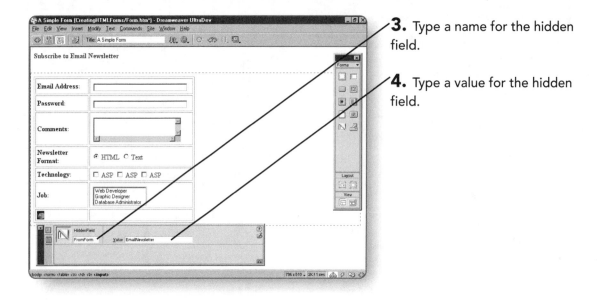

3. Type a name for the hidden field.

4. Type a value for the hidden field.

Submitting a Form

Submitting a form involves transferring all of the data entered by a user to a server where it will be retrieved and processed. Before a form can be submitted, you need to set the Action and Method attributes of the form. The Method attribute defines how the data is sent, while the Action attribute tells the browser where to send the form data.

1. Click on the Form border (a dashed red line). The entire contents of the form will be highlighted.

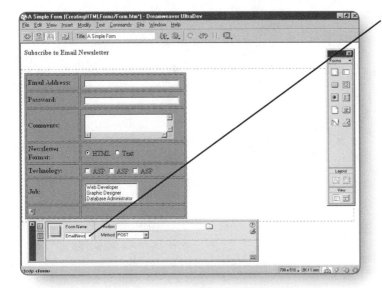

2. Type a name for the form.

3. Click the down arrow of the Method drop-down list. A list of options will appear.

4a. Click on Post. The Post method will be selected.

OR

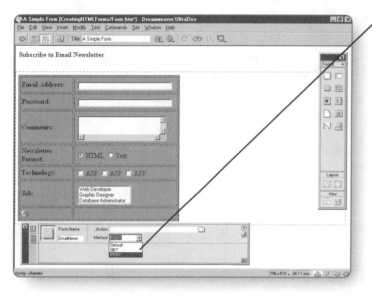

4b. Click on Get. The Get method will be selected.

- The Get method tells the browser to append all of the submitted form data to the URL. The appended data is known as the QueryString. The Get method is restricted by the maximum amount of characters allowed for a Web address. This varies form server to server. Your data will be truncated if it exceeds this limit. You will also be able to see the contents of the form in the address field of your browser. For example: http://www.yoursite.com/sample.asp?formfield1=value1&formfield2=value2

- The Post method sends all of the form data in the body of the HTTP Post command. You will not be able to read the posted data in the URL. There is no limit on the amount of data that can be transferred. This should be your preferred method for submitting form data.

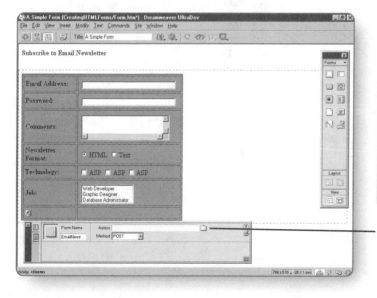

NOTE

The method you select will affect the way you retrieve the posted information on the server. Both methods are covered in Chapter 6, "Validating and Retrieving Form Data."

5. Click on the Folder icon. The File dialog box will open.

6. Click on the file that will process the form. Any simple Web page will do at the moment.

7. Click on OK. The file name will be entered into the Action field.

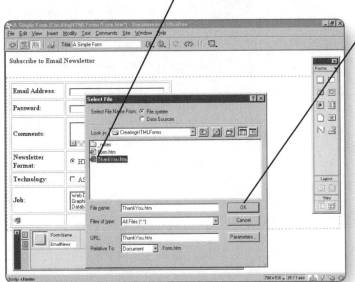

NOTE

The Action attribute tells the browser where to send the form data. This is usually a Web page that can process the form data. You will learn to create such a file in the next chapter.

Using a Button to Submit a Form

A Submit button, once pressed, will collect all of the information and send it to the server.

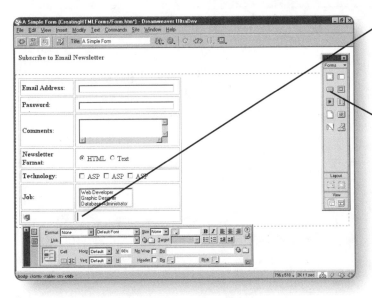

1. Click inside a table cell where you would like to insert a Submit button. The cursor will appear where you click.

2. Click on Insert button. A Submit button will be inserted. The button will have a default name and label.

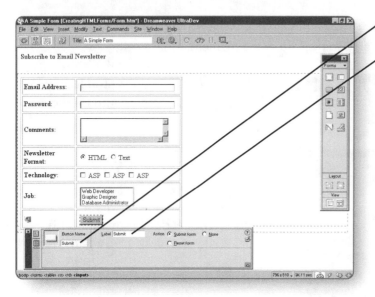

3. Type a name for the button.

4. Type a label for the button. This will appear when the button is displayed in a Web browser. The label must describe the purpose of the button, which in this case is to send the information entered to the server.

Using an Image to Submit a Form

Sometimes an ordinary grey button may not conform to the rest of your Web page design. Luckily, an image can also be used to submit form data.

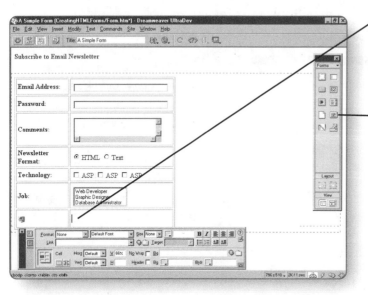

1. Click inside the table where you want to insert an image. The cursor will appear where you click.

2. Click on the Image Field button. A Select Image Source dialog box will open.

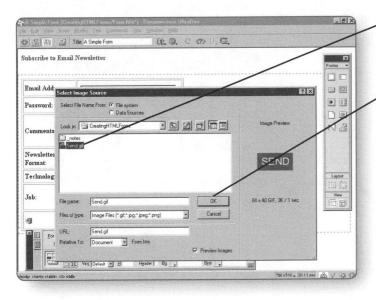

3. Click on the image you want to use to submit the form. The file name will be highlighted.

4. Click on OK. The image is inserted.

Resetting a Form

Resetting a form clears all the data that has been entered by a user and returns the form to its default settings.

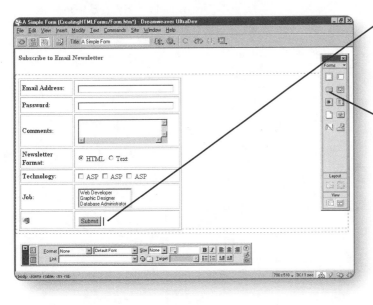

1. Click inside the table cell where you want to insert a Reset button. The cursor will appear where you click.

2. Click on Insert button. A Submit button will be inserted.

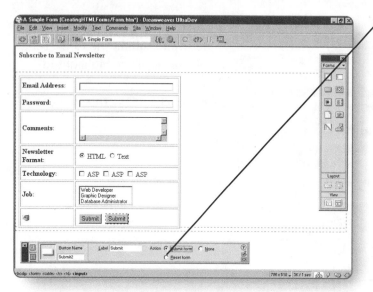

3. Click on Reset Form. The option will be selected. The label will be changed to Reset.

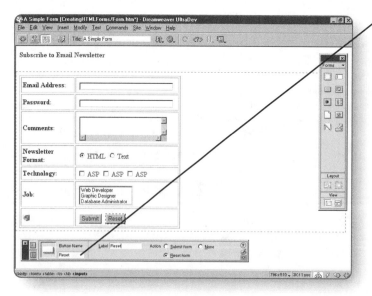

4. Type a name for the Reset button. When the user clicks this button, any data in his or her form will be cleared from the screen.

6

Validating and Retrieving Form Data

To create a powerful Web site, you need to be able to process and respond to data sent by users. The first step in this process involves retrieving the data. It is also useful to verify that the information entered by the users is in the correct format before it gets processed. This will prevent errors from occurring. In this chapter, you'll learn to:

- Validate form data
- Retrieve form data posted using the Get method
- Retrieve form data posted using the Post method
- Retrieve server/environment

Validating Form Data

Before you process data, you must make sure that data has been entered and is in the correct format. This process is known as form validation and can be performed before the information is submitted to the server. We will use a behavior to insert JavaScript code to validate the data from the form before it is submitted. JavaScript is a scripting language that runs within a Web browser on the client's machine. This is known as client-side scripting (as opposed to server-side scripting, which runs on the server). You can also perform validation on the server, but using a client-side behavior is faster and more efficient.

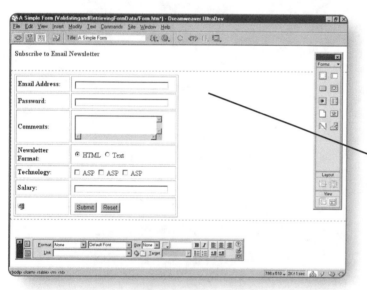

1. Open the Web page that contains a form you wish to validate. All the form fields must be named. The previous chapter covered the basics of creating a form in UltraDev. Please refer to Chapter 5, "Creating HTML Forms," if you are not familiar with creating a form.

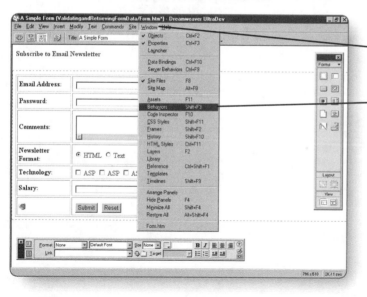

2. Click on Window. The Window menu will appear.

3. Click on Behaviors. The Behaviors floating palette will open.

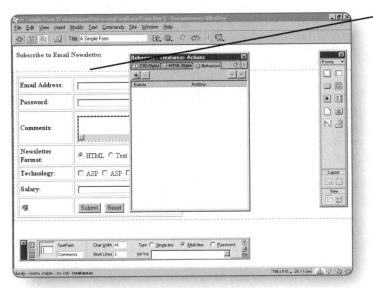

4. Click on the form border, a dashed red line. The form will be highlighted.

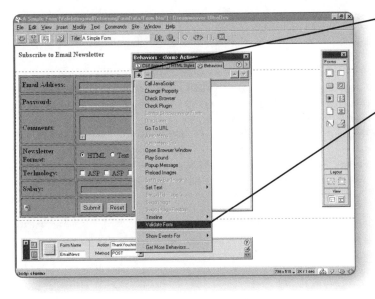

5. Click on the + sign. A submenu containing available client-side behaviors is displayed.

6. Click on Validate Form. The Validate Form dialog box will open. A list of all named form element fields will be displayed in the Named Fields list.

NOTE

The Validate Form Behavior only allows you to verify the data entered into text fields.

7. Click on the name of a form object you want to make mandatory. Users must enter a value in the field before the form is submitted to the server for processing.

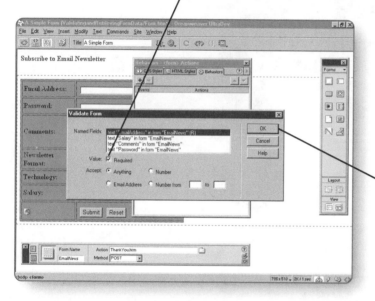

8. Click inside the Required check box. A check will be placed inside the check box. (R) will appear next to the form object name. This indicates that the form will not be submitted if the field is left blank.

9. Click on OK. The Validate Form dialog box will close.

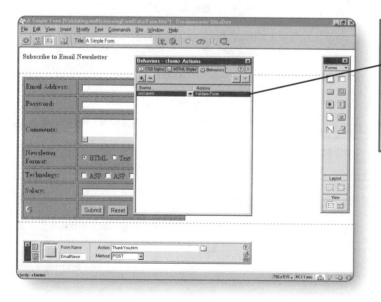

NOTE

The Validate Form action has been added to the OnSubmit form event. UltraDev does all of this automatically.

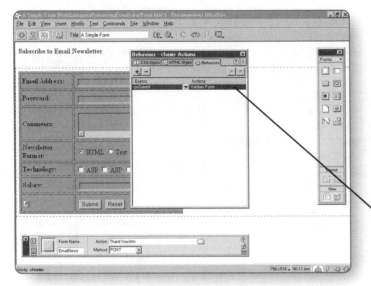

Validating Numeric Data

Sometimes you require only numeric data in a field. To prevent the user from entering other data, you need to make sure that the field can only contain numbers.

1. Double-click on the Validate Form Action in the Behaviors floating palette. The Validate Form dialog box opens.

2. Click on the name of the field that must contain numeric data. The field name is highlighted.

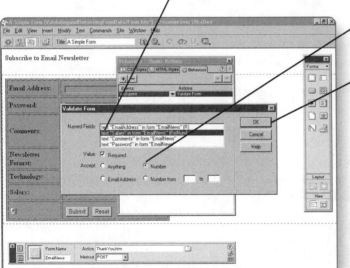

3. Click on the Number option button. The option is selected.

4. Click on OK. The field is set to receive only numeric data from users.

Validating E-mail Addresses

A valid e-mail address must contain the @ sign and no invalid characters (such as /:,;'). Users might accidentally include a space or colon when typing their e-mail addresses. You should validate e-mail addresses if you don't want to encounter any problems when sending messages back to the users.

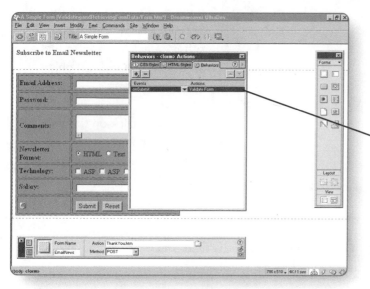

1. Double-click on the Validate Form Action in the Behaviors floating palette. The Validate Form dialog box opens.

2. Click on the name of the field that must contain an e-mail address. The field name will be highlighted.

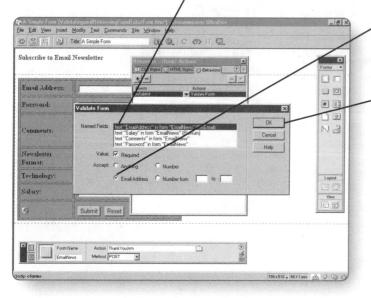

3. Click on the E-mail Address option button. The option will be selected.

4. Click on OK. The field is set to receive only an e-mail address entry from users.

Retrieving Form Data

Once data is posted to a server, it must be retrieved and processed. This is achieved by using a server-side script that is embedded within the Web page. The Web page that will process the information must be specified in the Action attribute of the form. UltraDev takes care of the scripting; all you have to do is tell it which form elements to retrieve. The process of retrieving data sent using the Post method is slightly different from retrieving data sent with the Get method. Both methods are explained below.

Retrieving Form Data Submitted with the Get Method

When a form is submitted using the Get method, the form data is appended to the URL of the file requested in the form action. A question mark (?) is inserted between the file name and the form data. The form data tagged onto the URL is known as a QueryString. The Get method appends data in name-pair values; i.e., each field is paired with the value that the user has entered. The Get method may truncate the data if it exceeds a certain limit, which varies from server to server. The Get method also encodes certain characters (&, +, and $) that are used to define a QueryString. URL encoding involves converting the character to ASCII and preceding it with a % symbol. The Request Variable behavior is used to retrieve data posted with the Get method.

1. Create a new Web page with an .asp extension. This Web page will process form data.

CAUTION

Don't use the Get method when you want your users to enter private information—it can be viewed in the address field of the Web browser.

Use the Get method when you want to allow users to bookmark the Web page. Data in the QueryString is also saved when a URL is bookmarked.

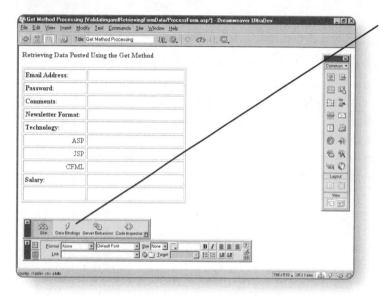

2. Click on the Data Bindings icon. The Data Bindings Inspector will open.

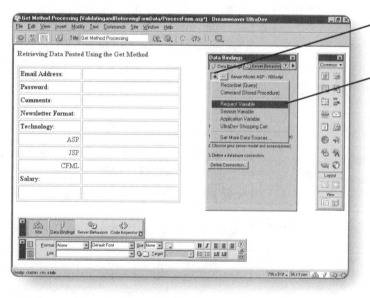

3. Click on the + button. A submenu will appear.

4. Click on Request Variable. The Request Variable dialog box will appear.

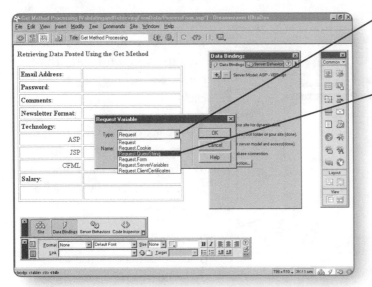

5. Click on the down arrow of the Type drop-down box. A list of request types will appear.

6. Click on Request.QueryString. The option will be selected.

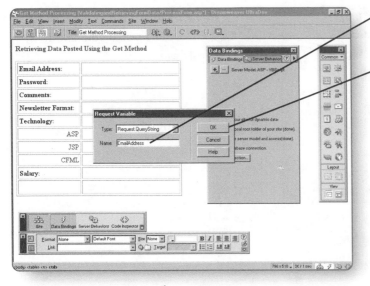

7. Type the name of the form object into the Name field.

8. Click on OK. The retrieved form element will be displayed in the Data Bindings palette. The form element name will be preceded by "QueryString."

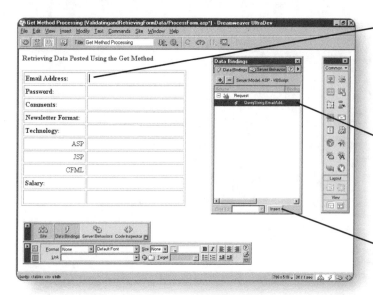

9. Click inside your document where you would like to insert the retrieved form data. The cursor will appear where you click.

10. Click on the form field whose contents you would like to retrieve in the Data Bindings palette. The form field will be highlighted.

11. Click on Insert. The field placeholder is inserted as dynamic text.

12. Repeat steps 3-11 for each field value you would like to retrieve.

Retrieving Form Data Submitted with the Post Method

The Post method allows unlimited amounts of data to be transferred to the server without appending anything onto the URL. The Post method is much more secure because the posted form data is not displayed. You should also use the Post method when you don't want users bookmarking or returning directly to the processing Web page.

1. Create a new Web page with an .asp extension. This Web page will process form data.

2. Click on the Data Bindings icon. The Data Bindings Inspector will open.

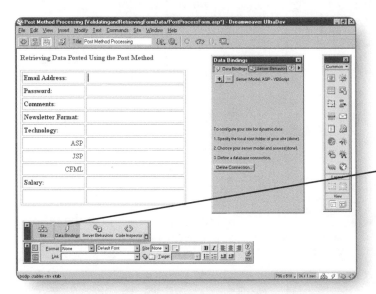

3. Click on the + button. A submenu will appear.

4. Click on Request Variable. The Request Variable dialog box will appear.

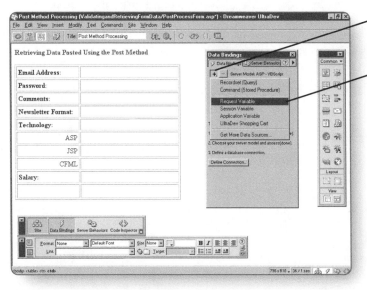

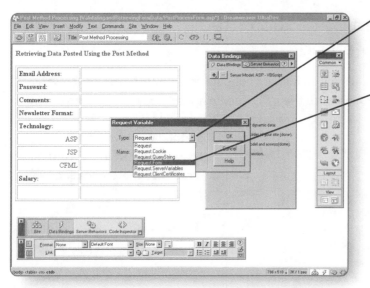

5. Click on the down arrow of the Type drop-down box. A list of request types will appear.

6. Click on Request.Form. The Request Variables dialog box will open.

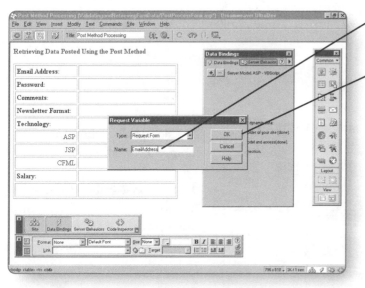

7. Type the name of the form field into the Name field.

8. Click on OK. The Retrieved form field will be displayed on the Data Bindings palette.

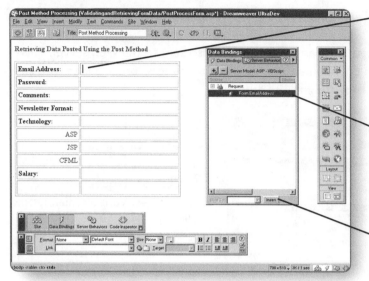

9. Click inside your document where you would like to insert the retrieved form data. The cursor will appear where you click.

10. Click on the form field whose contents you would like to retrieve in the Data Bindings palette. The form field will be highlighted.

11. Click on Insert. The field placeholder is inserted as dynamic text.

12. Repeat steps 3-11 for each field value you would like to retrieve.

Retrieving Environment/Server Variables

When a form is submitted, data about the user is also sent to the Web server. This data is referred to as an Environment/Server Variable. Among other things, you can retrieve the user's Web browser and IP address.

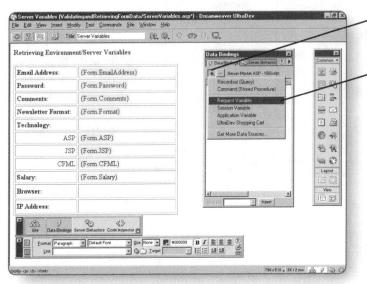

1. Click on the + button. A submenu will appear.

2. Click on Request Variable. The Request Variable dialog box will open.

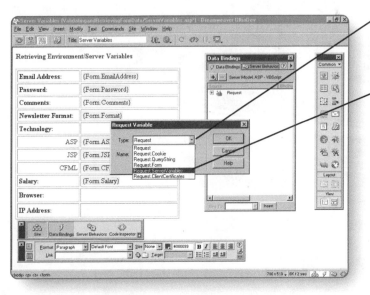

3. Click on the down arrow of the Type drop down box. A list of request types will appear.

4. Click on Request.ServerVariables. The Request Variables dialog box will open.

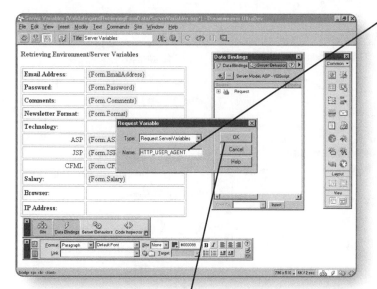

5. Type the name of the Server Variable into the Name field.

Environment Variables include:

TABLE 6.1 Environment Variables

Description	Variable Name
Virtual Path of Script	SCRIPT_NAME
Length of Posted Content	CONTENT_LENGTH
Browser Name	HTTP_USER_AGENT
Referring Web Page Address	HTTP_REFERER
Client's IP Address	REMOTE_ADDR
QueryString	QUERY_STRING

6. Click on OK. The Retrieved Environment Variable will be displayed in the Data Bindings palette.

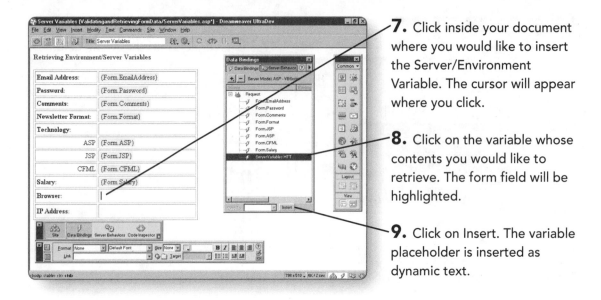

7. Click inside your document where you would like to insert the Server/Environment Variable. The cursor will appear where you click.

8. Click on the variable whose contents you would like to retrieve. The form field will be highlighted.

9. Click on Insert. The variable placeholder is inserted as dynamic text.

10. Repeat steps 1-9 for each variable you would like to retrieve.

NOTE

All you have done thus far is retrieve the form data and display it on a Web page. In later chapters, you will learn to:

- Insert, update, and delete the data in a database (Chapter 13, "Inserting, Updating, and Deleting Records")
- Manipulate the data using string and mathematical functions (Chapter 15, "Writing Your Own ASP Code")
- Send the data as an e-mail message (Chapter 17, "Sending E-mail Messages")
- Store data in cookies and as session variables (Chapter 18, "Maintaining State")
- Save the data to a file (Chapter 19, "Working with Files and Folders")

7

Designing
a Database

You have probably figured out by now that you first need a database before you can create a dynamic database-driven Web site. UltraDev has revolutionized the manner in which database-enabled Web sites are built. The process is much simpler and you don't need to write a line of code unless you require complex functionality. The irony, though, is that you still need to know how to design a relational database. Relational databases are not very complex. You only need to know some basic background theory and you'll be on your way. In this chapter, you'll learn:

- About relational databases
- To create a Microsoft Access database
- To create a System DSN (Data Source Name) for your database

Understanding Relational Databases

RDMS (Relational Databases Management Systems) store data in tables. A database table is not much different from a table in Word or a spreadsheet in Excel. A table is made up of columns and rows.

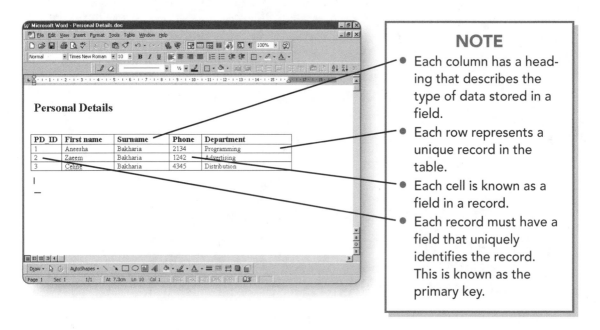

NOTE

- Each column has a heading that describes the type of data stored in a field.
- Each row represents a unique record in the table.
- Each cell is known as a field in a record.
- Each record must have a field that uniquely identifies the record. This is known as the primary key.

At this stage, you're probably wondering why you need a database to store data when you can already use both Word and Excel. The answer is simple: Word and Excel are not capable of handling large amounts of data in an efficient manner. A relational database, on the other hand, is designed to store and manage large amounts of information. A relational database has powerful query capabilities and the ability to extract meaningful information. Relational databases are also flexible and easy to maintain.

A relational database comprises one or more tables. Each table must contain unique data that is not duplicated in another table. This ensures that you only need to search and update data in one place. Tables are linked. The link between two tables is known as a relationship. A relationship is established by linking common fields from both tables.

Designing Database Tables and Relationships

After you have determined the purpose of your database, you need to determine what tables are required. Each table should contain information about one subject, and no two tables should contain duplicate information. I can't stress this point enough. It is key to creating a database that can be maintained easily and does not contain duplicate data. There should only be one place to update data.

Each table should be normalized. Data normalization simply means that you are optimizing the storage of data in tables. Normalization will help you to eliminate duplication and store data in an efficient way. Here are some guidelines:

- A field can't contain multiple values. Each field can only contain a single value. You should also avoid repeating columns of similar data stored in a table.

- Every field that makes up a record in a table must be dependent upon the primary key. All fields that are not dependent upon the primary key should be stored in another table.

- A field that is not a primary key should not be linked to another field that is also not a primary key.

When you design required tables, you need to determine:

- The type of data that each field in a table will store. A field could store numeric, text, or date information.

- Which field to use as the primary key in each table. The primary key must be unique for each record.

- How tables will be related in your database. You can store another table's primary key to identify the linked record stored in another table. This is known as a foreign key.

Creating a Microsoft Access Database

Microsoft Access is a relational database that is very easy to learn. If you have never created a database before, this section is just for you. You'll learn to create

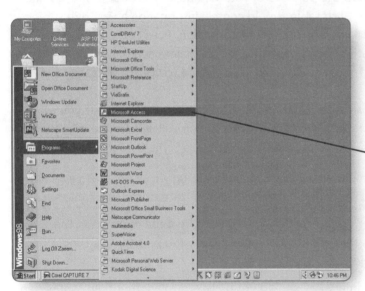

and relate tables in Access. As you become comfortable with designing databases and relational theory, you should consider scaling up to a client/server database like Microsoft SQL Server.

1. Open Microsoft Access from the Start menu. Access is part of Microsoft Office but can also be purchased separately. Chances are that Access will already be installed on your computer.

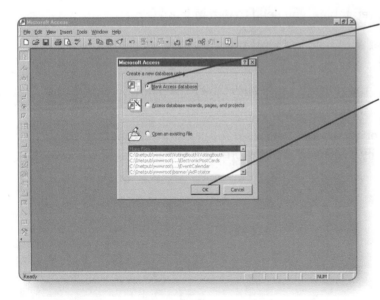

2. Click on the Blank Database option button. The option will be selected.

3. Click on OK. The File New dialog box will open.

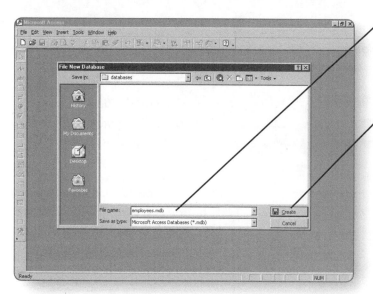

4. Enter the database name into the File name field. The file name must have an .mdb extension.

5. Click on Create. The database will be created.

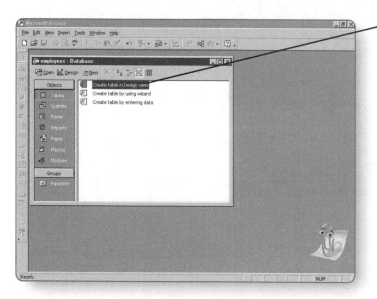

6. Click on Create tables in Design View. The Table Design View window will open.

7. Type in a field name in the Field Name column. The first field is usually the primary key. Don't include spaces, periods, exclamation marks, or square brackets in field names. Use an underscore to replace spaces.

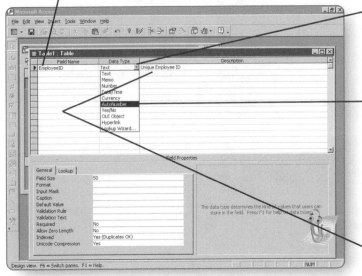

8. Click on the down arrow of the Data Type column. All the types of data that Access can store are displayed.

9. Click on Autonumber. The option is selected. Autonumber is a sequential number that is automatically inserted when a new record is added to a table. This is ideal for creating a primary key.

10. Type in a description for the field. This will help you when you return to modify the database.

11. Click on the Field Selection button. The field will be selected.

12. Click on the Primary Key button in the toolbar. The selected field will be converted to a primary key.

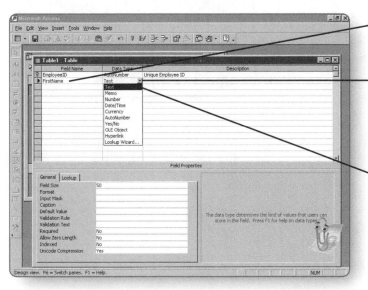

13. Type in a field name in the Field Name column.

14. Click on the down arrow of the Data Type column. All the types of data that Access can store are displayed.

15. Click the appropriate data type. The data type will be selected.

NOTE

The Hyperlink and the Ole Data Types are not utilized in Web-enabled databases.

NOTE

The following data types are available:

- Text. A text field can hold up to 255 alphanumeric characters.
- Memo. A memo field can store about 64,000 alphanumeric characters.
- Number. A number field stores numeric data that can be included in calculations.
- Date/Time. A date/time field stores date- and time-formatted data.
- Currency. A currency field stores data with a currency sign, but allows you to perform calculations.
- Yes/No. A yes/no field stores logical values (true/false, yes/no, 1/0).

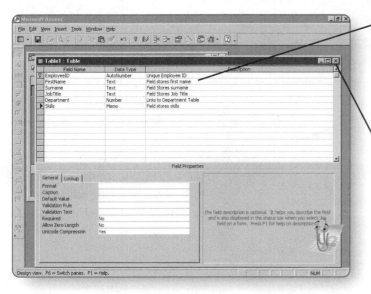

16. Type in a description for the field.

17. Repeat steps 13-16 for each field in the table.

18. Click on the Close icon. The Save As dialog box will open.

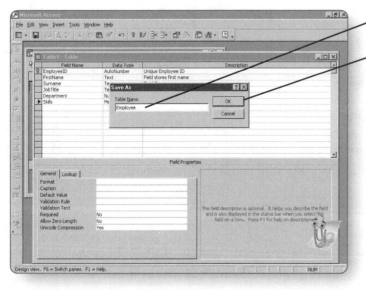

19. Type in the table name.

20. Click on OK. The table will be saved.

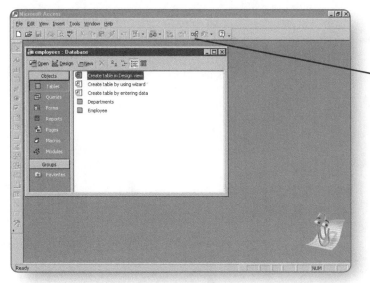

21. Repeat steps 6-20 for each table in your database.

22. Click on the Relationships button in the toolbar. The Show Table dialog box will open.

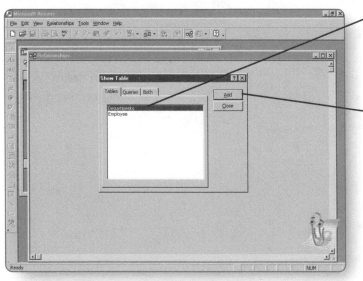

23. Ctrl+click on the tables you would like to relate to each other. The tables will be selected.

24. Click on Add. The tables will be added to the Relationships window.

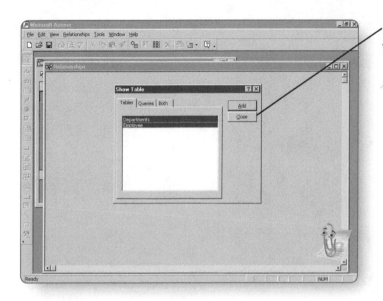

25. Click on Close. The Show Table dialog box will close.

26. Click on the field that you would like to link to another table.

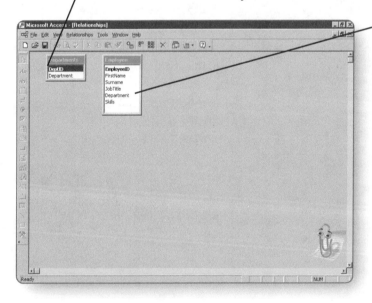

27. Drag the field that you want to relate from one table to the related field in the other table. The Relationships dialog box will open.

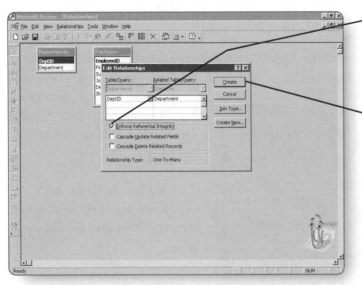

28. Click inside the Enforce Referential Integrity check box. A check (✔) will be placed in the box.

29. Click on Create. A one-to-many relationship will be created. This means that each record links to many related records in the linked table. You can also use one-to-one and many-to-many relationships.

NOTE

The connection between the tables will be displayed in the Relationships window.

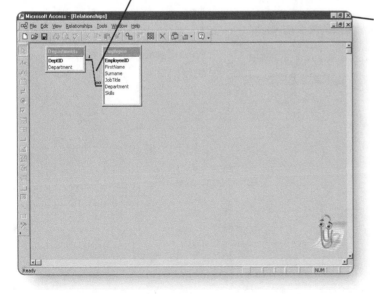

30. Click on the Close icon. Access will close.

Creating a System DSN

A System DSN (Data Source Name) is a shortcut to your database. It contains the path to your database, the driver, user name, and password required to access your

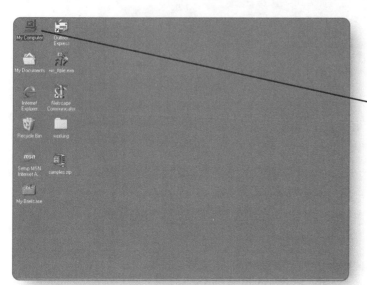

database. When your database is Web-enabled in UltraDev, all you need to do is specify the DSN name.

1. Double-click on the My Computer icon on your desktop. Your My Computer window will open.

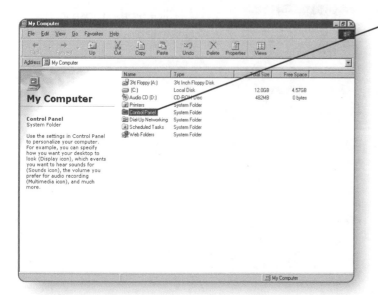

2. Double-click on the Control Panel folder or icon. The contents will be displayed.

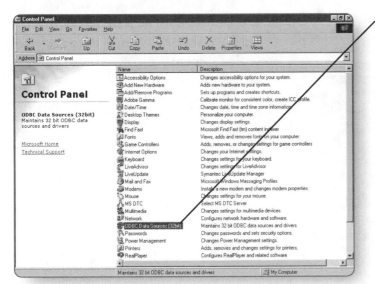

3. Double-click on ODBC Data Sources (32bit). The ODBC Database Administrator dialog box will open.

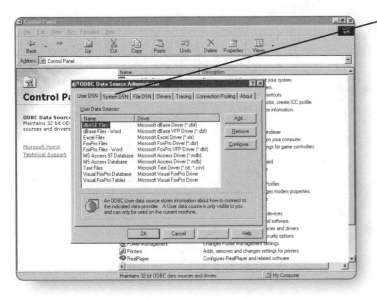

4. Click on the System DSN tab. The system DSN page will come to the front.

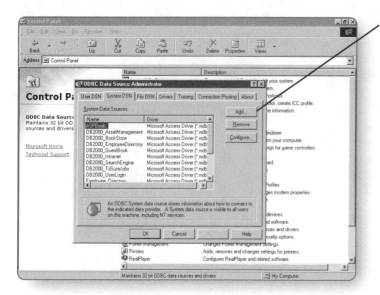

5. Click on Add. The Create New Data Source dialog box will open.

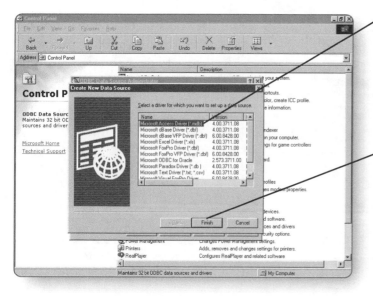

6. Click on the driver that matches your database. If you created an Access database, then click on Microsoft Access Driver (*.mdb). The option will be selected.

7. Click on Finish. The ODBC Microsoft Access Setup dialog box will open.

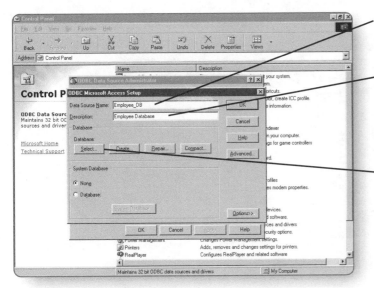

8. Type the DSN name into the Data Source Name field.

9. Type in a description for the DSN. This should be a description of what the database stores.

10. Click on Select. The Select Database dialog box will be displayed.

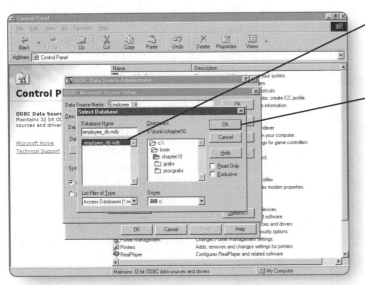

11. Click on the database file. The file name will be highlighted.

12. Click on OK. The Select Database dialog box will close.

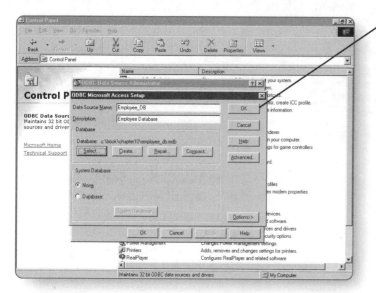

13. Click on OK. The ODBC Microsoft Access Setup dialog box will close.

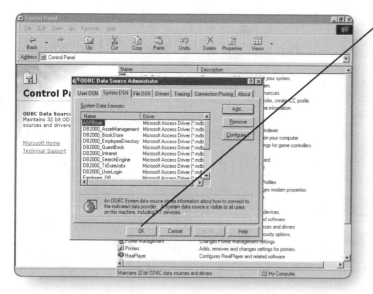

14. Click on OK. The ODBC Database Administrator dialog box will close.

NOTE

That's all that is required to create a System DSN. You will need to create a System DSN for each database that will be Web-enabled.

8

Retrieving Data from a Database

You are now ready to create your first dynamic, database-driven Web site. This used to be a tedious process before UltraDev came to the rescue. You can now bind data to a Web page in a totally visual environment. In this chapter, you'll learn to:

- Define a database connection
- Create recordsets
- Bind data to a Web page
- Use the Live Data window
- Create simple database queries

Defining a Database Connection

When you create a database connection, you have to specify the DSN (Data Source Name) of the database and the type of connection required. UltraDev allows you to set up separate connections for your run-time and design-time environments. This means that you can easily publish your dynamic Web site without having to change the connection settings manually.

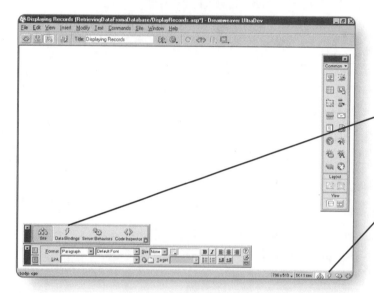

If you're using ASP as a server-side technology, you must create an ADO (ActiveX Data Objects) connection.

1a. Click on the Data Bindings icon on the Launcher. The Data Bindings palette will open.

OR

1b. Click on the Data Bindings icon on the Mini-Launcher at the bottom of the Document window. The Data Bindings palette will open.

2. Click on Define Connection. The Define Connection dialog box will open. The Connections for Site dialog box will open.

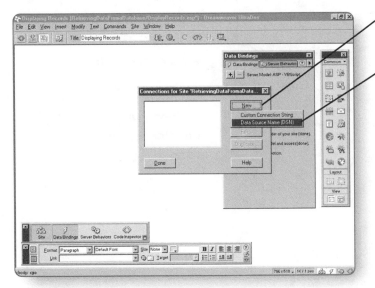

3. Click on New. A submenu will appear.

4. Click on Data Source Name (DSN). The Data Source Name dialog box will open.

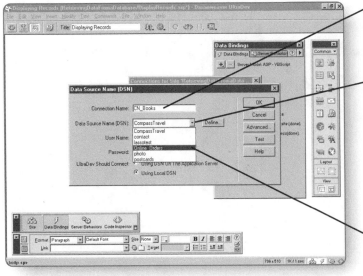

5. Type a name for the database connection into the Name field.

6. Click on the down arrow of the Data Source Name drop-down list. A list of all available system DSNs on your local machine is displayed. Chapter 7, "Designing a Database," covers creating a DSN for a database.

7. Click on a DSN. The option will be selected.

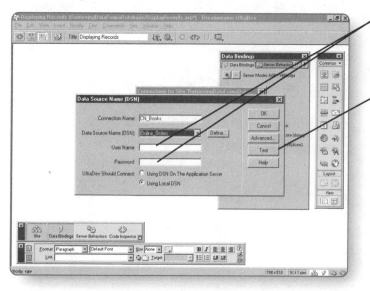

8. Enter the user name and password if the database is password-protected.

9. Click on Test. An information dialog box will confirm whether or not the test has been a success.

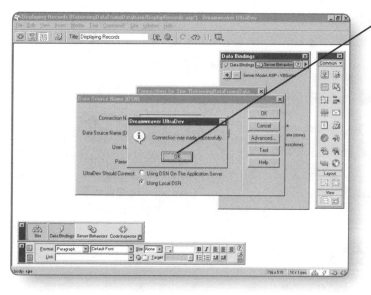

10. Click on OK. The information dialog box will close. The database connection will be set up.

NOTE

Your local DSN settings should mimic the settings on your Application Server. This makes development easier and allows you to test database connectivity comprehensively. It is up to you to make sure that the DSNs have identical settings on both the run-time and design-time environments. UltraDev does, however, allow you to choose which connection it should use.

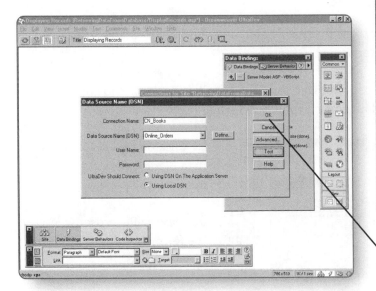

11. Click on OK. The database connection will be created.

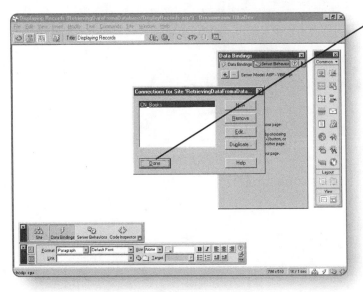

12. Click on Done. The Connections for Site dialog box will close.

Data Binding

Data binding means retrieving data from a database and displaying it on a Web page. A recordset must be created before data can be bound to a Web page.

Creating Recordsets

A recordset contains records that have been retrieved from a database because they match specific criteria.

1. Create a new Web page with an .asp file extension. The Web page must have an .asp extension for data binding to be successful.

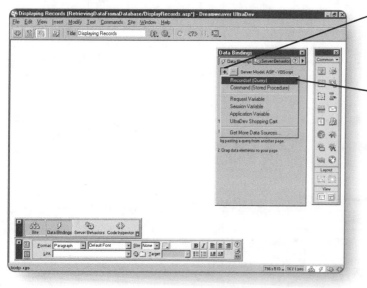

2. Click on the + sign on the Data Bindings palette. A submenu will appear.

3. Click on Recordset(Query). The Recordset dialog box will open.

4. Type a name for the recordset.

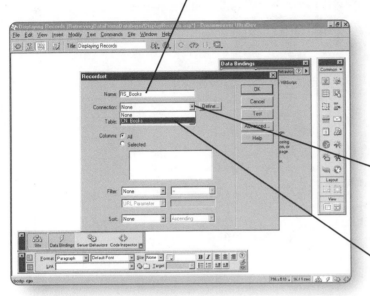

TIP

It is handy to name all recordsets with an Rs prefix. This allows you to identify recordsets easily.

5. Click on the down arrow of the Connection drop-down list. A list of available database connections will appear.

6. Click on a connection. The connection will be selected. All the tables in the database will be loaded.

7. Click on the down arrow of the Table drop-down list. A list of tables in your database is displayed.

8. Click on the name of the table you want to include in the query. The table will be selected.

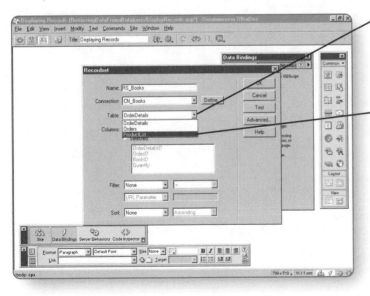

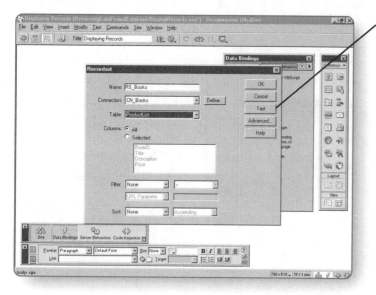

9. Click on Test. The Test SQL Statement dialog box will be displayed.

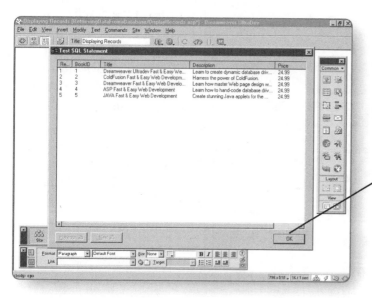

NOTE

The table column names and their contents will be displayed. Each row represents a record retrieved from the database.

10. Click on OK. The Test SQL Statement dialog box will close.

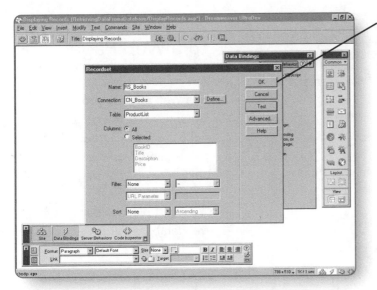

11. Click on OK. The Recordset dialog box will close. A Recordset node will be added to the Data Bindings palette.

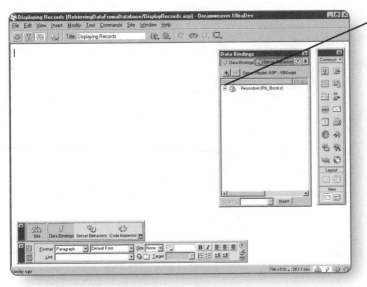

12. Click on the + sign to open the Recordset node. A list of all retrieved fields will be displayed.

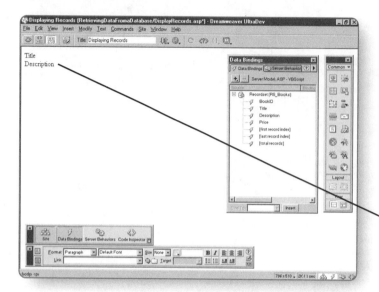

Binding Data to a Web Page

A recordset field can be bound to a Web page to produce dynamic text. You can drag fields from the Data Bindings palette and drop them anywhere on your page.

1. Insert placeholder text for the database fields.

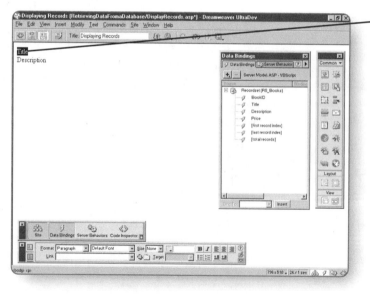

2. Select a placeholder field. The selected text will be highlighted.

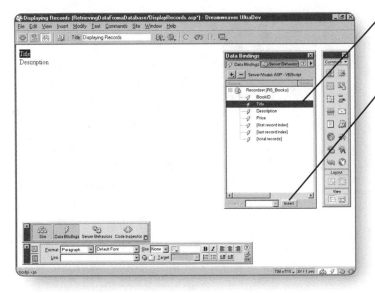

3. Click on the field you want to display. The field will be highlighted.

4. Click on Insert. The placeholder text will be replaced by dynamic text.

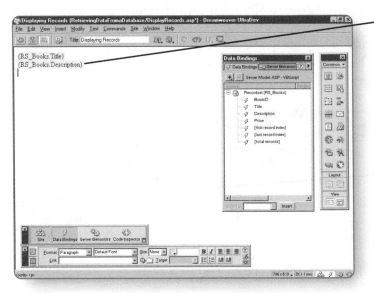

5. Repeat steps 2-4 for each field you want to bind to the Web page.

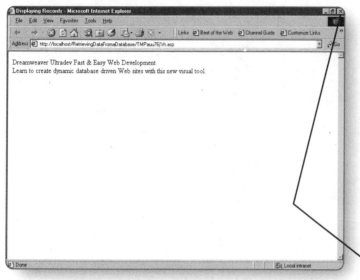

6. Press F12 to preview the Web page in a browser. The Browser will open and load the Web page.

> **NOTE**
>
> Only the first record in the recordset is displayed. You'll use the Repeat Region server behavior to display multiple records.

7. Click on the Close icon. The Web browser will close.

Using the Repeat Region Server Behavior

When data is bound to a Web page only the first record that was returned by the recordset is displayed. The Repeat Region server behavior must be used to specify the number of records that need to be displayed on a page.

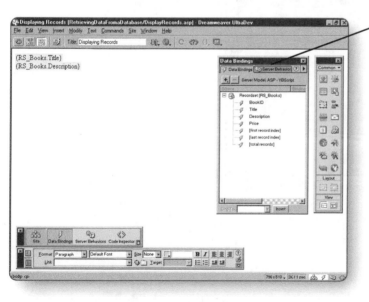

1. Click on the Server Behaviors tab. The Server Behaviors palette will be displayed.

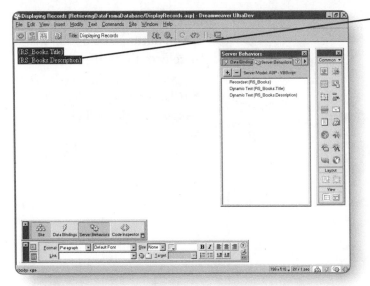

2. Select the region you want to repeat. The selection will be highlighted.

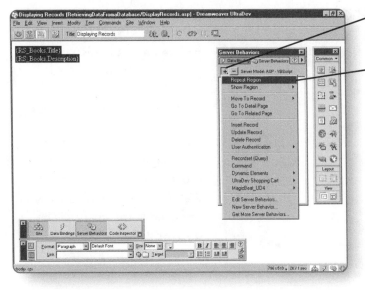

3. Click on the + sign. A submenu will appear.

4. Click on Repeat Region. The Repeat Region dialog box will open.

NOTE

The recordset that is bound to the region will automatically be selected in the Recordset drop-down list.

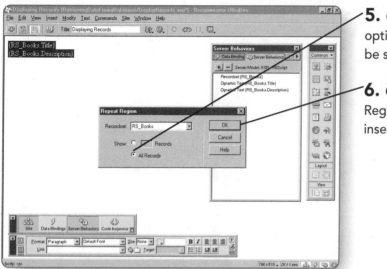

5. Click on the All Records option button. The option will be selected.

6. Click on OK. The Repeat Region behavior will be inserted.

NOTE

The Repeat Region code is enclosed in a tabbed grey outline.

7. Press F12 to preview the Web page in a browser. The browser will open and load the Web page. All the records retrieved in the query will be displayed.

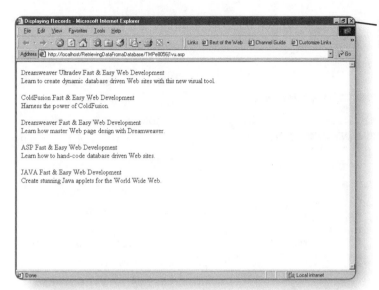

8. Click on the Close icon. The Web browser will close.

Dynamic Data Formatting

You can apply formatting to retrieved data so that it can be displayed in a user-friendly manner. Dynamic Data Formatting can also be used to format numbers, date/time, text, and percentages.

1. Click on the Data Bindings tab. The Data Bindings palette will be displayed.

2. Click on a dynamic text element. A dynamic text element is a database field that has been bound to a Web page. The field name will be selected in the Data Bindings palette.

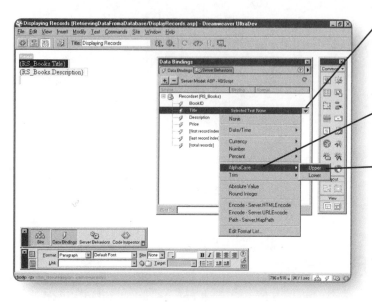

3. Click the down arrow in the Format column. A list of all available formatting options will be displayed.

4. Click on AlphaCase. A submenu will appear.

5. Click on Upper. This option will convert the text to uppercase when it is previewed in a Web browser.

6. Press F12 to preview the Web page in a browser. The Web browser will open and load the Web page.

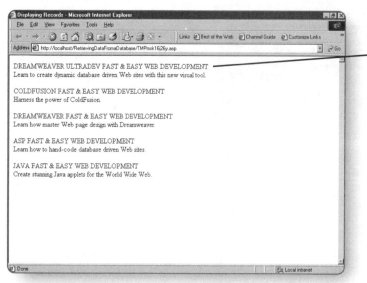

NOTE

The field in which you applied Dynamic Data Formatting is displayed in uppercase for all records.

7. Click on the Close icon. The Web browser will close.

Live Data Preview

There is no need to preview your Web page in a browser each time you need to test your dynamic Web page. You can preview and format data within the UltraDev interface.

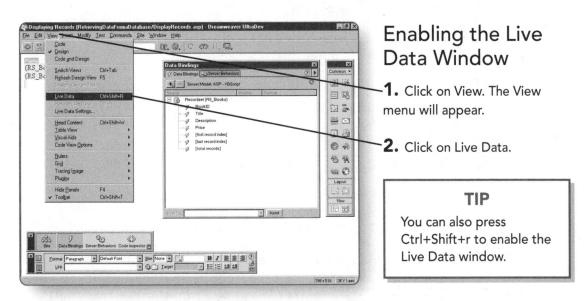

Enabling the Live Data Window

1. Click on View. The View menu will appear.

2. Click on Live Data.

TIP

You can also press Ctrl+Shift+r to enable the Live Data window.

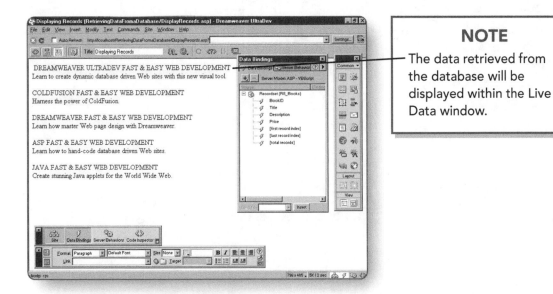

NOTE

The data retrieved from the database will be displayed within the Live Data window.

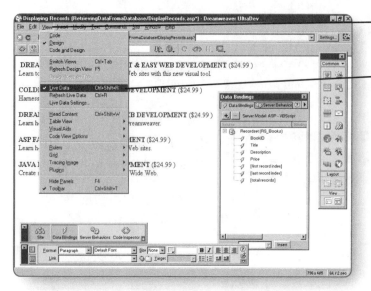

3. Click on View. The View menu will appear.

4. Click on Live Data. The Live Data window will close.

Binding Data in Live Data Window

1. Click on View. The View menu will appear.

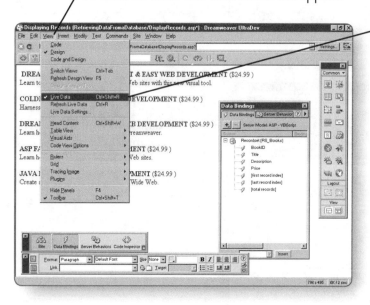

2. Click on Live Data. The Live Data window will be displayed.

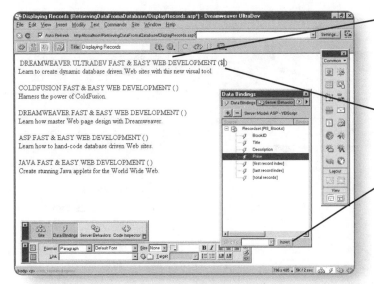

3. Click on the field you would like to insert in the Data Bindings palette. The selection will be highlighted.

4. Click where you would like the field to be inserted. The cursor will appear.

5. Click on Insert. The field will be inserted.

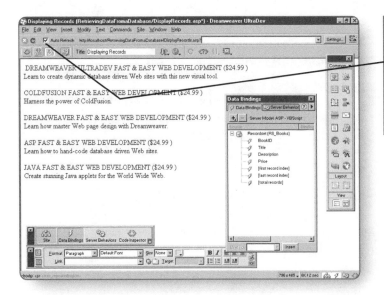

NOTE

The contents of the field will automatically be displayed if the Auto Refresh checkbox is checked.

Applying Formatting in Live Data Preview

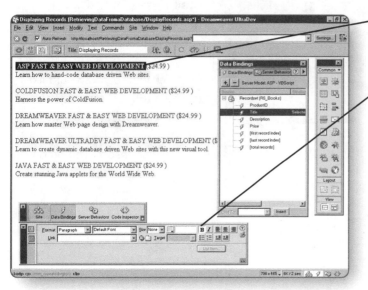

1. Select the text you would like to format. The text will be highlighted.

2. Apply formatting by setting the properties found on the Properties palette. There is no difference between applying formatting in the Document or Live Data windows. Chapter 1, "UltraDev HTML Basics," covers formatting in detail.

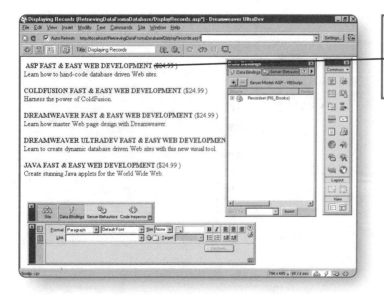

NOTE

The formatting of the selected text will change.

3. Click on View. The View menu will appear.

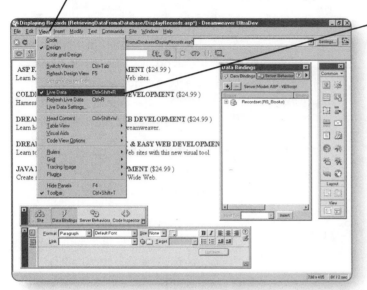

4. Click on Live Data. The Live Data window will close.

Creating Simple Queries

Queries retrieve the records you require from a database. The Recordset dialog box allows you to create simple queries intuitively, without writing a single line of code.

Editing a Recordset

The Recordset dialog box is opened by creating a new Recordset(Query) in the Data Bindings palette. You can edit a recordset at any time.

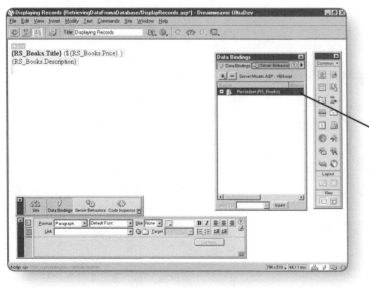

1. Double-click on the Recordset node. The Recordset dialog box will open.

2. Follow the steps in the following sections depending on the type of selection you want to make.

Selecting Table Fields to Be Queried

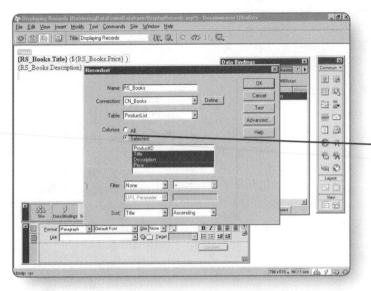

It is wise to include only tables containing data that will be inserted in a Web page when creating a query. This will improve the speed at which your pages are generated.

1. Click on the Selected option button. The list containing the table fields is enabled.

2. Click on a field to select it. (Ctrl+click to select multiple fields.) The selection will be highlighted.

Filtering Data

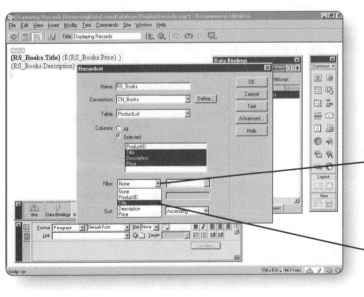

A filter allows you to search for specific field values and can be placed on any field in your database. You can enter the value that the filter must match manually, or retrieve it from a form.

1. Click on the down arrow of the Filter drop-down box. A list of all fields in the table will be displayed.

2. Click on the field you want to filter. The field will be highlighted.

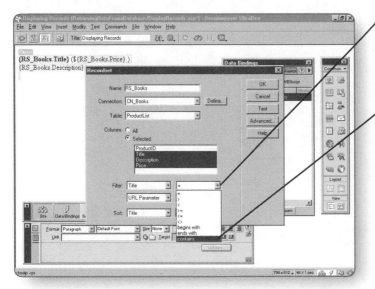

3. Click on the down arrow of the comparison operators. All the comparison operators are displayed.

4. Click on a comparison operator sign. The option is selected.

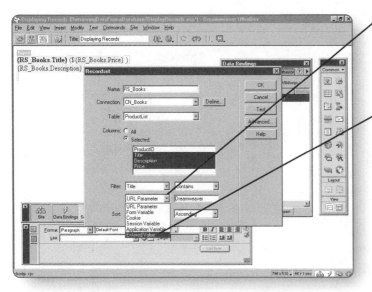

5. Click on the down arrow of the Parameter drop-down list. All the filter options will be displayed.

6. Click on Entered Value. The option will be selected. The Entered value filter option allows you to enter the filter criteria manually. In Chapter 10, "Advanced Database Queries," you will learn to create dynamic queries.

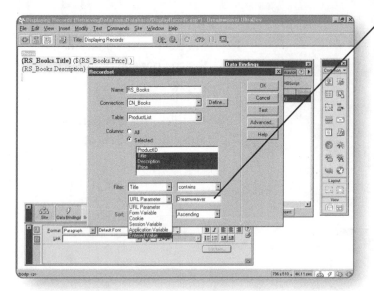

7. Type the value that the field must match. Records that match the filter will be returned in the Recordset.

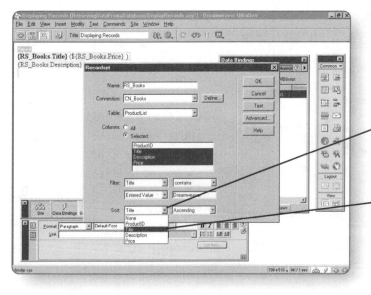

Sorting Data

The records returned in a recordset can be sorted in ascending or descending order.

1. Click on the down arrow of the Sort drop-down list. A list of all table fields will be displayed.

2. Click on the field you would like to use sort records. The field will be highlighted.

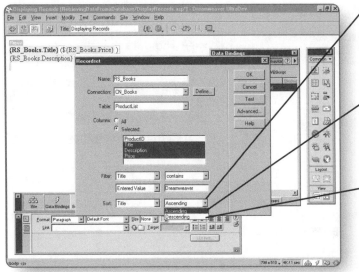

3. Click on the down arrow of the Sort Order drop-down list. Records can be sorted in Ascending or Descending order.

4a. Click on Ascending. The option will be selected.

OR

4b. Click on Descending. The option will be selected.

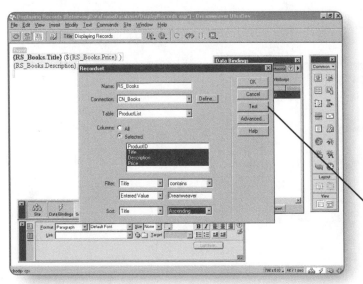

Testing a Query

It is always a good idea to check whether a query can be executed successfully before you bind data to a Web page. The Test SQL Statement window allows you to view the results of a query.

1. Click on Test. The Test SQL Statement dialog box will open.

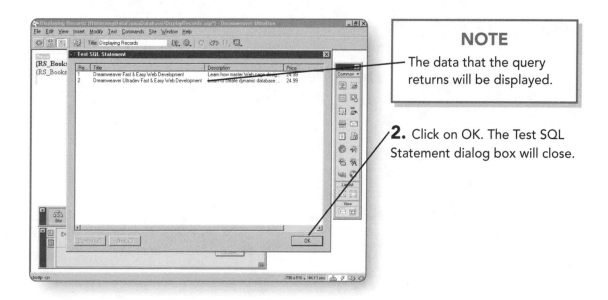

NOTE

The data that the query returns will be displayed.

2. Click on OK. The Test SQL Statement dialog box will close.

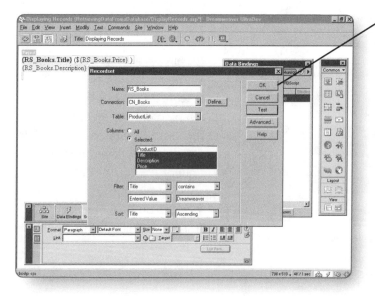

3. Click on OK. The Recordset dialog box will close.

9

Using Live Data Objects

There are common features that most database-driven Web applications require. These include displaying search results, linking to more specific information, inserting new records, and updating existing records in a database. Server behaviors can certainly be used to incorporate this functionality but Live Data Objects can automate the whole process. Live Data Objects are just wizards that insert server behaviors into the current Web page to perform a particular task. You still have control over page layout and the ability to modify the server behaviors. You can now spend more time developing complex solutions. In this chapter you'll learn to:

- Use Live Data Objects
- Insert a record counter
- Insert Recordset Navigation Panel
- Create a master-detail page set
- Insert new records into a database
- Update existing records in a database

Using Live Data Objects

Live Data Objects are wizards that automatically insert server behaviors to perform common database functionality. You can insert Recordset navigation panels, Recordset statistics, and Master/Detail page sets. Forms that insert and update data in a database can also be created.

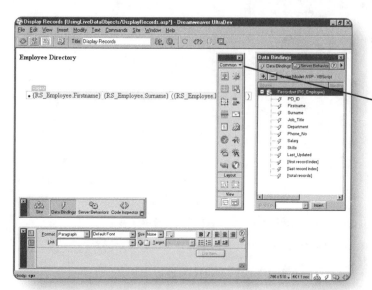

1. Click on the drop-down arrow at the top of the Objects palette. A submenu containing all available panels will be displayed.

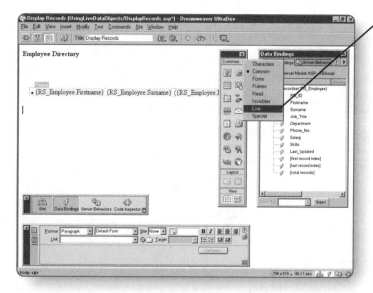

2. Click on Live. The Live Data Object panel will open.

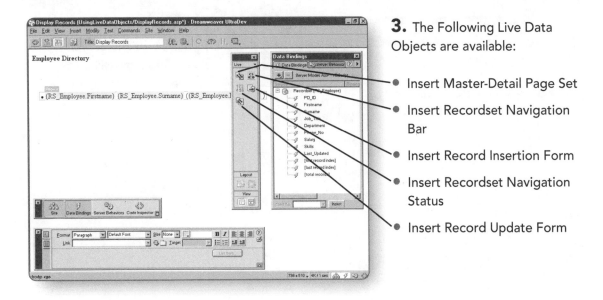

3. The Following Live Data Objects are available:

- Insert Master-Detail Page Set

- Insert Recordset Navigation Bar

- Insert Record Insertion Form

- Insert Recordset Navigation Status

- Insert Record Update Form

Inserting a Record Counter

The Insert Recordset Navigation Status object is used to display the number of records returned in a search and the location of the records currently being viewed.

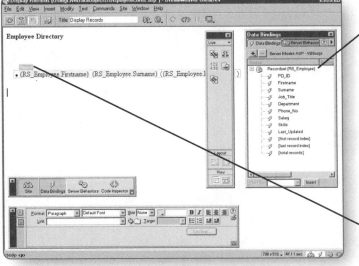

1. Create a search results page.

- Use the Recordset(Query) data source from the Data Bindings palette to create a Recordset. The retrieved Recordset must be bound to the search results page. The steps involved in creating a Recordset are covered in Chapter 8, "Retrieving Data from a Database."

- Use the Repeat Region server behavior to display multiple records.

2. Click on the Server Behaviors tab. The Server Behaviors palette will be displayed.

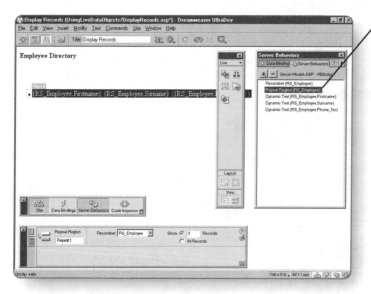

3. Double-click on Repeat Region in the list of utilized server behaviors. The Repeat Region dialog box will open.

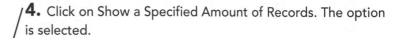

4. Click on Show a Specified Amount of Records. The option is selected.

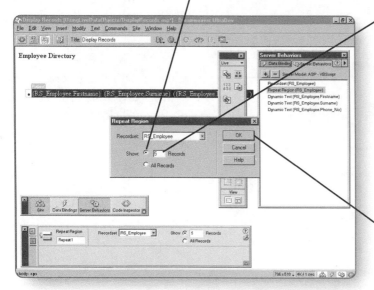

5. Type the number of records to display on a page. You will have to make a decision about the amount of records that should be displayed at any one time. The value you select will depend upon the layout of your search result Web page. You should generally try to prevent too much scrolling.

6. Click on OK. The Repeat Region dialog box will close.

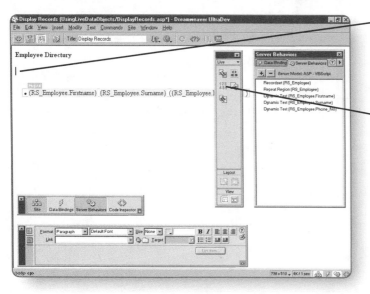

7. Click inside the Document window where you would like to insert the Recordset Navigation Status Bar.

8. Click on the Insert Recordset Navigation Status object. The Insert Navigation Status dialog box will open.

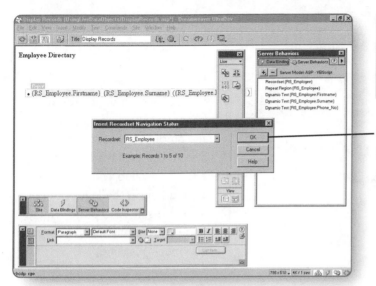

NOTE

The current Recordset will automatically be selected.

9. Click on OK. The Insert Recordset Navigation Status dialog box will close.

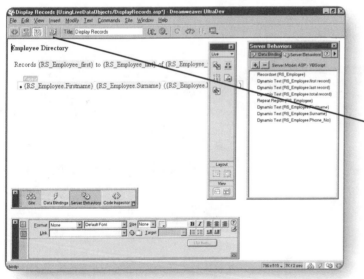

NOTE

A Recordset Navigation Status Bar will be inserted.

10. Click on the Live Data View icon. Live Data View will be enabled.

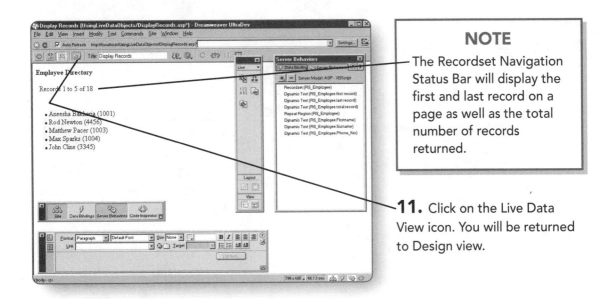

NOTE
The Recordset Navigation
Status Bar will display the
first and last record on a
page as well as the total
number of records
returned.

11. Click on the Live Data
View icon. You will be returned
to Design view.

Inserting a Navigation Panel

Databases can contain millions of records. When you display the results of a
database search, you should always split the results across multiple pages and
allow users to easily navigate between pages. This technique is employed by most
popular Internet search engines. The Insert Navigation Panel object creates a set of
text or image links to the first,
last, next, and previous pages.

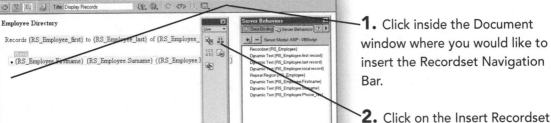

1. Click inside the Document
window where you would like to
insert the Recordset Navigation
Bar.

2. Click on the Insert Recordset
Navigation Bar object. The
Insert Recordset Navigation Bar
dialog box will open.

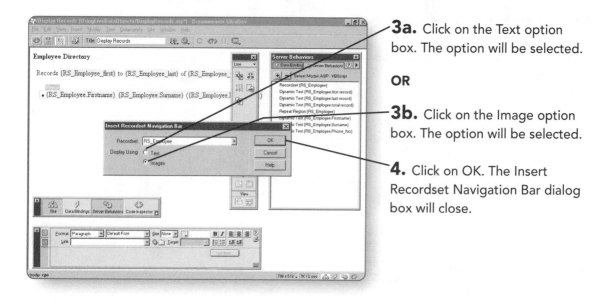

3a. Click on the Text option box. The option will be selected.

OR

3b. Click on the Image option box. The option will be selected.

4. Click on OK. The Insert Recordset Navigation Bar dialog box will close.

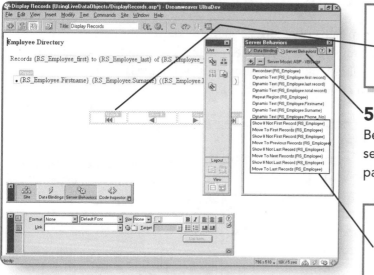

NOTE

The Recordset Navigation Bar will be inserted.

5. Click on the Server Behaviors tab, if it is not already selected. The Server Behaviors palette will be displayed.

NOTE

You can see that the Show and Move To server behaviors have been used to create the navigation panel. In Chapter 11, you will learn to use these server behaviors and create a custom navigation panel.

Testing the Recordset Navigation Bar

1. Press F12 to preview the current Web page in a browser. The browser will open and display the Web page.

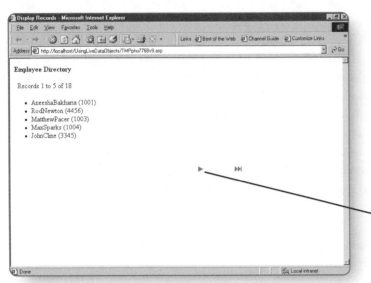

NOTE
The first page of records does not contain a link to the First page and Previous page. The last page will also not contain a link to the Last page and the Next page.

2. Click on the Next button. The Next page containing results will be displayed.

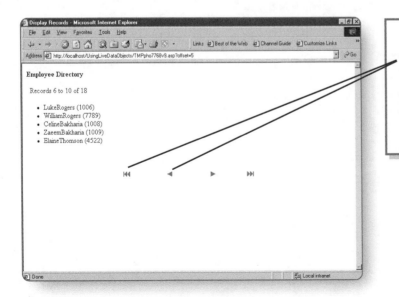

NOTE
The First and Previous buttons are only displayed when you are not viewing the first page of results returned by a Recordset.

Creating a Master-Detail Page Set

A Master page only displays summary data for each record returned in a search. A Master page also contains a link, which the user must click on to view the record in detail. This allows users to view multiple records on a single page and then decide which record they would like to display in full.

The Master page displays the results in a table. You decide on the amount of records that can be displayed on a single page. The object will automatically insert a navigation panel and Recordset status information if the search results span multiple pages. The resulting Master and Detail pages are both fully editable.

1. Create a new Web page to display Master records. Use the Recordset(Query) data source from the Data Bindings palette to create a Recordset. The steps involved in creating a Recordset are covered in Chapter 8, "Retrieving Data from a Database."

2. Click inside the Document window where you would like to insert the master records table.

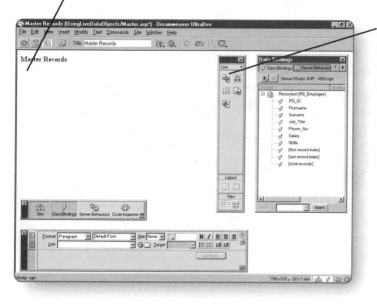

3. Click on the Insert Master Detail Page Set object. The Insert Master Detail Page Set dialog box will open.

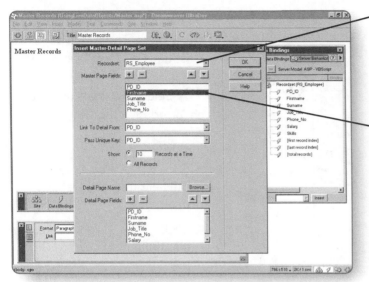

4. Select the Recordset that will be used to create the Master-Detail page set. The fields retrieved will be included in the Master and Detail pages.

5. Include only essential fields on the Master page. Select the table column/field name. You can:

- Click on the – sign to remove the field from the Master page.

- Click on the + sign to include additional fields on the Master page.

- Use the up and down arrows to change the order in which the fields will be displayed.

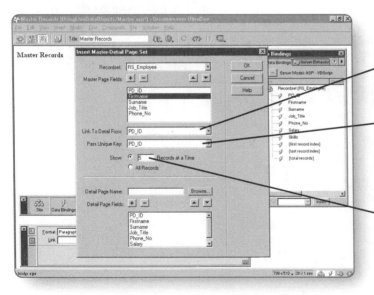

6. Select the field that must link to the Detail page.

7. The unique record id/primary key is automatically selected. It will be passed to the Detail page via the QueryString.

8. Type in the number of records that can be displayed on the Master page at any one time.

NOTE

If you are limiting the number of records displayed per page of search results, a Recordset Navigation Bar will be inserted.

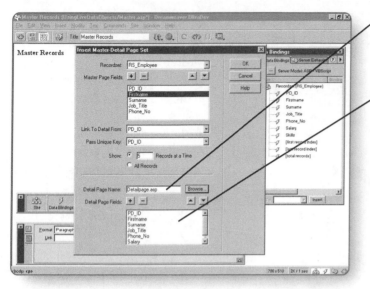

9. Type in the name of the Detail page. The Detail page must have an ".asp" extension.

10. Select the fields that must be included in the Detail page. You can:

- Click on the – sign to remove the field from the Detail page.

- Click on the + sign to include additional fields on the Detail page.

- Use the up and down arrows to change the order in which the fields will be displayed.

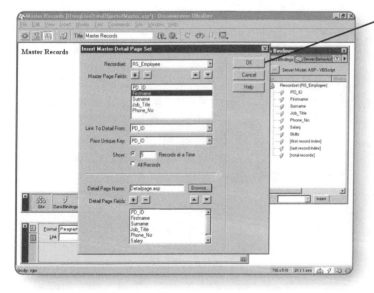

11. Click on OK. Both the Master and the Detail pages will be created.

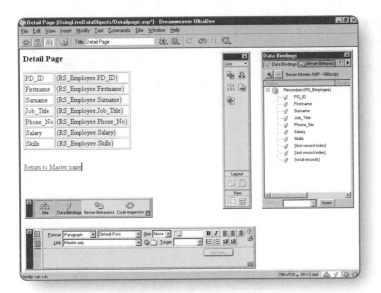

NOTE

The Detail record will be displayed in a table.

12. Create a link back to the Master page so that the user can view detail pages for other records as well.

Testing the Master-Detail Page Set

You can only test a Master-Detail Page Set from a browser because Live Data view does not support links.

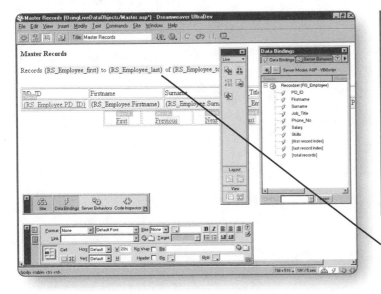

NOTE

The Master page will display summary records in a table and link to a Detail page for each record. A Recordset Navigation and Status Bar will both be included if all records are not displayed on a single page.

1. Press F12 to preview the Master page in a Web browser. The Master page will be displayed in a Web browser.

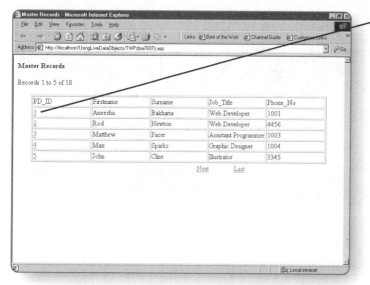

2. Click on the Link for a record that you want to view in detail. The Detail page that contains the full record will be displayed.

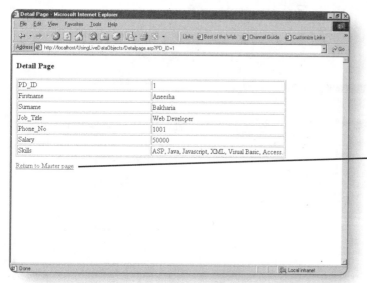

NOTE

You can see the record's unique id number passed to the Detail page in the QueryString.

3. Click on the link to return to the Master page from which you can choose to view more records in detail.

Inserting a New Record in a Database

The Insert Record object creates a form in the current Web page that allows users to insert new records in a database. You need to select the appropriate form objects and the database columns where the data will be inserted. Common form objects like text fields, drop-down lists, radio buttons, and check boxes can all be used.

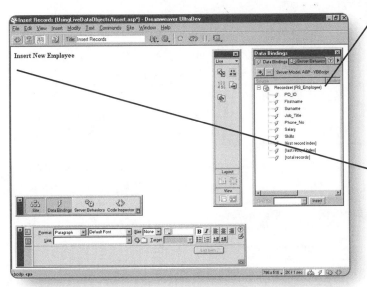

1. Create a database connection. Records will be inserted into a table within this database. The steps involved in creating a database connection are covered in Chapter 8, "Retrieving Data from a Database."

2. Click inside the Document window where you would like to insert the form generated by the Insert Record object.

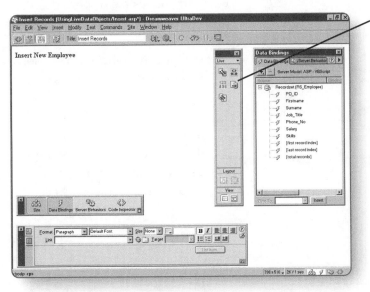

3. Click on the Insert Record Insertion object. The Insert Record Insertion Form dialog box will open.

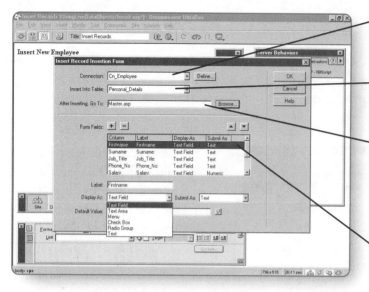

4. Select the database connection.

5. Select the table where the new record will be inserted.

6. Type in the name of the Web page, which must be displayed after the record has been successfully inserted.

7. Click on a database table column name. You can:

- Click on the + sign to add a field to the Insertion Form.

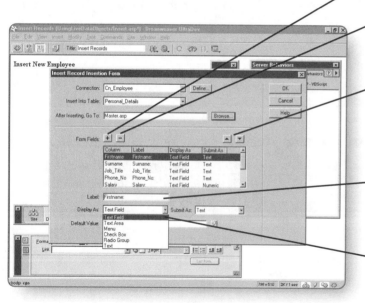

- Click on the – sign to remove the field from the Insertion Form.

- Use the up and down arrows to change the order in which the fields are displayed in the Insertion Form.

8. Type in a label for the field. The table column name is used by default.

9. Select the form object that the user will use to enter the data. You could select a text field, text area, menu, check box, or a radio button group.

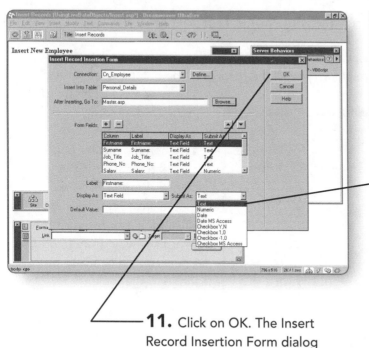

TIP

You could even specify a default value for each field, which will be displayed when the page loads. This could aid data entry.

10. Select the format of the data that will be inserted into the table column.

NOTE

Repeat steps 7–10 for each field that must be included in the Insertion form.

11. Click on OK. The Insert Record Insertion Form dialog box will close.

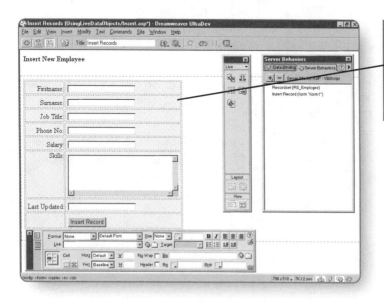

NOTE

The Insertion form will be created. A table is used to format the form.

Selecting a Record to Update

We need to allow the user to select the record that he wants to update. The Master page already contains a summary of all the records in the database, so for each record we will just insert a link to the Update form.

1. Open the Master page that we created earlier in this chapter. We will insert an update link for each record. This will allow a user to select the record she would like to update. A new column needs to be added to the table.

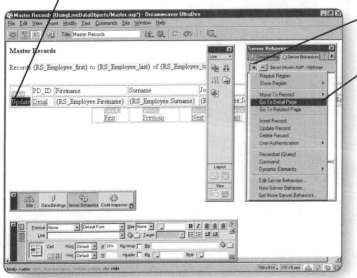

2. Select the update link. The text will be highlighted.

3. Click on the + sign. A submenu will appear.

4. Click on Go To Detail Page. The Go To Detail Page dialog box will open.

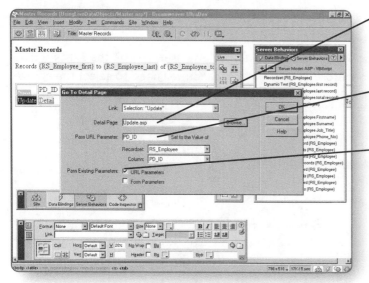

5. Type in the name of the Web page that will contain the Update form.

6. Type in the primary key/ unique id field.

7. Click inside the URL Parameters check box. A check will be placed inside the box. The unique identifier of the current record will be passed to the Update form as a URL Parameter. This means that it will be appended to the URL as a QueryString.

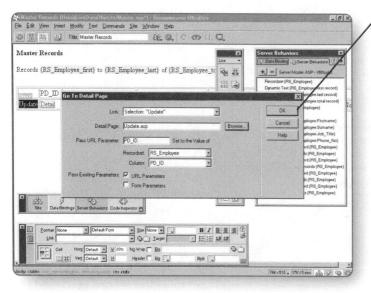

8. Click on OK. The Go To Detail dialog box will close and the Update link will be created.

9. Press Ctrl+s. The Master page will be saved.

Updating an Existing Record

The Update Record object will create a form that allows users to edit the existing data and then update the record stored in the database. You will need to select the appropriate form object for each field that needs to be updated in the database table.

1. Create the Web page that will contain the Update form.

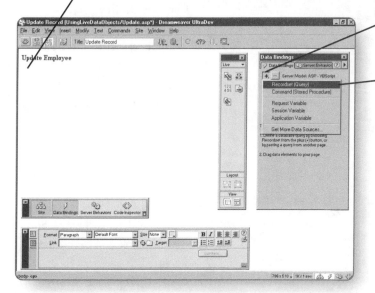

2. Click the + sign. A submenu will appear.

3. Click on Recordset(Query). The Recordset dialog box will open.

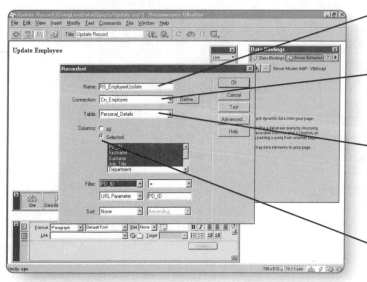

4. Type a name for the Recordset.

5. Select a database connection. The option will be selected.

6. Select the table that contains the record you need to retrieve. The option will be selected.

7. Click on the Selected option box. The option will be selected.

8. Select the fields that must be included in the Update form. To select more than one field, hold down the Ctrl key, and then click the fields you want to include. Only select the fields that the user will be allowed to update. These fields will be bound to the form objects on the Update form.

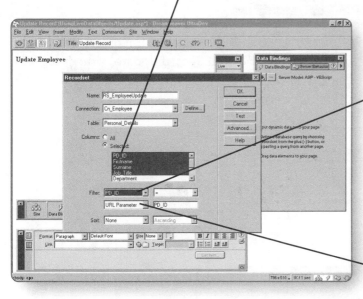

9. Select the field that corresponds to the value that is being passed to the Update form via the QueryString. In this case it must be the unique ID field also known as the primary key. The field will be highlighted.

10. Select URL Parameter, because the ID number must be retrieved from the QueryString. The option will be selected.

11. Click on OK. The Recordset dialog box will close.

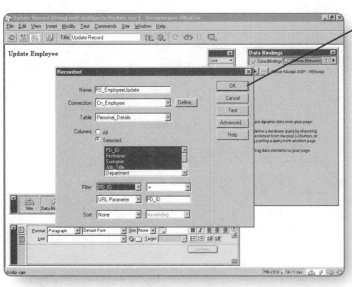

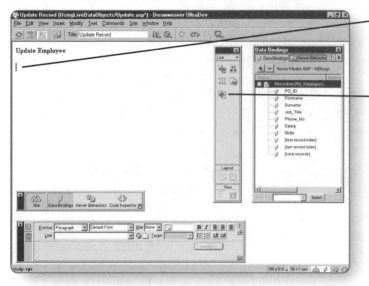

12. Click inside the Document window where you would like to place the Update form.

13. Click on the Insert Record Update Form object. The Insert Record Update Form dialog box will open.

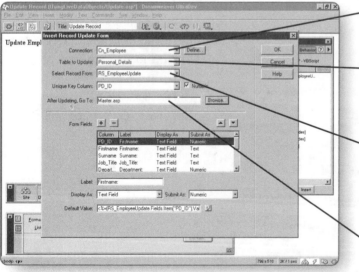

14. Select the database connection.

15. Select the table that contains the records that will be updated.

16. Select the Recordset that retrieves the unique id value for the record that must be updated.

17. Type in the name of the Web page that must be displayed after the record has been updated.

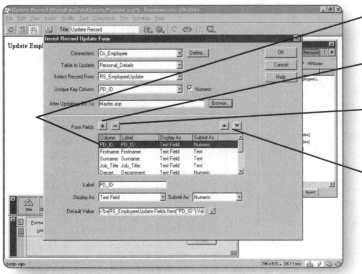

18. Click on a database table column name. You can

- Click on the + sign to add a field to the Update Form.

- Click on the − sign to remove the field from the Update Form.

- Use the up and down arrows to change the order in which the fields are displayed in the Update Form.

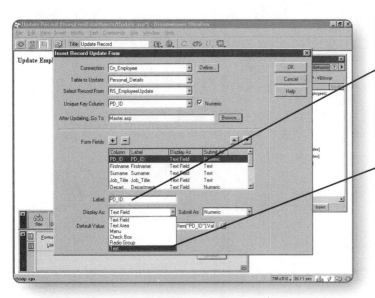

NOTE

The table column name by default will be used as the field label. You can change the label.

19. Select the form object that the user will use to enter the data. You could select a text field, text area, menu, check box, or a radio button group.

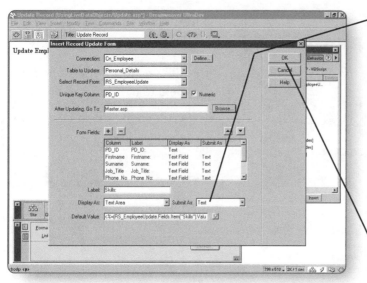

20. Select the format of the data that will be inserted into the table column.

NOTE

Repeat steps 18–20 for each field that must be included in the Insertion Form.

21. Click on OK. The Insert Record Update Form dialog box will close.

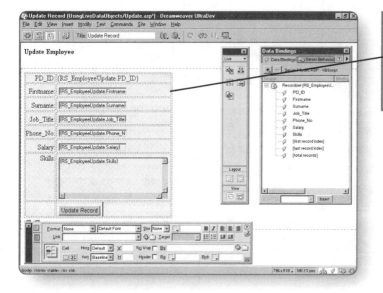

NOTE

The Update Form will be created. A table will be used to format the form.

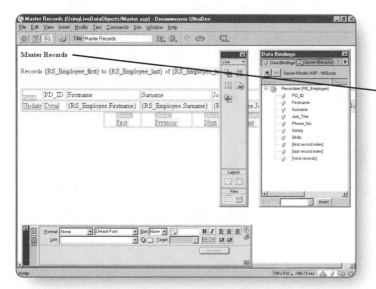

Testing the Update Form

1. Open the Master page and press F12 to preview the page in a Web browser. The Master page will be displayed.

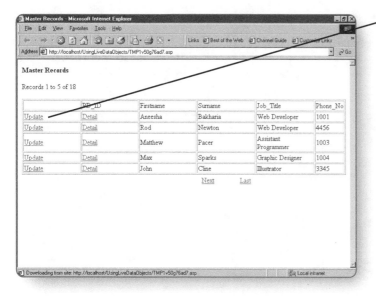

2. Click on an Update link. The Update form will be displayed.

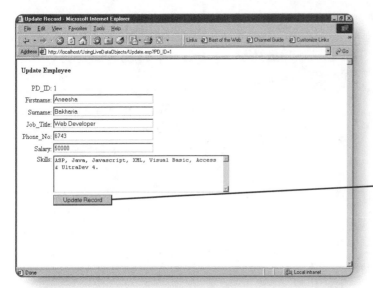

3. Edit the data.

4. Click on Update. After the record is updated, you will be returned to the Master page.

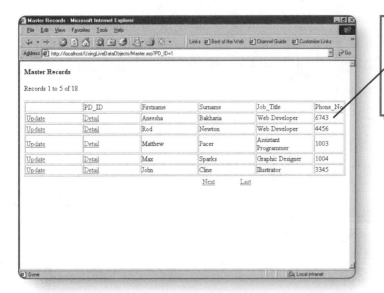

10

Advanced Database Queries

In Chapter 8, "Retrieving Data from a Database," you learned to create simple queries that returned all the available records in a table. However, to create truly powerful database-enabled Web applications, you need to learn to select and retrieve only specific data from a database. In simple terms, you need to build customized queries in SQL (Structured Query Language). UltraDev will help you generate the SQL commands for manipulating data, but you will still have to customize the statements it generates. In this chapter, you'll learn to:

- Create SQL queries
- Define search criteria
- Use Boolean operators
- Retrieve distinct records
- Use wildcards to search strings
- Retrieve summary data from a table
- Work with related tables

Generating SQL Statements

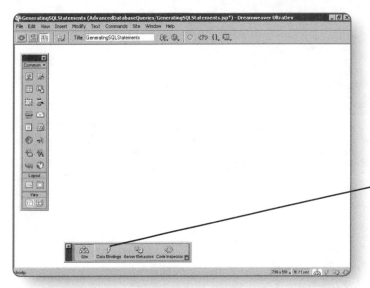

SQL is used to build database queries. It is a simple yet powerful language that allows databases to be queried based upon specific criteria. The Advanced Recordset dialog box allows you to generate and test SQL queries intuitively.

1. Click on the Data Bindings icon on the Launcher. The Data Bindings palette will be displayed.

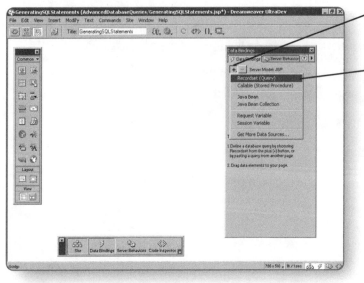

2. Click on the + sign. A submenu will appear.

3. Click on Recordset(Query). The Recordset dialog box will open.

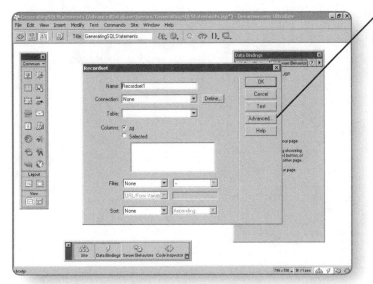

4. Click on Advanced. The dialog box will be expanded.

5. Type the name of the recordset.

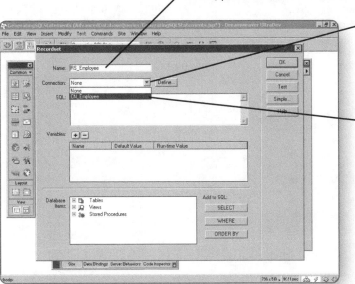

6. Click on the down arrow of the Connection drop-down box. The DSNs available on your local computer will be displayed.

7. Click on a DSN title. The connection will be selected.

> ### NOTE
>
> If you would like to follow the example in this chapter, create a System DSN for the Employee Directory Microsoft Access database (employee_directory.mdb) that is located in the Chapter 10 folder on the CD-ROM that accompanies this book.

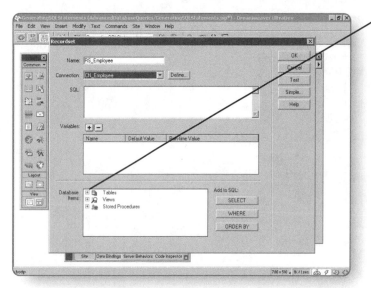

8. Click on the + sign to expand the Tables tree. A list of tables will be displayed.

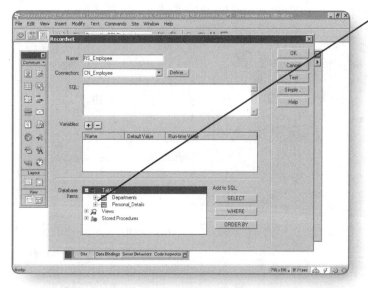

9. Click on the + sign next to the name of a table. All of the fields in the table will be displayed.

Selecting Fields and Tables

The SELECT clause is used to specify the fields to be returned in the recordset. Only the fields that are required on a Web page should be included in the SELECT clause.

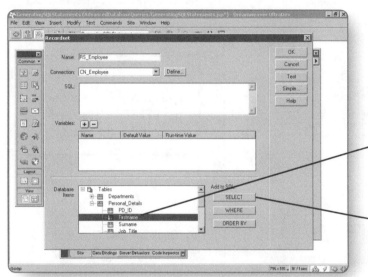

The FROM clause specifies the tables that are included in the query. A list of tables is automatically inserted after the FROM clause when the SELECT button is clicked.

1. Click on the name of a field that you would like to retrieve. The field will be highlighted.

2. Click on SELECT. The SQL statement will be created and displayed in the SQL text area.

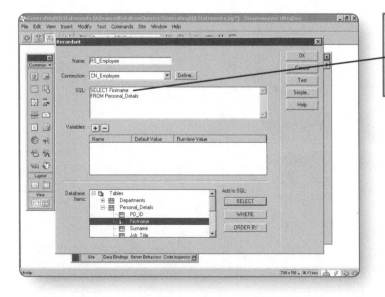

NOTE

The field name is inserted after the SELECT clause.

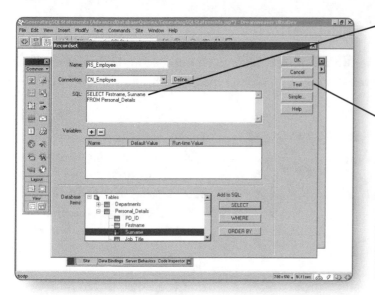

3. Repeat steps 1 and 2 to include more fields in the query. A comma separates fields returned in the recordset.

4. Click on Test. The Test SQL Statement dialog box will open.

TIP

Only the fields included in the SELECT clause are returned in the query.

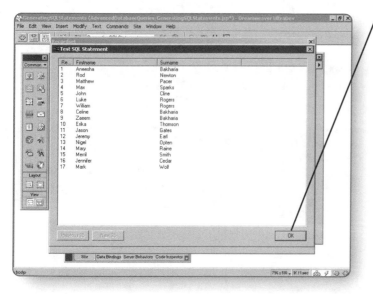

5. Click on OK. The Test SQL Statement dialog box will close.

Defining Search Criteria

The number of records returned can be limited by filtering the data. The WHERE clause is used to set search criteria.

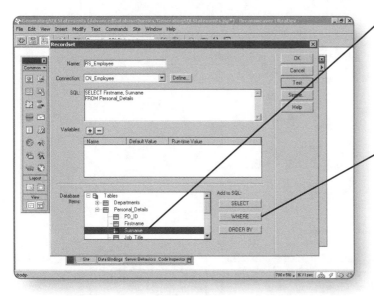

1. Click on the field you would like to use as a filter. You will need to expand the branches of the Tables tree until you find the required table and field. The field will be highlighted.

2. Click on WHERE. The WHERE clause will be inserted into the SQL text area.

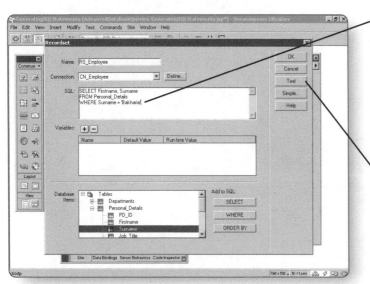

3. Type the search criteria into the SQL text area. Search criteria are made up of a comparison operator and the value with which the field should be compared. The value must be surrounded by apostrophes.

4. Click on Test. The Test SQL Statement dialog box will open.

Table of Comparison Operators

Operator	Description
=	Equal to (case sensitive)
LIKE	Equal to (not case sensitive)
<>	Not Equal to (case sensitive)
NOT LIKE	Not Equal to (not case sensitive)
<	Less Than
>	Greater Than
<=	Less Than or Equal to
>=	Greater Than or Equal to

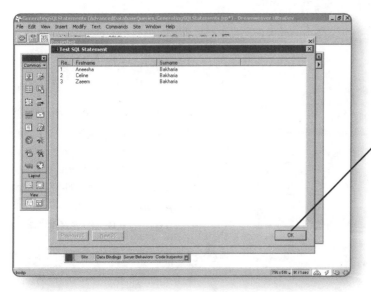

NOTE

Only records that meet the specified criteria are displayed.

5. Click on OK. The Test SQL Statement dialog box will close.

Using Boolean Operators

Boolean operators provide a way to specify multiple criteria in a query. The AND operator is used when each criteria must be met before a record will be returned. The OR operator will return records if any of the specified criteria are matched.

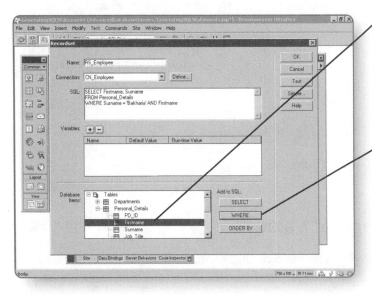

1. Click on another field that you would like use as a filter. You will need to expand the branches of the Tables tree until you find the required table and field. The field will be highlighted.

2. Click on WHERE. The field is added to the WHERE clause. The AND Boolean operator is automatically inserted between the fields. Records will only be returned if the criteria for all fields are met. If you want records to be returned if any of the set criteria are met, replace AND with OR.

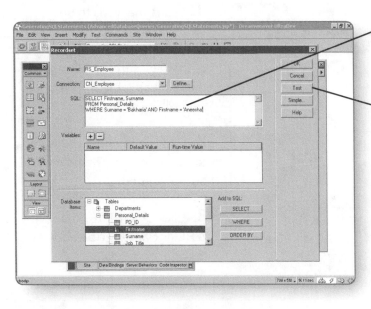

3. Type the value for the field's search criteria.

4. Click on Test. The Test SQL Statement dialog box will open.

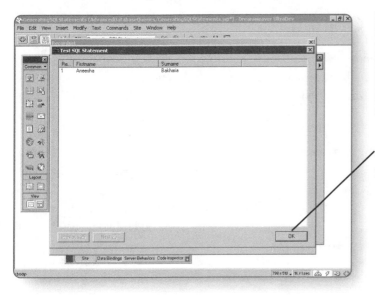

NOTE

Only records that meet the specified criteria are returned.

5. Click on OK. The Test SQL Statement dialog box will close.

Matching a Range of Values

Sometimes it's handy to search for records that contain values within a specified range. You could use comparison operators (<, >, <>, <=, and >=), but using the BETWEEN keyword is much easier.

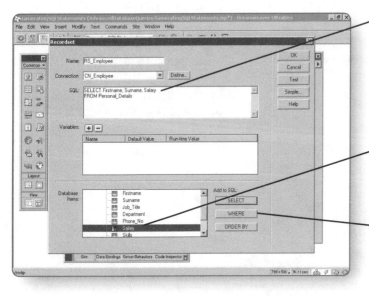

1. Select the fields to be included in the recordset. You will need to expand the branches of the Tables tree until you find the required table and field. The field will be highlighted.

2. Click on the field you want to use as a filter. The field will be highlighted.

3. Click on WHERE. The WHERE clause will be added in the SQL text area.

4. Type BETWEEN after the field name.

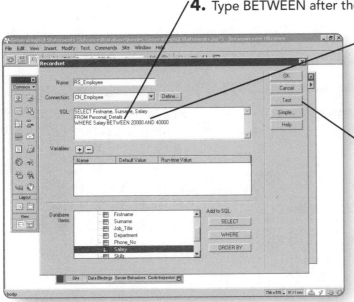

5. Type the values, separated by the AND Boolean operator. In this example, we are trying to find all employees that earn between $20,000 and $40,000.

6. Click on Test. The Test SQL Statement dialog box will open.

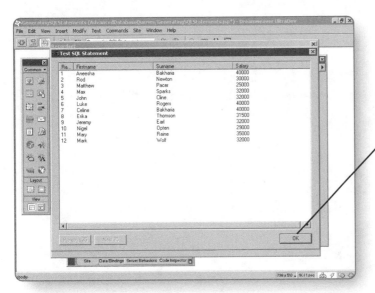

NOTE

Only records that match the specified range are returned.

7. Click on OK. The Test SQL Statement dialog box will close.

Ordering Results

SQL allows for returned records to be sorted in either ascending or descending order. You'll use the ORDER BY clause to specify which fields to sort.

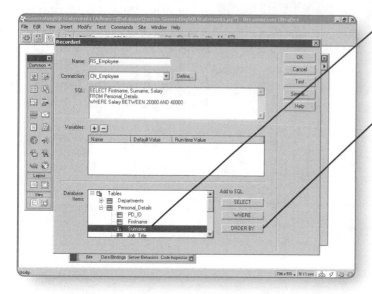

1. Click on the field on which you want to order the returned records. The field will be highlighted.

2. Click on ORDER BY. The ORDER BY clause will be inserted in the SQL text area.

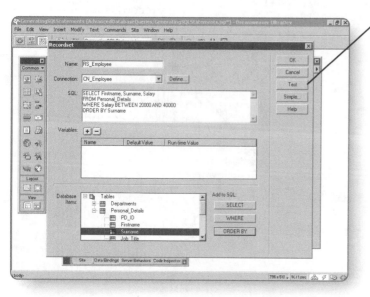

3. Click on Test. The Test SQL Statement dialog box will open.

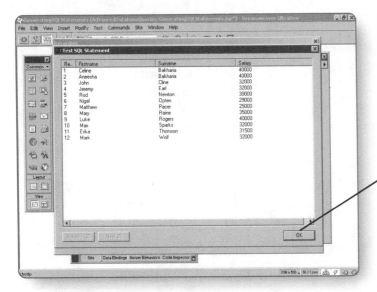

4. Click on OK. The Test SQL Statement dialog box will close.

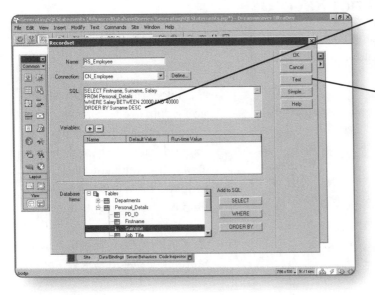

5. Type DESC after the field name. This will return records in descending order.

6. Click on Test. The Test SQL Statement dialog box will open.

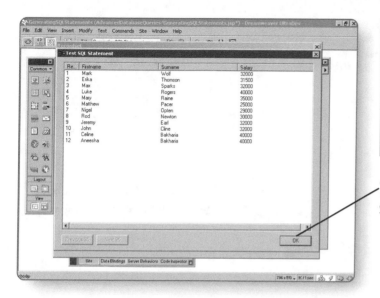

NOTE

The records will be returned in descending order based upon the field that was specified in the ORDER BY clause.

7. Click on OK. The Test SQL Statement dialog box will close.

Retrieving Distinct Records

Sometimes a table column contains duplicate values. The DISTINCT keyword is used to retrieve all unique values in a column.

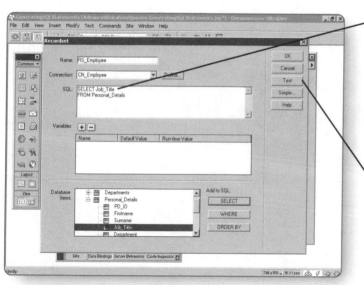

1. Select the field from which you would like to retrieve distinct values. You will need to expand the branches of the Tables tree until you find the required table and field. The field will be highlighted.

2. Click on Test. The Test SQL Statement dialog box will open.

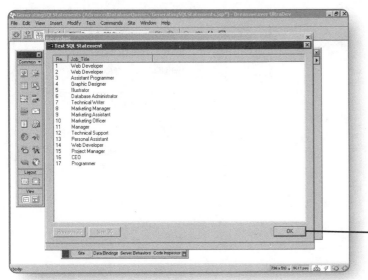

3. Click on OK. The Test SQL Statement dialog box will close.

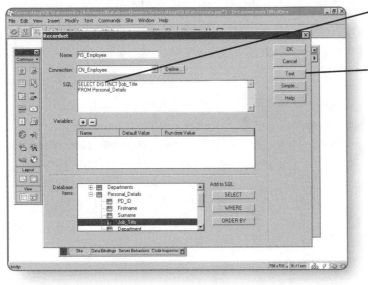

4. Type DISTINCT after the SELECT clause.

5. Click on Test. The Test SQL Statement dialog box will open.

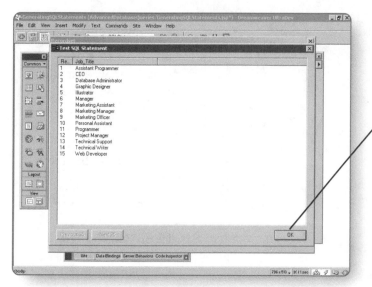

6. Click on OK. The Test SQL Statement dialog box will close.

Using Wildcards to Search Strings

Wildcards can be used as placeholders for other characters when querying fields. Wildcards will help you find data when you only know part of a value or are searching for a specific pattern.

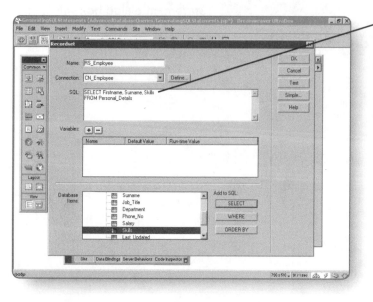

1. Select the fields to be returned in the recordset. You will need to expand the branches of the Tables tree until you find the required table and field. The field will be highlighted.

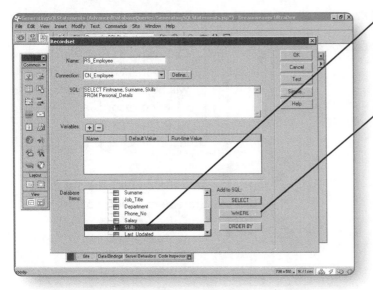

2. Click on the field you want to use as a filter. The field must not be numeric. The field will be selected.

3. Click on WHERE. The WHERE clause will be added to the SQL text area.

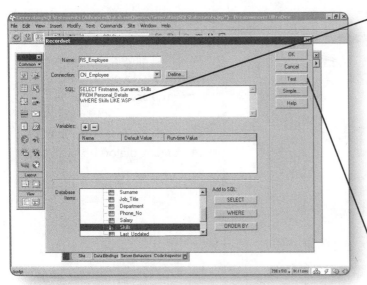

4. Type search criteria into the SQL text area. In this example, we are searching for employees that have ASP skills. The skill field contains a list of skills, separated by commas. ASP could be anywhere within the string. The Equal To (LIKE) operator will return all employees who can create ASP applications.

5. Click on Test. The Test SQL Statement dialog box will open.

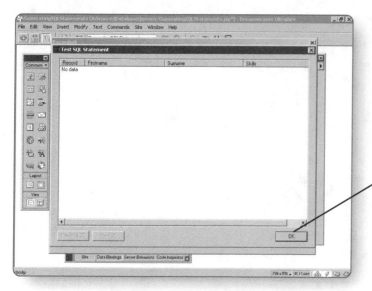

6. Click on OK. The Test SQL Statement dialog box will close.

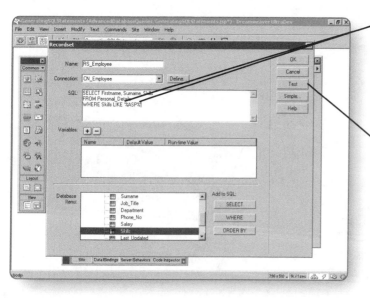

7. Type % before and after the value to be searched. The % wildcard allows any number of characters to occur before and after the search value.

8. Click on Test. The Test SQL Statement dialog box will open.

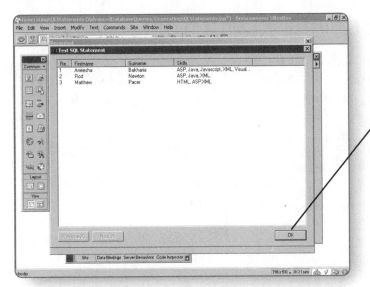

NOTE

Records that contain the search string are returned.

9. Click on OK. The Test SQL Statement dialog box will close.

TIP

Other wildcard characters:

- ? Match a single character:

  SELECT firstname,lastname FROM Employees WHERE skills = '? SP'.

- [ ] Match all characters found between the braces:

  SELECT firstname FROM Employees WHERE surname LIKE '[ab]%' returns surnames that begin with A or B.

- - can be used to define a range of characters within braces:

  SELECT firstname FROM Employees WHERE surname LIKE '[a-d]%' returns all surnames from A to D.

Retrieving Summary Data from a Table

The SQL Aggregate function can be used to return summary data such as the number of records in a table, the average value of a column, the sum of column values, or the maximum/minimum values in a column.

Counting Records

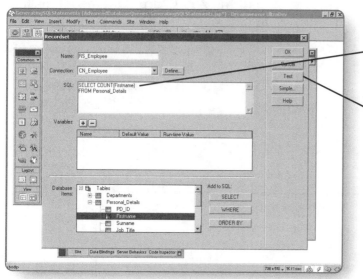

1. Type Count('field name') into the SQL text area.

2. Click on Test. The Test SQL Statement dialog box will open.

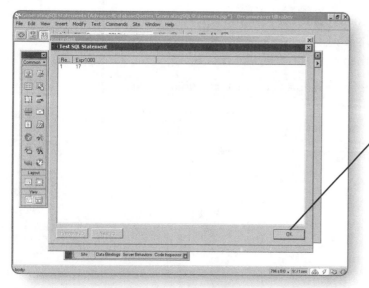

> ### NOTE
> The total number of records in the table is returned.

3. Click on OK. The Test SQL Statement dialog box will close.

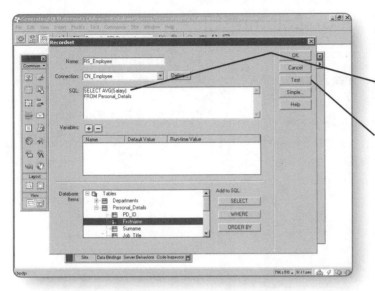

Average Column Value

1. Type AVG('field name') into the SQL text area.

2. Click on Test. The Test SQL Statement dialog box will open.

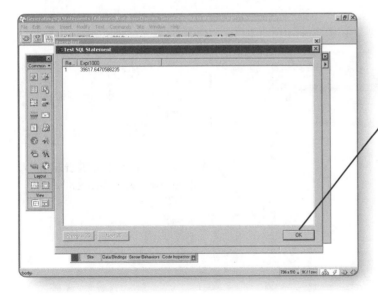

NOTE

The average column value is returned.

3. Click on OK. The Test SQL Statement dialog box will close.

Sum of Column Values

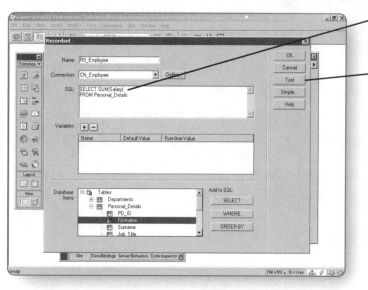

1. Type SUM('field name') into the SQL text area.

2. Click on Test. The Test SQL Statement dialog box will open.

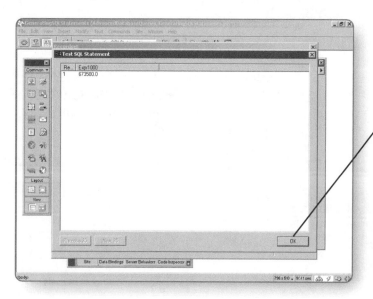

NOTE

The sum of column values is returned.

3. Click on OK. The Test SQL Statement dialog box will close.

Maximum Column Value

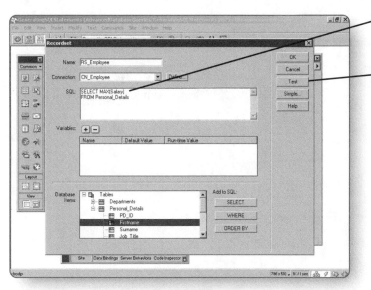

1. Type MAX('field name') into the SQL text area.

2. Click on Test. The Test SQL Statement dialog box will open.

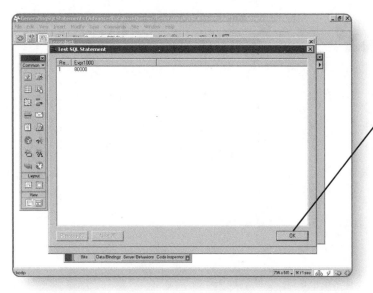

NOTE
The maximum column value is returned.

3. Click on OK. The Test SQL Statement dialog box will close.

Minimum Column Value

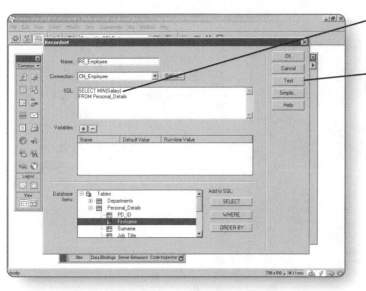

1. Type MIN('field name') into the SQL text area.

2. Click on Test. The Test SQL Statement dialog box will open.

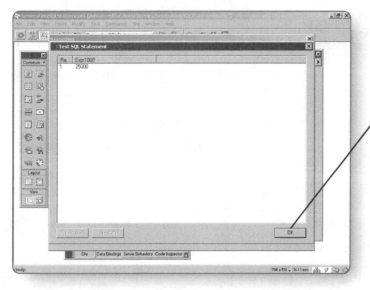

NOTE

The minimum column value is returned.

3. Click on OK. The Test SQL Statement dialog box will close.

Working with Related Tables

When working with a database that has related tables, you will need to define the table connection in the SQL statement. This is achieved by establishing a relationship between columns from each table.

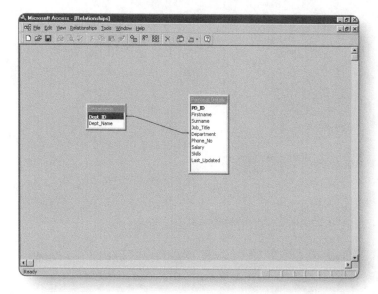

In this Microsoft Access example, there is a relationship between the Department field from the Personal_Details table and the Dept_ID field from the Department table. This allows the titles to be updated in a single location. If the Department field is retrieved, users will have to look up department titles manually in the Departments table. You can avoid this by writing a SQL statement that joins the Department and the Dept_ID fields and retrieves the Dept_Name field.

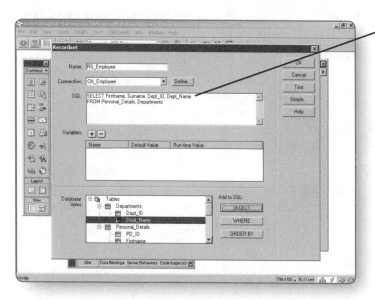

1. Select the fields to be retrieved. You will need to expand the branches of the Tables tree until you find the required table and field. The field will be highlighted.

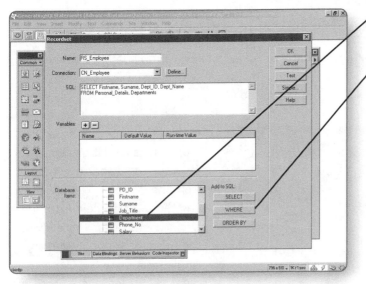

2. Select the related field. The field will be highlighted.

3. Click on WHERE. A WHERE clause will be inserted.

4. Type a comparison operator.

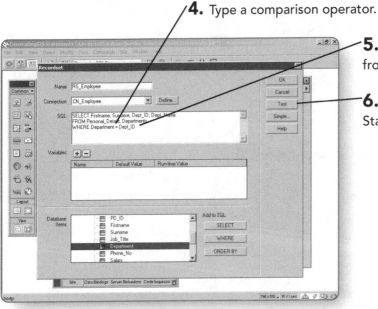

5. Type the name of the field from the related table.

6. Click on Test. The Test SQL Statement dialog box will open.

NOTE

The contents of the related field are displayed.

7. Click on OK. The SQL Statement dialog box will close.

NOTE

Dot Notation can be used to avoid ambiguity by prefixing table names with column names:

- SELECT Personal_Details.Firstname, Personal_Details. Surname, Departments.Dept_Name

- FROM Personal_Details, Departments

- WHERE Personal_Details.Department = Departments. Dept_ID

11

Searching a Database

It's time you stopped hard-coding search criteria and developed a forms-based interface to collect and process search requests. This technique provides a much more efficient way for users to find exactly what they need. It is also essential that you display search results in a visually appealing and user-friendly manner. In this chapter, you'll learn to:

- Create a simple search form
- Process a search form
- Search multiple database fields
- Display paged search results
- Link to a Detail Page

Creating a Simple Search Form

In the following steps, you will create a form that enables the user to enter a search request in a text box. It is useful to indicate which field will be searched. The search request will be sent to the server for processing when the Search button is clicked.

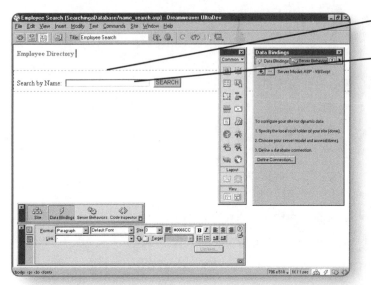

1. Create a search form.

2. Type a name for the search that describes the type of search being performed.

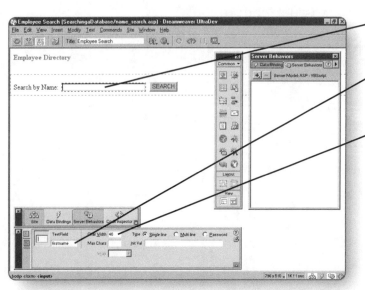

3. Insert a text field for the user to enter his search request.

4. Type a name for the text field.

5. Type in the character width of the text field. You should use the type of data stored in the field that the user can search as a guide when defining the width. Be sure to give users ample room to enter their search request.

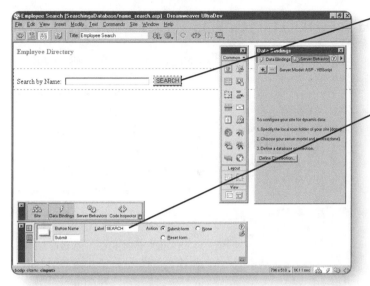

6. Insert a Submit button. The user will click on this button to send his search request to the server for processing.

7. Type in a name for the button in the Label field. The label should clearly describe the purpose of the button, which in this case is to search the database.

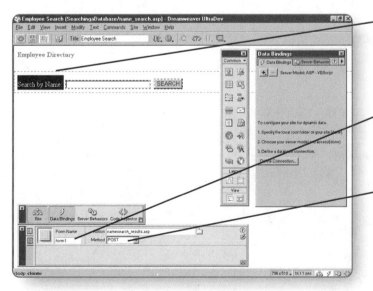

8. Click on the dashed red line that surrounds the form. The contents of the form will be highlighted.

9. Type the name of the page that will process the search request into the Action field.

10. Select Post from the Method drop-down box. The Post option will be selected.

Processing a Search Form

To process a search request, you will need to include the retrieved form data and include it in the database query.

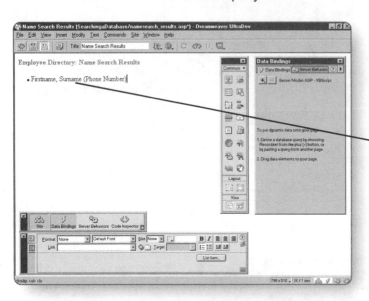

1. Create a new Web page using the name you assigned the search page in step 9 of the previous section. The page should have an .asp extension.

2. Type in placeholder text for the fields. Each record will be displayed in a bulleted list. Later in this chapter, you'll learn to display search results in a table.

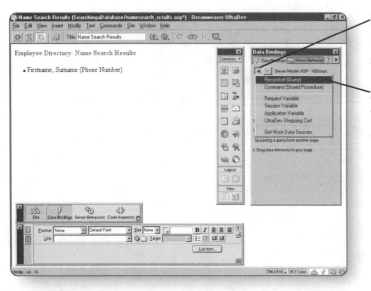

3. Click on the + sign in the Data Bindings palette. A submenu will appear.

4. Click on Recordset(Query). The Recordset dialog box will open.

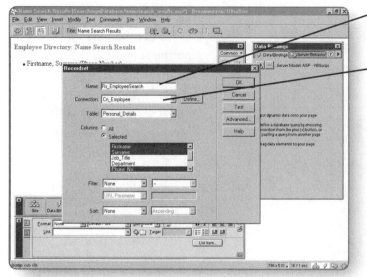

5. Type in a name for the Recordset.

6. Select a database connection. All the tables in the database will be loaded.

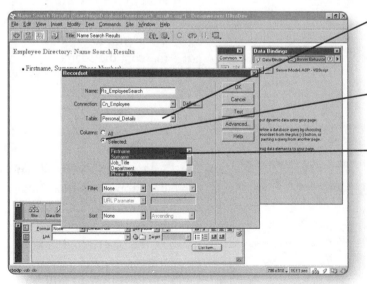

7. Select the table that contains the field that must be searched.

8. Click on the Selected option box.

9. Select the fields that must be returned by the query. To select more than one field, hold down the Ctrl key and then click the fields you want to include. Only select fields that will be bound to the search results Web page.

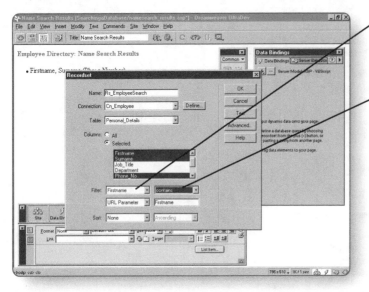

10. Using the Filter drop-down box, select the field that will limit the search.

11. Select Contains as the comparison operator. This will allow the search criteria to be matched to any portion of the field.

NOTE

You could also select:

- Begins With to return a match if the search criteria are found at the start of the text stored in the field.

- Ends With to return a match if the search criteria are found at the end of the text stored in the field.

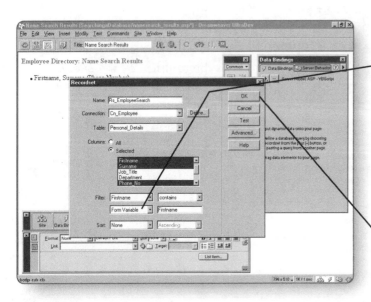

12. Select Form Variable from the Filter drop-down box. This option will retrieve the search request from the form. Type the name of the search text field from your form page into the text field next to the Form Variable selection.

13. Click on OK. The Recordset dialog box will close.

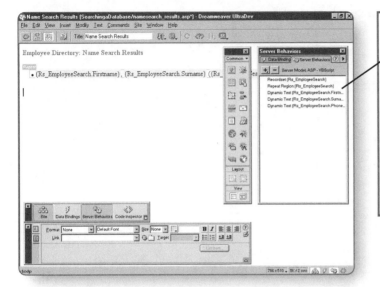

NOTE

You will now have to bind the fields returned in the Recordset to the Web page and use the Repeat Server behavior to display multiple records. Chapter 8, "Retrieving Data from a Database," covers this topic in depth.

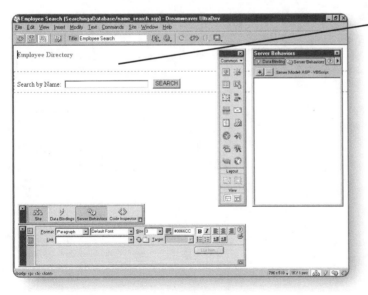

14. Open the search form that you created in the previous section.

15. Press F12 to preview the Web page in a browser. The Web browser will open and load the search form.

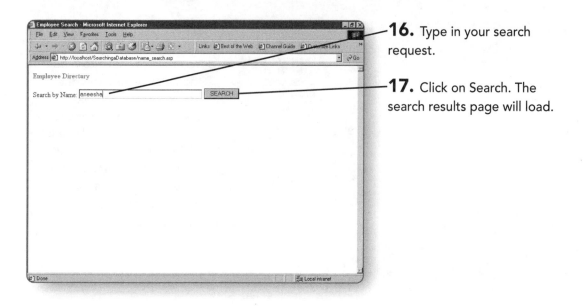

16. Type in your search request.

17. Click on Search. The search results page will load.

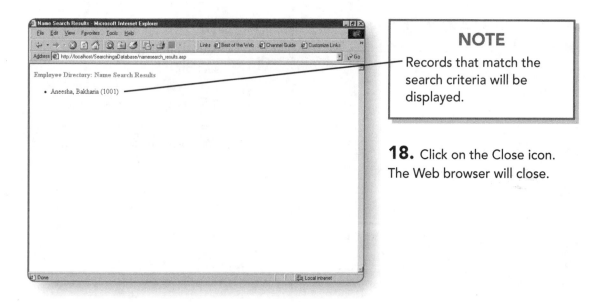

NOTE

Records that match the search criteria will be displayed.

18. Click on the Close icon. The Web browser will close.

Searching Multiple Database Fields

Because a table is usually made up of several search fields, it might be useful to perform a search across multiple fields. Data entered into a text field can be compared with numerous fields in a database. You will need to retrieve the form data, store it in a variable, and then include it in the SQL query.

NOTE

In the previous section, you were searching for an employee by name, but only searched the firstname field. The name entered could either be a first name or a surname. This is why we need to search both fields.

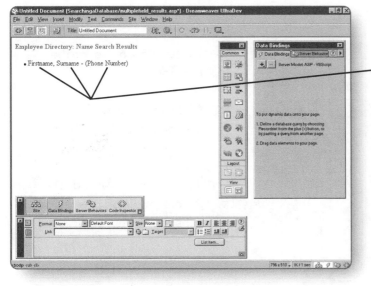

1. Create a new Web page with an .asp extension.

2. Type in placeholder text for the fields. Each record will be displayed in a bulleted list.

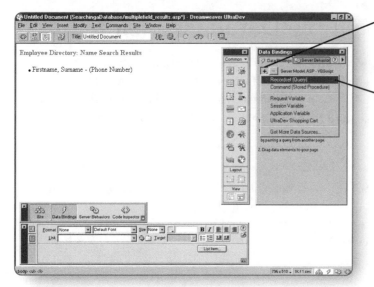

3. Click on the + sign in the Data Bindings palette. A submenu will appear.

4. Click on Recordset(Query). The Recordset dialog box will open.

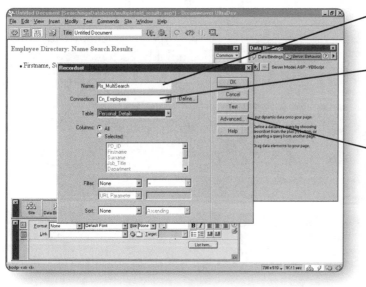

5. Type in a name for the Recordset.

6. Select a database connection. All the tables in the database will be loaded.

7. Click on Advanced. The Recordset dialog box will be expanded.

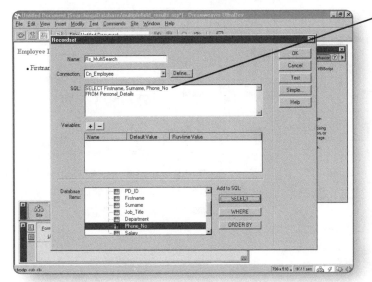

8. Select the fields to be included in the query. You will have to expand the Tables tree until you find the fields that need to be included in the query and then click on SELECT for each field.

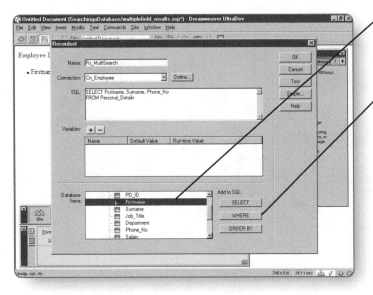

9. Click on the field that the user will be able to search. The field will be highlighted.

10. Click on WHERE. The WHERE clause will be added to the SQL statement.

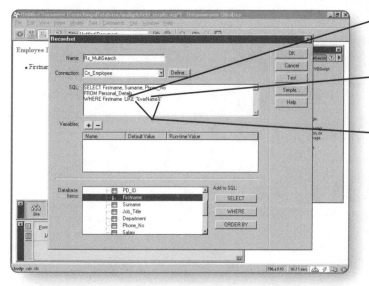

11. Type LIKE after the field name in the WHERE clause.

12. Type in a variable name enclosed by apostrophes.

13. Type the % wildcard before and after the variable name. This will allow the search criteria to be matched to any portion of the field.

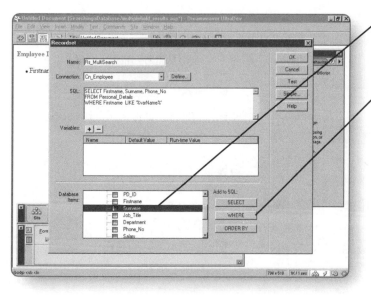

14. Click on the other field that needs to be searched. The field will be highlighted.

15. Click on WHERE. The fields will be separated by AND in the WHERE clause.

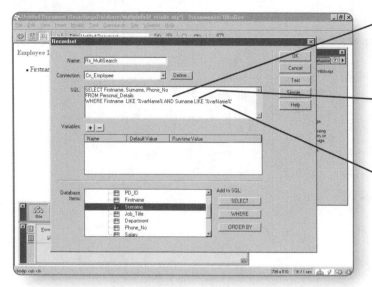

16. Replace AND with OR, because the search criteria can match any of the fields.

17. Type the Equal To (LIKE) operator after each field in the WHERE clause.

18. Type in the variable name used in step 12 between apostrophes after the Equal To operator for both fields. Be sure to include the % wildcard.

19. Click on the + sign. A new field will be created in the Name column of the Variables grid.

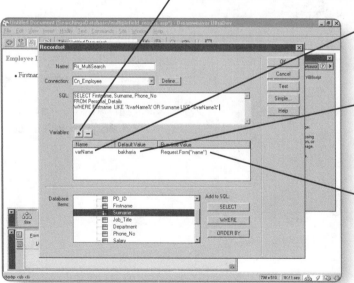

20. Type in the name of the variable entered in steps 12 and 18 in the SQL statement.

21. Type in a default value. This is used when you test the query by clicking on the Test button.

22. Type in a run-time value. This will be retrieved from a form using the Request.Form object.

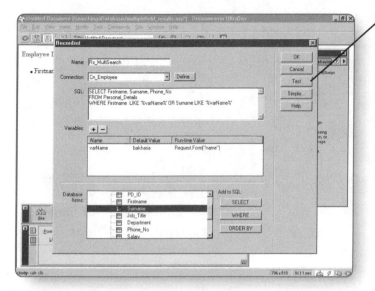

23. Click on Test. The Test SQL Statement dialog box will open.

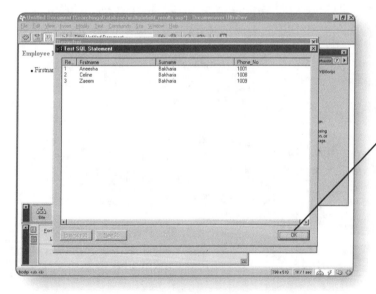

NOTE

You have just created a query that will search multiple database fields.

24. Click on OK. The Test SQL Statement dialog box will close.

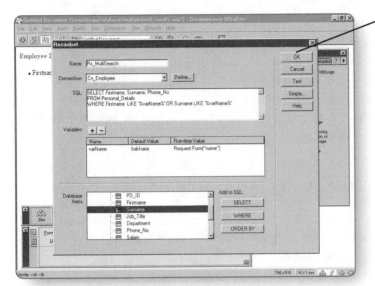

25. Click on OK. The Recordset dialog box will close.

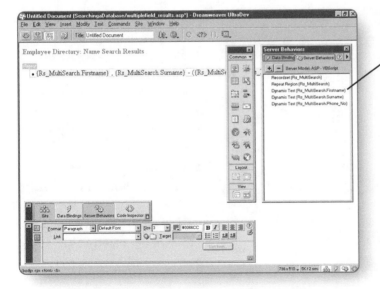

NOTE

You will now have to bind the fields returned in the Recordset to the Web page, and use the Repeat Server behavior to display multiple records. Chapter 8, "Retrieving Data from a Database," covers this topic in depth.

Displaying User-Friendly Search

Databases can hold thousands of records. When enabling users to search a database, you never know how many records will be returned. You can easily achieve this goal by displaying a reasonable amount of records on a page and letting users page through the returned results at their own pace. Search engines take a similar approach by splitting results across multiple pages.

Displaying Search Results in a Table

Tables provide a handy way to display multiple records from a database because they have a grid-like structure. Each column within the table can represent a field in the database. In Chapter 1, you learned to use UltraDev as a visual tool to create and modify tables. You will now learn how to bind data to a table cell.

1. Create a new Web page with an .asp extension.

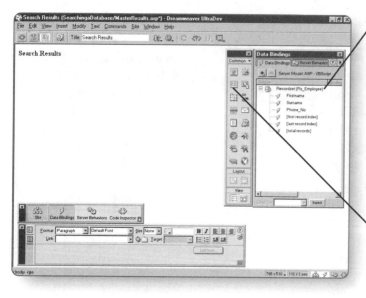

2. Use the Recordset(Query) data source from the Data Bindings palette to create a recordset. The retrieved recordset will be bound to the table cells. The steps involved are fully explained in Chapter 8, "Retrieving Data from a Database," and Chapter 10, "Advanced Database Queries."

3. Click on the Insert Table icon on the Object palette. The Insert Table dialog box will open.

4. Type in the number of rows required. You only need to include a row that will be used to display the column headings and another that will be bound to the database. The Repeat Server Behavior will be used to create a new row for each record retrieved from the database.

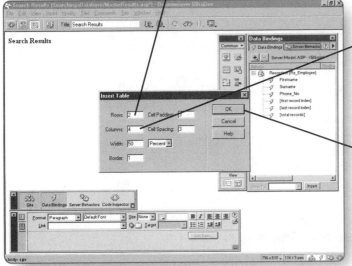

5. Type in the number of columns required. This value will depend upon the number of fields you have retrieved in your recordset and wish to display.

6. Click on OK. The table will be inserted.

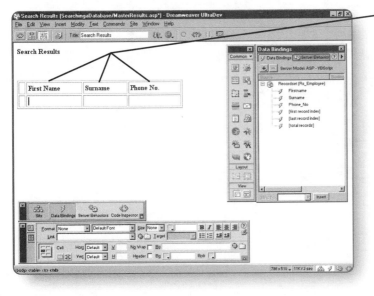

7. Label the table columns. The column headings should reflect the data that will be displayed. Refer to Chapter 1, "UltraDev HTML Basics," for information on adding text to a table cell.

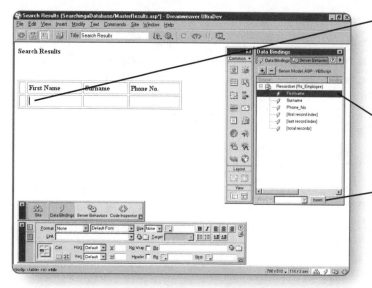

8. Click inside the table cell where the field should be bound. The cursor will appear where you click.

9. Click on a field in the Data Bindings inspector. The field will be selected.

10. Click on Insert. The field placeholder will be inserted as dynamic text in the table cell.

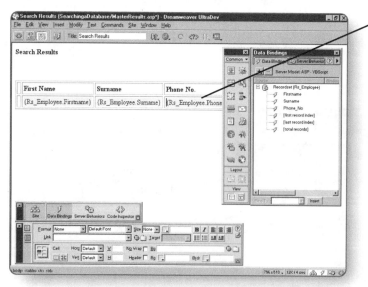

11. Repeat steps 8-10 for each field you want to bind to a table cell. Make sure the cells are all within the same table row.

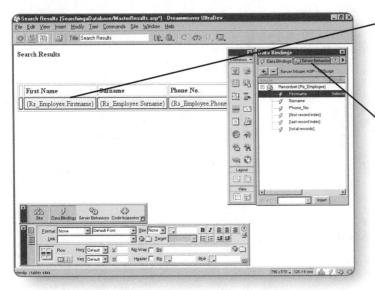

12. Select the row that contains the dynamic text elements. The row will be highlighted.

13. Click on the Server Behaviors tab. The Server Behaviors palette will be displayed.

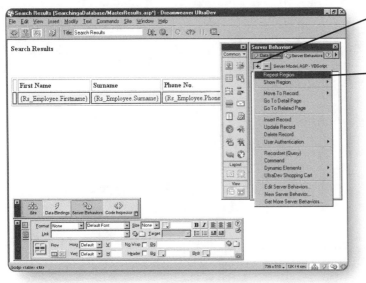

14. Click on the + button. A submenu will appear.

15. Click on Repeat Region. The Repeat Region dialog box will open.

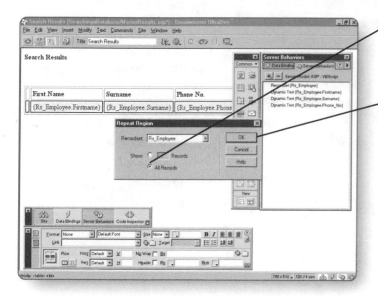

16. Click on the All Records option button. The option will be selected.

17. Click on OK. The Repeat Region dialog box will close. A tabbed grey outline will appear around the table row. This signifies a Repeat Region.

18. Click on the Live Data View icon. Live Data view will be enabled.

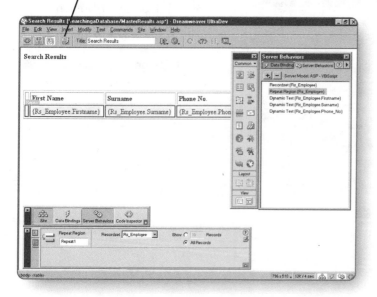

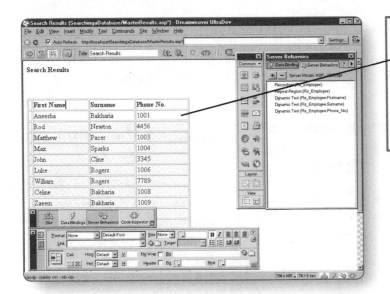

19. Click on the Live Data View icon. Design view will be enabled.

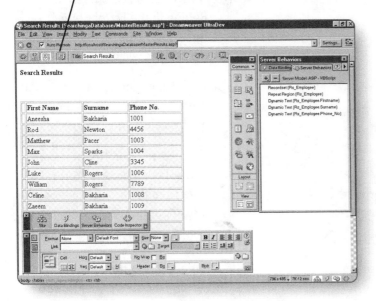

Displaying Paged Search Results

You will now learn how to display results in smaller groups and allow users to step through the results at their own pace. This is essential when a search can return hundreds of records.

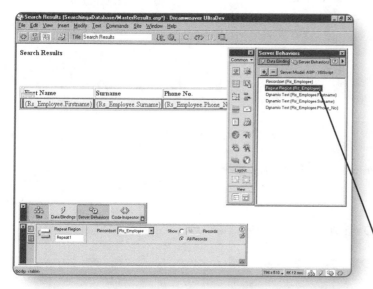

Limiting the Number of Records

Reducing the number of records displayed on a page will save server resources and decrease the time it takes a page to load. The Repeat Region Server Behavior is used to specify the number of records that can be displayed on a page.

1. Double-click on Repeat Region in the list of Server Behaviors. The Repeat Region dialog box will open.

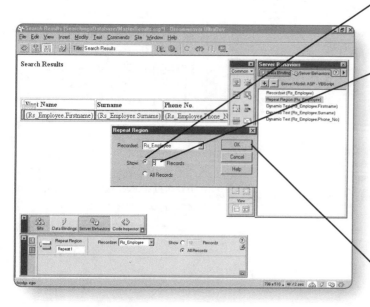

2. Click on Show a Specified Amount of Records. The option will be selected.

3. Type the number of records to display on a page. You will have to make a decision about the amount of records that should be displayed at any one time. The value you select will depend upon the layout of your search results Web page. You should generally try to prevent too much scrolling.

4. Click on OK. The Repeat Region dialog box will close.

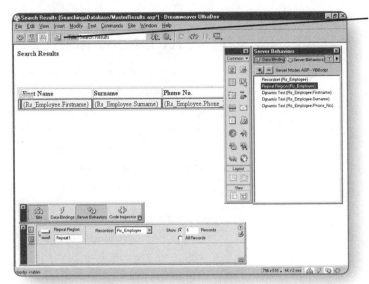

5. Click on the Live Data View icon. Live Data view will be enabled.

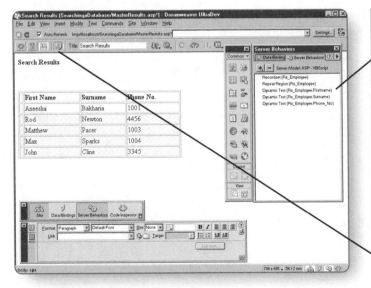

NOTE

Only the specified number of records is displayed on the page. But what if more results are returned in the search? In the next section, you will create a navigation panel so that users can page through returned results.

6. Click on the Live Data View icon. Design view will be enabled.

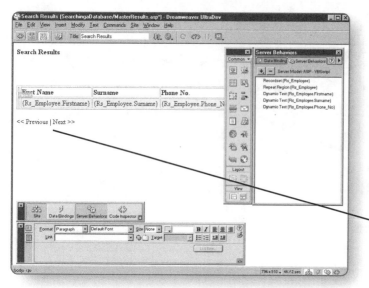

Creating a Navigation Panel

A navigation panel allows users to navigate quickly through paged search results. The navigation panel must contain a link/button to move forward to the next page and a link/button to return to the previous page.

1. Insert text for the recordset navigation panel. Ideally, you will have placeholder text for Previous and Next links.

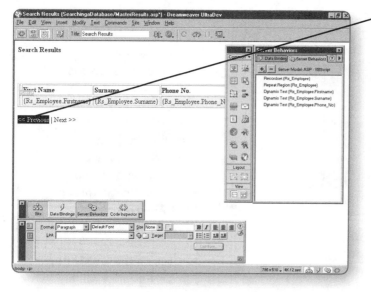

2. Select the Previous link. The text will be highlighted.

3. Click on the Server Behavior tab, if not already selected. The Server Behaviors palette will be displayed.

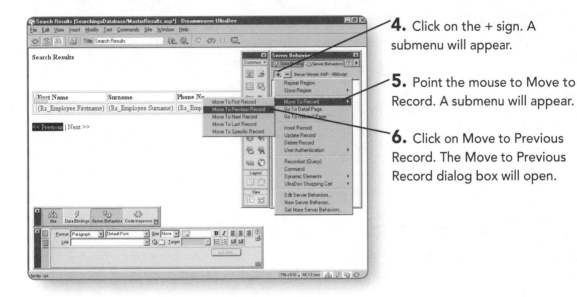

4. Click on the + sign. A submenu will appear.

5. Point the mouse to Move to Record. A submenu will appear.

6. Click on Move to Previous Record. The Move to Previous Record dialog box will open.

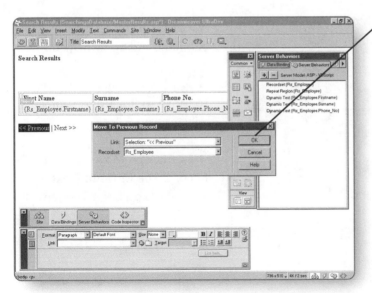

7. Click on OK. There is usually no need to change the default settings. The Move to Next Record dialog box will close.

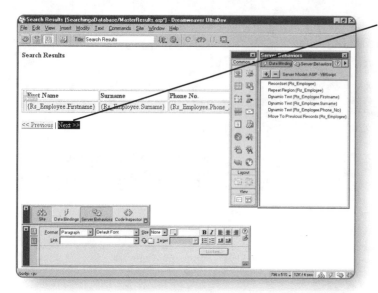

8. Select the Next link. The text will be highlighted.

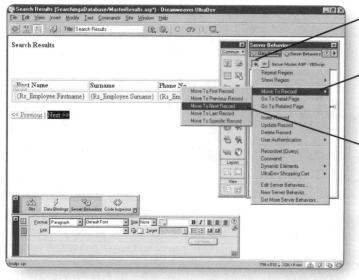

9. Click on the + sign. A submenu will be displayed.

10. Move the mouse pointer to Move to Record. A submenu will appear.

11. Click on Move to Next Record. The Move to Next Record dialog box will open.

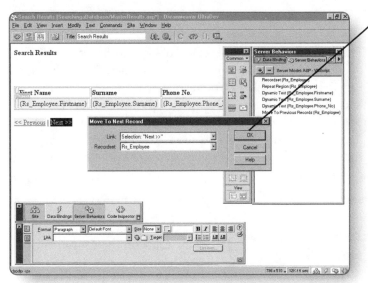

12. Click on OK. There is usually no need to change the default settings. The Move to Next Record dialog box will close.

NOTE

You can't follow links while in Live Data Mode. The functionality of the navigation panel must be tested in a browser.

---

13. Press F12 to preview the current Web page in a browser. The browser will open and display the Web page.

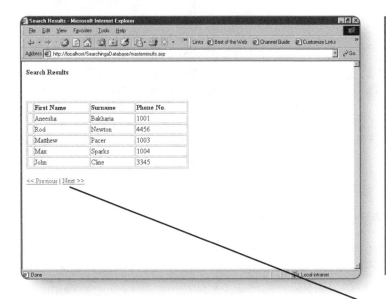

NOTE

The recordset navigation panel has been created. You will be able to page through the results using the Next and Previous links. When the user clicks the Next link, the Web page will display the next set of records. When the user clicks the Previous link, the previous set of records will be displayed.

---

14. Click on the Next link. The Next page of search results will be displayed.

NOTE

The Next and Previous links will always be displayed, even if there are no more records to display. The Previous link should not be displayed on the first page and the Next link should not be displayed on the last page. We will have to disable the Previous link when the first record is displayed and the Next link when the last record is displayed. This will make the navigation panel more intuitive.

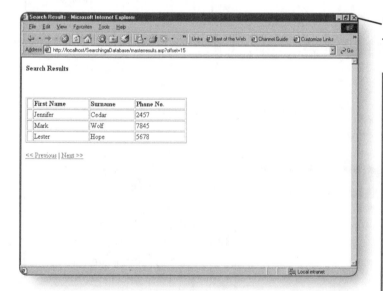

15. Click on the Close icon. The browser will close.

TIP

Download the Links List server behavior from the UltraDev Exchange Web site at **http://www.macromedia.com/exchange/ultradev**. This server behavior inserts a link to each page that contains search results. This drastically improves navigation between result pages.

Disabling Navigation Links

We will use the Show Region Server Behavior to disable the links when there are no more records to display. The Show Region Server Behavior must be applied to both the Next and Previous links.

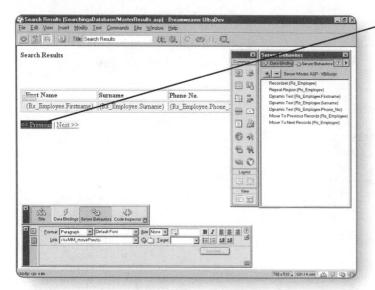

1. Select the Previous link. The text will be highlighted.

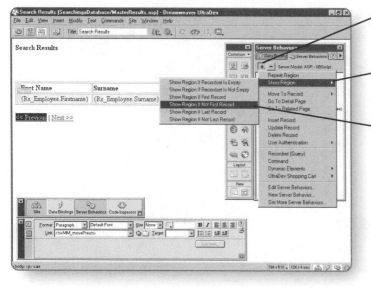

2. Click on the + sign. A submenu will appear.

3. Click on Show Region. A submenu will appear.

4. Click on Show Region If Not First Record. The Show Region If Not First Record dialog box will open.

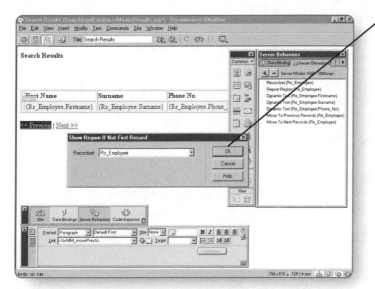

5. Click on OK. The Show Region If Not First Record dialog box will close.

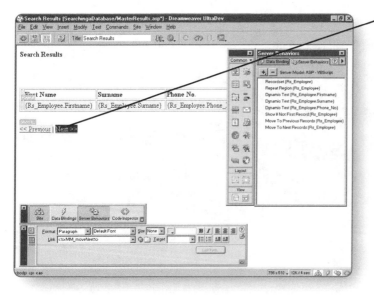

6. Select the Next link. The text will be highlighted.

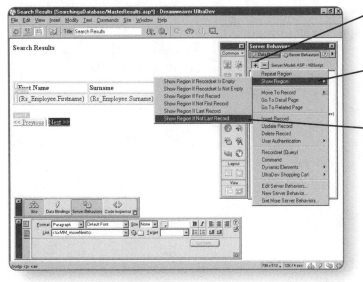

7. Click on the + sign. A submenu will appear.

8. Click on Show Region. A submenu will appear.

9. Click on Show Region If Not Last Record. The Show Region If Not Last Record dialog box will open.

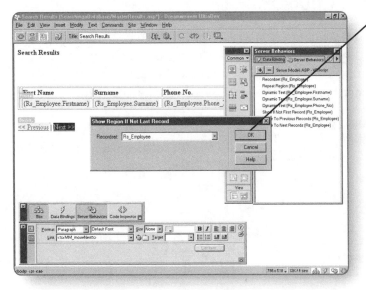

10. Click on OK. The Show Region If Not Last Record dialog box will close.

11. Press F12 to preview the current Web page in a browser. The browser will open and load the Web.

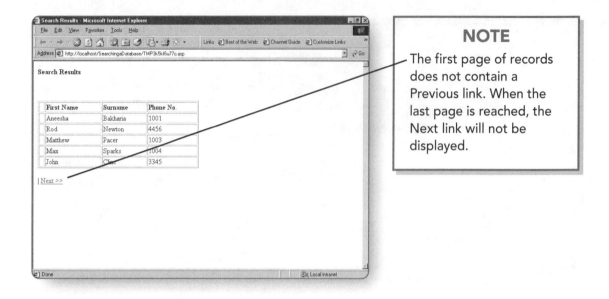

NOTE

The first page of records does not contain a Previous link. When the last page is reached, the Next link will not be displayed.

Creating a Record Counter

Recordset statistics are always returned in a recordset and can be used to create a record counter. Every query returns the index of the first record on a page, the index of the last record on a page, and the total number of records returned. A record count informs users about the amount of search results returned.

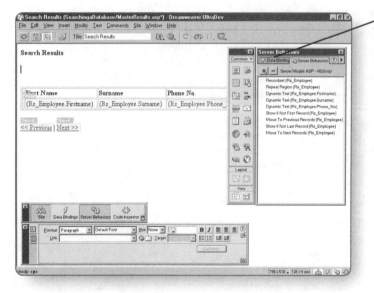

1. Click on the Data Bindings tab. The Data Bindings palette will be displayed.

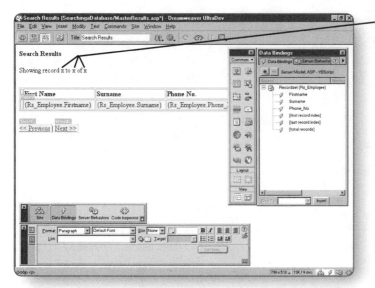

2. Insert placeholder text for the record counter. Ideally, you will have placeholder text to display the first record, the last record, and the total number of records.

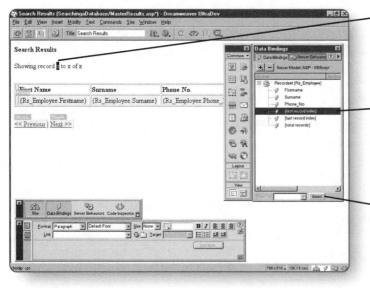

3. Select the text that should be replaced by the index of the first record on a page. The text will be highlighted.

4. Click on [first record index] in the Data Bindings palette. The [first record index] will be highlighted.

5. Click on Insert. The [first record index] placeholder will be inserted as dynamic text.

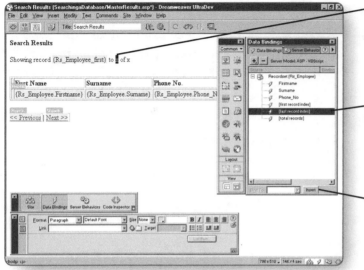

6. Select the text that should be replaced by the index of the last record on a page. The text will be highlighted.

7. Click on [last record index] in the Data Bindings palette. The [last record index] will be highlighted.

8. Click on Insert. The [last record index] placeholder will be inserted as dynamic text.

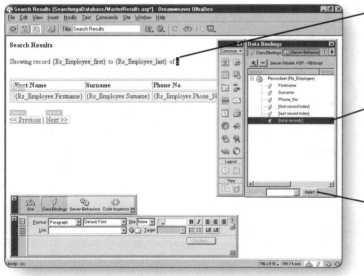

9. Select the text that should be replaced by the total number of records returned. The text will be highlighted.

10. Click on [total records] in the Data Bindings palette. The [total records] will be highlighted.

11. Click on Insert. The [total records] placeholder is inserted as dynamic text.

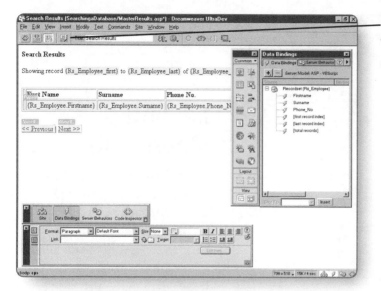

12. Click on the Live Data View icon. Live Data view will be enabled.

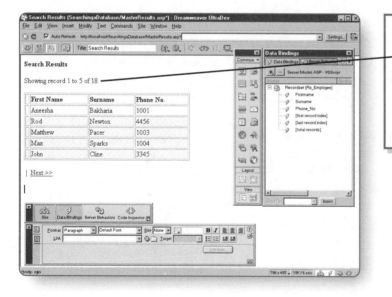

NOTE

The record counter will be displayed. The record counter indicates the user's position in the paged recordset.

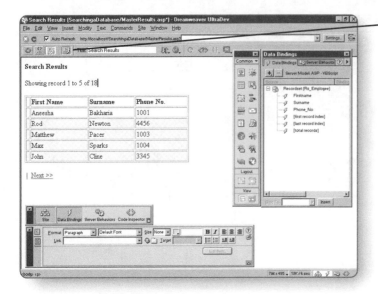

13. Click on the Live Data View icon. Design view will be enabled.

Linking to a Detail Page

The search results pages should ideally display only summary data from each record and provide a link which the user can click on to view detailed information. This allows the user to evaluate the search results and then decide which result he wants to view in full.

Creating a Detail Link

A detail link must pass the unique ID number of the record to the detail page. The best way to achieve this is to append the ID number to the detail page URL, i.e. the QueryString. Move To Specific Record takes care of all the hard work.

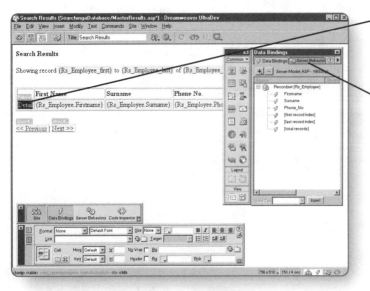

1. Select the text that must link to a detail page. The text will be highlighted.

2. Click on the Server Behaviors tab, if not already selected. The Server Behaviors palette will be displayed.

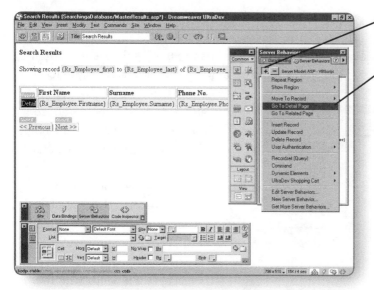

3. Click on the + sign. A submenu will appear.

4. Click on Go To Detail Page. The Go To Detail Page dialog box will open.

5. Type the name of the file that will display the full record. This is known as the Detail Page. The file name will be inserted into the name field.

NOTE

The primary key/unique ID of the record is detected by UltraDev.

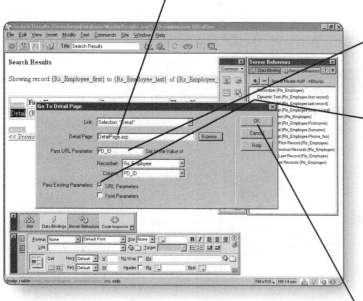

6. Click inside the URL Parameters check box. A check mark will be placed in the box. This means that the record ID will be passed to the Detail Page as a QueryString; i.e., it will be appended to the URL. Refer to Chapter 5, "Creating HTML Forms," for more information about the QueryString.

7. Click on OK. The Go To Detail Page dialog box will close.

Creating a Detail Page

A Detail Page must retrieve the record that matches the unique ID passed to it in the QueryString. In this section, you will set up a query that will retrieve the ID

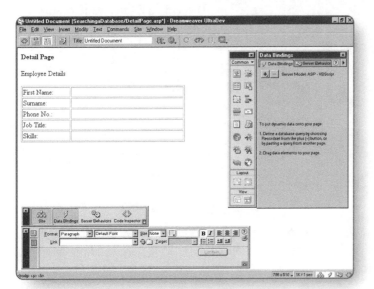

number from the QueryString and then search the database for the record that matches the ID number. Obviously, a Detail Page must display comprehensive information about a record. Users will be expecting the full record to be displayed.

1. Create a new file with the name assigned in step 5 of the previous section with an .asp extension.

2. Click on the Data Bindings tab, if not already selected. The Data Bindings palette will be displayed.

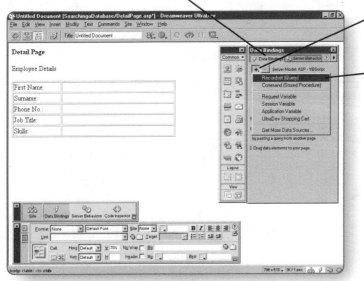

3. Click on the + sign. A submenu will appear.

4. Click on Recordset(Query). The Recordset dialog box will open.

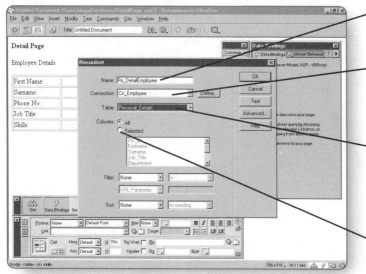

5. Type a name for the recordset.

6. Select a database connection. The option will be selected.

7. Select the table that contains the record that you need to retrieve. The option will be selected.

8. Click on the Selected option box. The option will be selected.

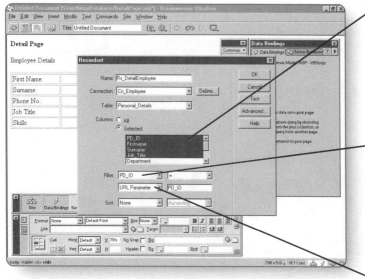

9. Select the fields that must be returned by the query. To select more than one field, hold down the Ctrl key, and then click the fields you want to include.

10. Select the field that corresponds to the value that is being passed to the Detail Page via the QueryString. It must be the unique ID field, also known as the primary key.

11. Select URL Parameter, because the ID number must be retrieved from the QueryString. The option will be selected.

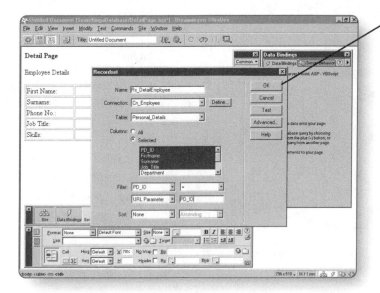

12. Click on OK. The Recordset dialog box will close.

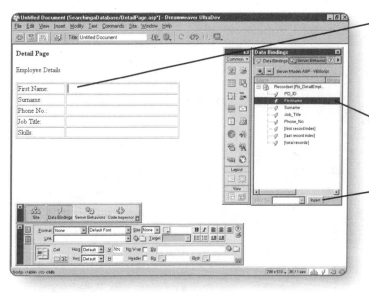

13. Click in the Document window where the field should be bound. The cursor will appear where you click.

14. Click on a field in the Data Bindings palette. The field will be selected.

15. Click on Insert. The field placeholder will be inserted as dynamic text.

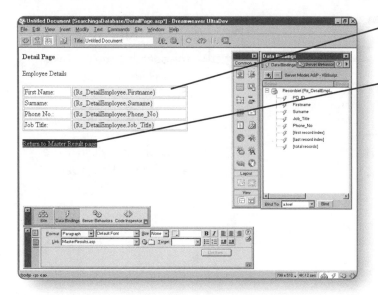

16. Repeat steps 13-15 for each field to be inserted.

17. Insert a link back to the Master results page.

Testing a Detail Link

A detail link can't be tested with the Live Data Preview. You will have to preview the Web page in a browser to test the detail links.

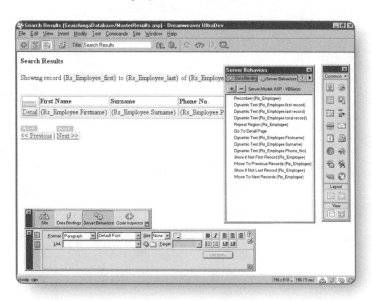

1. Open the search results page that contains the detail link. This page was created in a previous section, "Creating the Detail Link."

2. Press F12 to preview the current Web page in a browser. The browser will open and display the Web page.

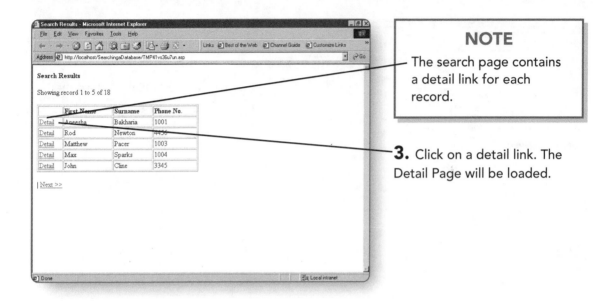

NOTE

The search page contains a detail link for each record.

3. Click on a detail link. The Detail Page will be loaded.

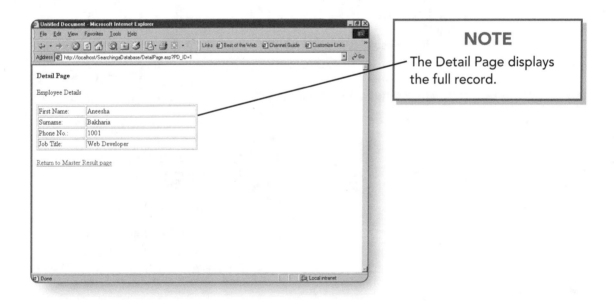

NOTE

The Detail Page displays the full record.

12

Creating Dynamic Form Objects

Forms play an important role in database maintenance. Form objects (text fields, check boxes, radio buttons, and drop-down lists/menus) must be populated with the contents of a record so that the user can view and edit the data before sending it back to the server for processing. In this chapter, you'll learn to make dynamic:

- Text fields
- Radio buttons
- Check boxes
- List/Menu boxes

Making Text Fields Dynamic

Text fields should only be bound to data that can be displayed in a single line. Text fields ideally are used to update fields that store data such as a name, phone number, or e-mail address. Use a multi-line text field if the stored data spans multiple lines.

1. Create an HTML form. Use form objects (text fields, radio buttons, check boxes and drop-down lists) that best suit your data entry needs. You will need to be familiar with creating forms in UltraDev; this was covered in Chapter 5, "Creating HTML Forms," and Chapter 6, "Validating and Retrieving Form Data."

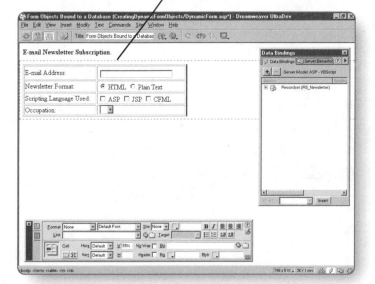

NOTE

All form objects must be named. The names given to form objects should match the table columns to which they will be bound.

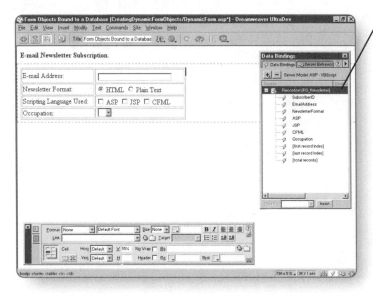

2. Use the Recordset(Query) Data Source from the Data Bindings palette to create a recordset. The retrieved recordset will be bound to form objects. You can only display one record at a time in a form. You must therefore create a query that only retrieves a single record from a database. The steps involved to create a recordset that retrieves a specific record are covered in Chapter 8, "Retrieving Data from a Database," and Chapter 10, "Advanced Database Queries."

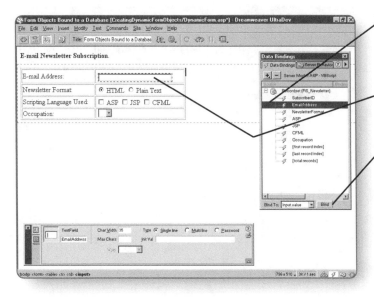

3. Click on the field that will be bound to a text field. The field name will be highlighted.

4. Click on the text field. The field will be selected.

5. Click on the Bind button. The field will be bound to the text field.

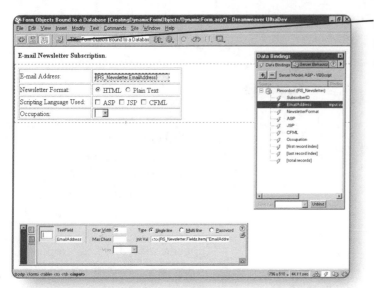

6. Click on the Live Data View icon. Live Data view will be enabled.

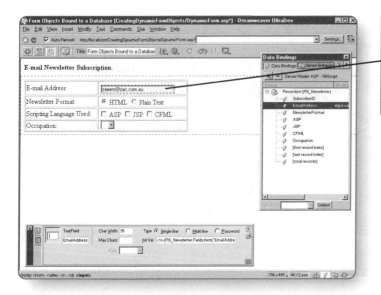

NOTE

The text field will display the data retrieved from the database.

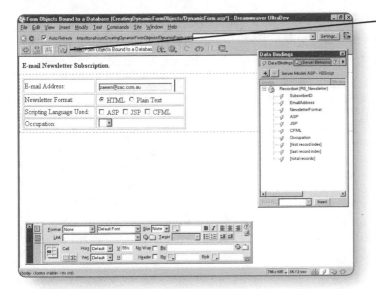

7. Click on the Live Data View icon. Design view will be enabled.

Making Radio Buttons Dynamic

Radio buttons can only be used correctly if more than one option is available to the user. You should use them to update data where the user has a number of options available but must only select one. A good example of this is a field that stores whether a person is under or over 18 years old. If the button group is dynamic, it will only appear when 'triggered' by information stored in the database. For

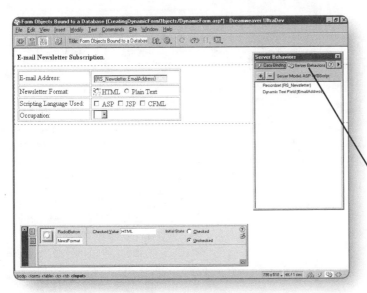

example, if the form is related to legally binding agreements, you may want the user to be prompted to state that he or she is over 18 years of age. Radio buttons must be grouped, and grouped radio buttons must all be given the same name.

1. Click on the Server Behaviors tab. The Server Behaviors palette will be displayed.

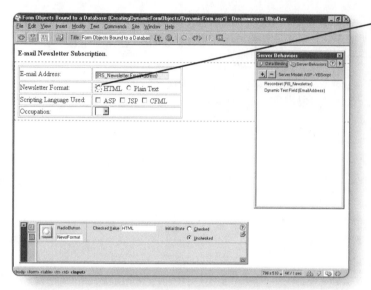

2. Click on a radio button that is part of a group of radio buttons. The radio button will be selected.

TIP

Make sure that all radio buttons in a group have the same name, but different values. Refer to Chapter 5, "Creating HTML Forms," to refresh your knowledge.

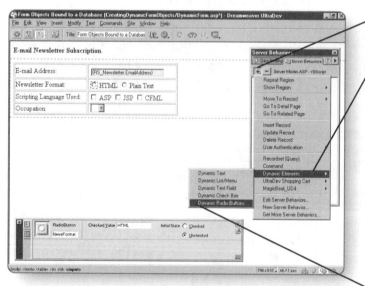

3. Click on the + sign. A submenu will appear.

4. Click on Dynamic Elements. A submenu will appear.

NOTE

The Dynamic Elements Server Behavior will help you bind data to all the different types of form objects.

5. Click on Dynamic Radio buttons. The Dynamic Radio buttons dialog box will open.

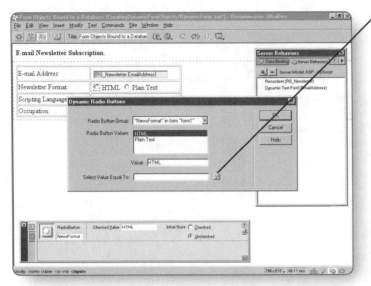

6. Click on the lightning bolt icon. The Dynamic Data dialog box will open.

NOTE

UltraDev detects the group to which the selected radio button belongs. All the radio button values are also inserted in the Radio Button Values list.

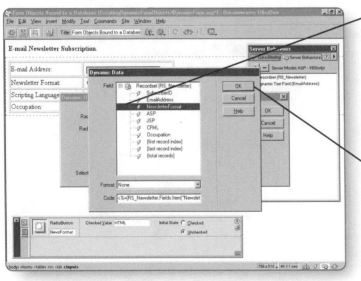

7. Click on the field that will be bound to the radio button. The Code field will be generated. The radio button that matches the data stored in the field will be selected when the page loads.

8. Click on OK. The Dynamic Data dialog box will close.

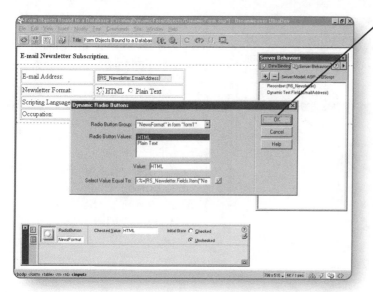

9. Click on OK. The Dynamic Radio Buttons dialog box will close. The group of radio buttons will be bound to the selected database field.

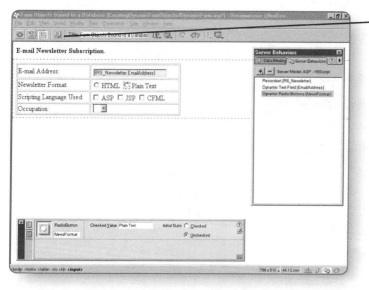

10. Click on the Live Data View icon. Live Data view will be enabled.

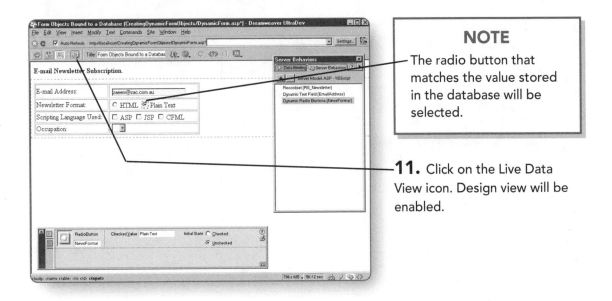

NOTE

The radio button that matches the value stored in the database will be selected.

11. Click on the Live Data View icon. Design view will be enabled.

Making Check Boxes Dynamic

Use check boxes for a list of fields that can be selected or deselected. The user is allowed to select any combination of fields. Typically, the field must contain data that can be represented in Boolean form, such as Yes/No or True/False. Boolean means that the form object is only capable of storing 2 values.

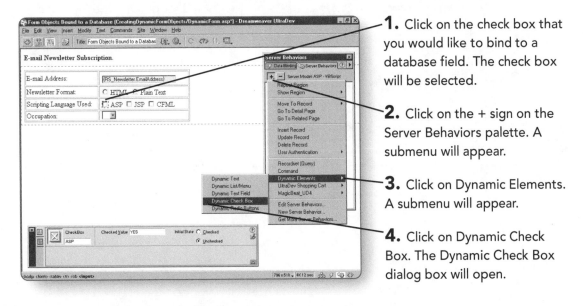

1. Click on the check box that you would like to bind to a database field. The check box will be selected.

2. Click on the + sign on the Server Behaviors palette. A submenu will appear.

3. Click on Dynamic Elements. A submenu will appear.

4. Click on Dynamic Check Box. The Dynamic Check Box dialog box will open.

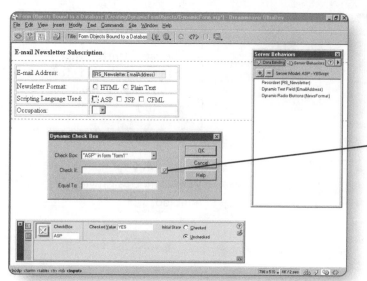

NOTE

The name and value of the check box will be detected.

5. Click on the Lightning Bolt icon. The Dynamic Data window will open.

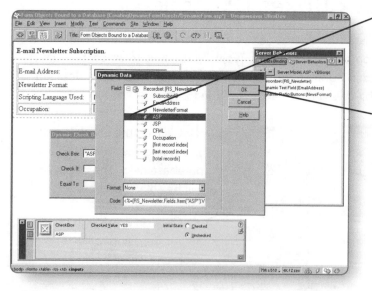

6. Click on the database field you want to bind to the check box. The Code field will be generated.

7. Click on OK. The Dynamic Data dialog box will close.

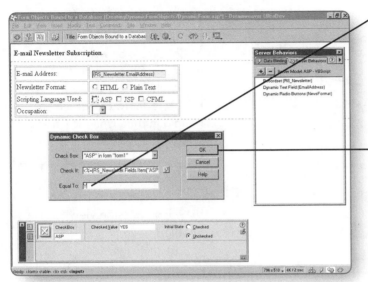

8. Type the value that must be stored in the database field for the check box to be selected by default when the Web page loads. This will usually be a Boolean value.

9. Click on OK. The Dynamic Check Box dialog box will close.

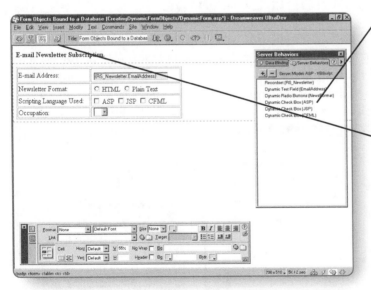

10. Repeat steps 1-9 for each check box on your form. A Dynamic Check Box Server Behavior will be added for each check box that you add.

11. Click on the Live Data View icon. Live Data view will be enabled.

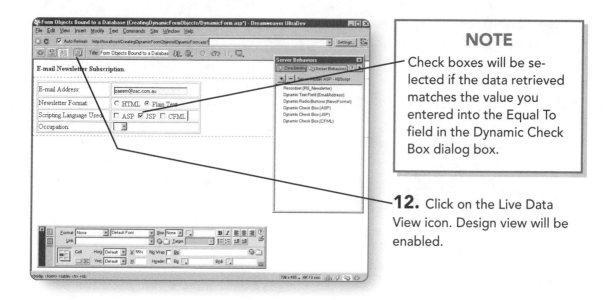

NOTE

Check boxes will be selected if the data retrieved matches the value you entered into the Equal To field in the Dynamic Check Box dialog box.

12. Click on the Live Data View icon. Design view will be enabled.

Making a List/Menu Dynamic

Dreamweaver menus are also commonly known as drop-down lists. They allow the user to make a selection from a long list of options without wasting valuable screen space. They are ideal if you want to restrict the values that can be stored in a database field to a pre-defined list. You can enter the options manually or dynamically populate the list with the results of a database query.

NOTE

You will need two recordsets to create a dynamic drop-down list.

The first recordset will be bound to the drop-down list. This means that the option that matches the data stored in the database will be selected when the Web page loads.

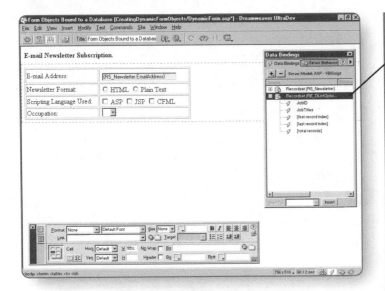

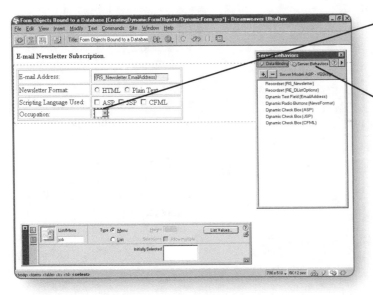

1. Click on the drop-down list. The drop-down list will be selected.

2. Click on the Server Behaviors tab. The Server Behaviors palette will be displayed.

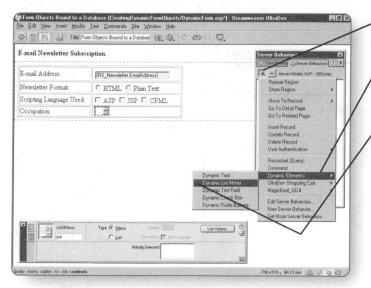

3. Click on the + sign. A submenu will appear.

4. Click on Dynamic Elements. A submenu will appear.

5. Click on Dynamic List/Menu. The Dynamic List/Menu dialog box will open.

6. Select the recordset that will be used to populate the drop-down list with options. This recordset must retrieve distinct records from the database. The recordset will be selected.

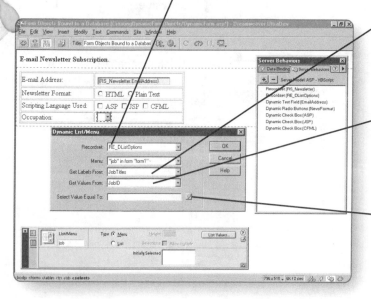

7. Select the field that will be used to set the labels of the drop-down list options. The field will be selected.

8. Select the field that will be used to set the values of the drop-down list options. The field will be selected.

9. Click on the lightning bolt icon. The Dynamic Data dialog box will open.

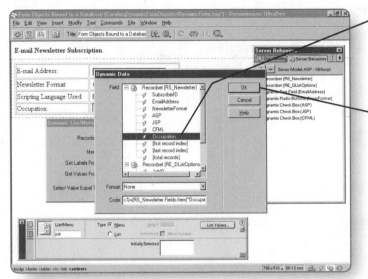

10. Click on the field that will be bound to the drop-down list. The Code field will be generated.

11. Click on OK. The Dynamic Data dialog box will close.

12. Click on OK. The Dynamic List/Menu dialog box will close.

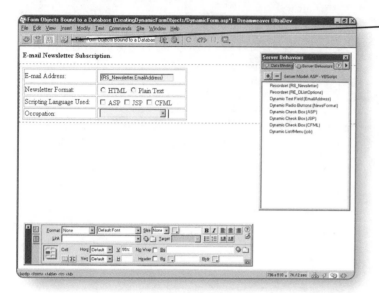

13. Click on the Live Data View icon. Live Data view will be enabled.

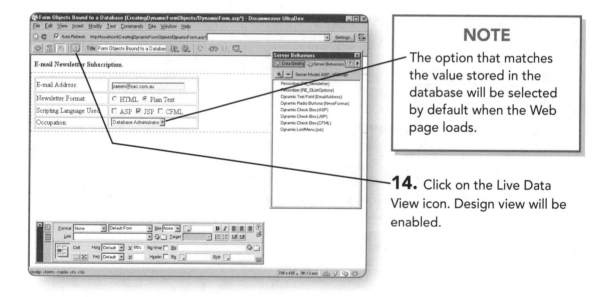

NOTE

The option that matches the value stored in the database will be selected by default when the Web page loads.

14. Click on the Live Data View icon. Design view will be enabled.

13

Inserting, Updating, and Deleting Records

It is rare that the data stored in a database will remain static over a long period of time. A Web-enabled database, in particular, has the potential to be accessed by millions of people and must be maintained to prevent invalid data from being displayed. You can easily insert, update, and delete records. UltraDev comes with a set of Server Behaviors that will allow you to incorporate all of this functionality in your Web site. In this chapter, you'll learn to:

- Insert records
- Update existing records
- Delete records

Inserting Records

You need to provide a means for users to populate a database in the first place, as well as to add to the database at a later stage. Adding a new record to a database is not as difficult as you might think. The Insert Record server behavior takes care of all the hard work.

Creating the Insert Form

A form must be created to gather the data to be inserted as a new record in the database table. The form should contain all the fields required to create a new record.

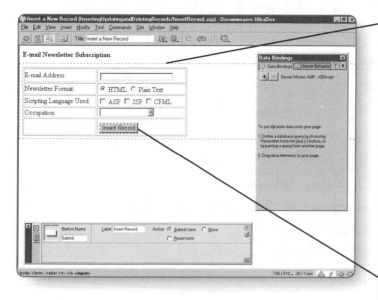

1. Create an HTML form. Use form elements (text fields, radio buttons, check boxes and drop-down lists) that best suit your data entry needs. Consult Chapter 5, "Creating HTML Forms," and Chapter 6, "Validating and Retrieving Form Data," if you do not feel comfortable with creating forms in UltraDev.

NOTE

The form must have a Submit button that indicates the purpose of the form, which in this case is to insert a new record in the database. This will be covered in the next section.

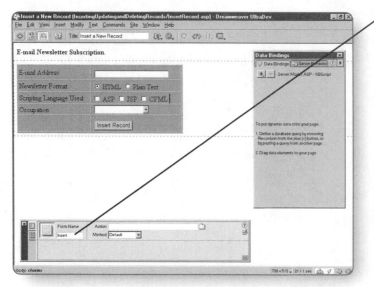

2. Type a name for the form, which indicates the purpose of the form.

> ### NOTE
> All form elements must be named. The names given to form elements must match the table columns where data will be inserted. This will make using the Insert Server Behavior a breeze.

Using the Insert Record Server Behavior

The Insert Record server behavior generates all of the code required to insert a new record. All you need to do is specify the database connection and the table where the record must be inserted then match the form elements to the table columns.

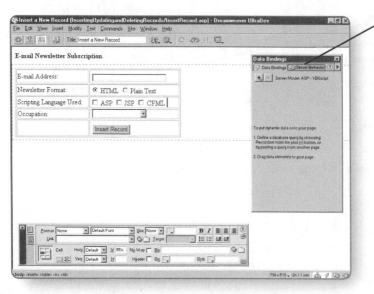

1. Click on the Server Behaviors tab. The Server Behaviors palette will be displayed.

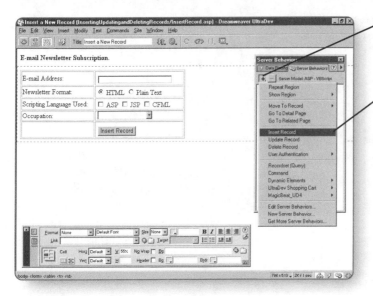

2. Click on the + sign in the Server Behaviors palette. A submenu will appear.

3. Click on Insert Record. The Insert Record dialog box will open.

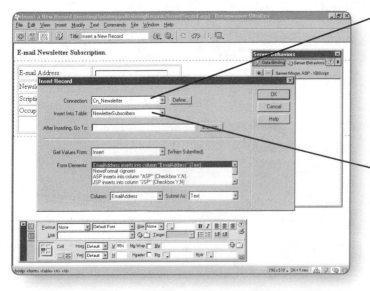

4. Select the connection for the database that needs a Web-based interface to insert data. Creating a connection is covered in Chapter 8, "Retrieving Data from a Database."

5. Select the table where the record will be inserted. The table name will be selected.

6. Type a file name in the After Inserting, Go To field. This file will be displayed after the record has been inserted.

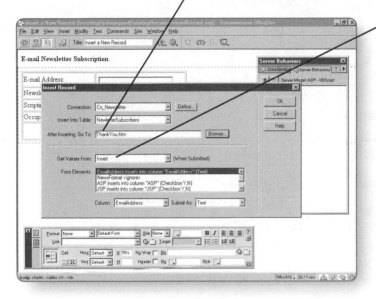

7. Select the form that will be used to insert data if the form that UltraDev has selected is incorrect. This will only happen if there is more than one form on your Web page.

NOTE

UltraDev will automatically match form elements to the database table columns where the data will be inserted, provided the form element and the database columns have the same names. This is why you should always label your form elements correctly. If UltraDev fails to match a form element to any column in the database table, <ignore> will be placed beside the field name. In this case, you will have to match the form elements to table columns manually.

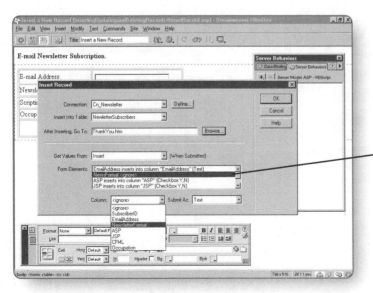

8. Select the column name where the data in the currently selected form element must be inserted. (You are really just matching the form elements to database columns/fields.)

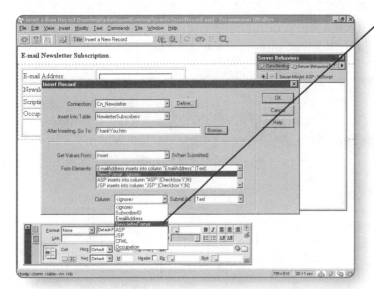

9. Click on the name of the form element that must be matched to a table column. The form object will be selected.

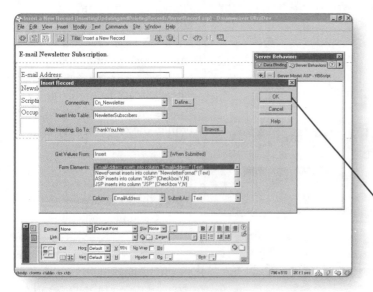

NOTE

Once a table column has been selected, the type of data that the column stores is detected. This column could hold text, numeric data, or a date.

10. Click on OK. The Insert Record dialog box will close.

Testing the Insert Record Server Behavior

You can only test the Insert server behavior from a Web browser. The Live Data window does not currently support this function.

1. Save the Web page and preview it in a Web browser. The Web page will be displayed in the Web browser. If you are not familiar with saving or previewing a page, please refer to Chapter 1.

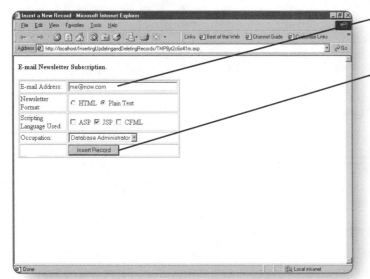

2. Enter relevant data into the form fields.

3. Click on the Insert Record button. The record will be inserted and the page that you specified in the After Inserting, Go To field in the Insert Server Behavior dialog box will be displayed.

Updating Records

Databases are very flexible in the way they allow records to be modified. In addition to adding new records, users often need to edit existing records. The Update Record server behavior incorporates this functionality into UltraDev.

Linking to an Update Form

Before a record can be updated, the user must first select it. You will therefore need to display a summary of records and create a detail link to the update form. The detail link will pass the unique ID number of the record to the update form.

1. Create a search results page that will display summary data from each record.

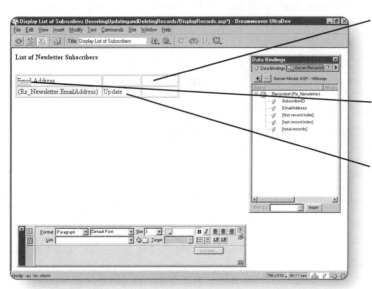

- Use a table to lay out the results. Chapter 11, "Searching a Database," covered the topic in detail.

- Use the Repeat Region server behavior to display multiple records in the result table.

- Each record must have an Update link, which the user can click on to open the appropriate form. The link will need to be within the Repeat Region, so that an Update link is inserted for each record displayed.

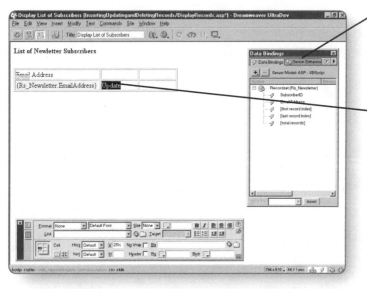

2. Click on the Server Behaviors tab. The Server Behaviors palette will be displayed.

3. Select the Update link. The text will be highlighted.

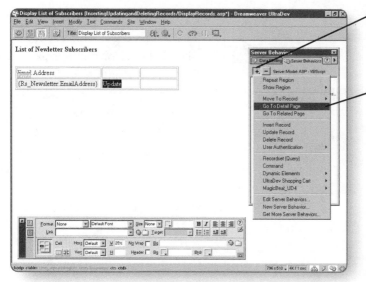

4. Click on the + sign of the Server Behaviors palette. A submenu will appear.

5. Click on Go to Detail Page. The Go To Detail Page dialog box will open.

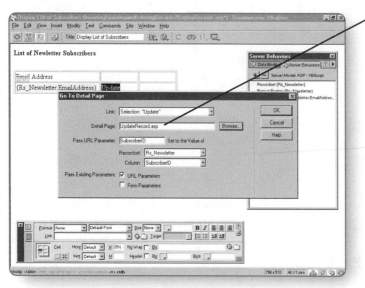

6. Type in the name of the Web page that will contain the update form.

NOTE

The primary key of the table will be detected. This value will be passed to the Web page that contains the update form.

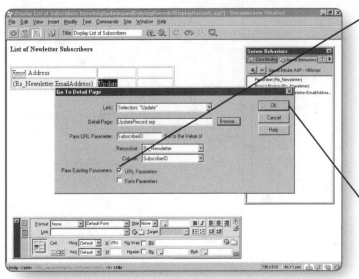

7. Click inside the URL Parameters check box. A check will be placed inside the box. The unique identifier of the current record will be passed to the update form as a URL parameter. This means that it will be appended to the URL as a QueryString.

8. Click on OK. The Go To Detail Page dialog box will close and the Update link will be created.

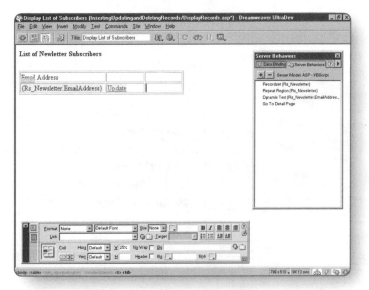

9. Press Ctrl+s. The search results Web page will be saved.

Creating an Update Form

The form objects that comprise the update form need to display the contents of the retrieved record. The update form should contain all of the fields that the user is allowed to update.

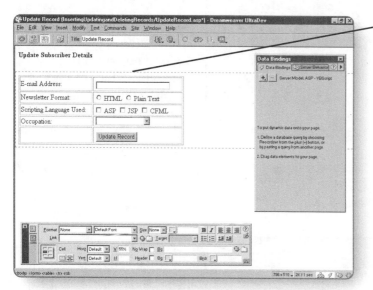

1. Create an HTML form. The update form must contain form objects (text fields, radio buttons, check boxes, and drop-down lists) that best suit your data entry requirements. Refer to Chapter 5, "Creating HTML Forms," and Chapter 6, "Validating and Retrieving Form Data," if you do not feel comfortable with creating forms in UltraDev.

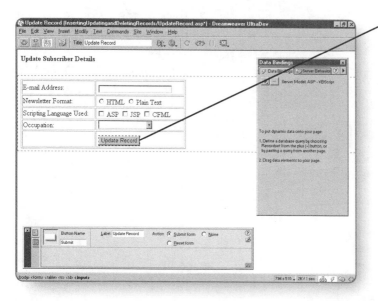

2. Create a Submit button. The form must have a Submit button that indicates the purpose of the form, which in this case is to insert a new record in the database.

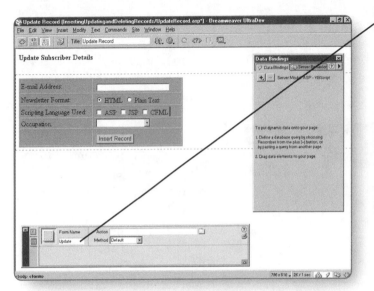

3. Type a name for the form, which indicates the purpose of the form.

NOTE

All form objects must be named. The names given to form objects must match the table columns to which they will be bound. This will make using the Update server behavior a breeze.

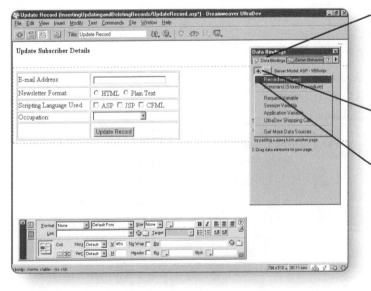

4. Click on the Data Bindings tab, if not already selected. The Data Bindings palette will be displayed.

5. Click on the 1 sign. A submenu will appear.

6. Click on Recordset(Query). The Recordset dialog box will open.

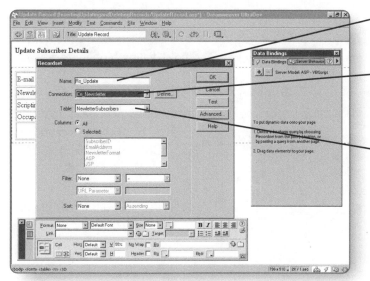

7. Type a name for the recordset.

8. Select a database connection. The option will be selected.

9. Select the table that contains the record you need to retrieve. The option will be selected.

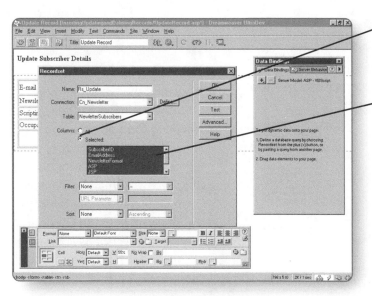

10. Click on the Selected option box. The option will be selected.

11. Select the fields that must be returned by the query. To select more than one field, hold down the Ctrl key, and then click the fields you want to include. Only select the fields that the user will be allowed to update. These fields will be bound to the form objects on the update form.

12. Select the field that corresponds to the value that is being passed to the update form via the QueryString. In this case it must be the unique ID field also known as the primary key. The field will be highlighted.

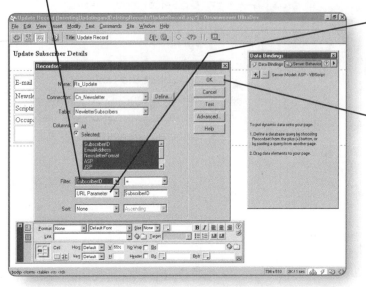

13. Select URL Parameter, because the ID number must be retrieved from the QueryString. The option will be selected.

14. Click on OK. The Recordset dialog box will close.

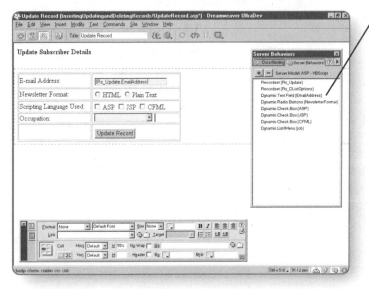

15. Bind the fields retrieved from the database to their matching form objects. You will need to use the Dynamic Elements server behavior. Chapter 12, "Creating Dynamic Form Objects," covers this topic comprehensively. The Dynamic Elements server behavior can be used to create dynamic text fields, radio buttons, check boxes and drop-down lists. Binding a form element to a database field means that when the Web page loads, the form objects will be populated with the contents of a record. This will allow the user to view and edit the data.

Using the Update Record Server Behavior

Using the Update Record server behavior is slightly more involved than using the Insert Record server behavior. In addition to specifying the database connection and the table where the record should be updated and matching form objects to table columns, you also need to specify the unique ID number of the record to be updated. This value is passed to the update form in the query string.

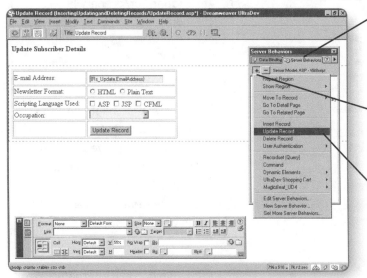

1. Click on the Server Behaviors tab, if not already selected. The Server Behaviors palette will be displayed.

2. Click on the + sign in the Server Behaviors palette. A submenu will appear.

3. Click on Update Record. The Update Record dialog box will open.

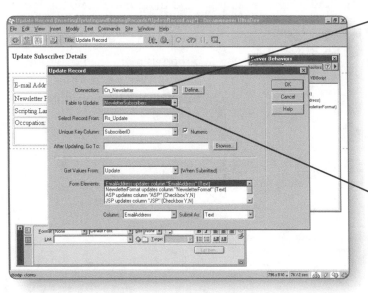

4. Select the database connection for the database that needs a Web-based interface to update data. Creating a connection is covered in Chapter 8, "Retrieving Data from a Database."

5. Select the table that will contain the record to be updated. The table name will be selected.

6. Select the recordset that is bound to the update form if the recordset that UltraDev has selected is incorrect. This will only happen if there is more than one recordset bound to the Web page.

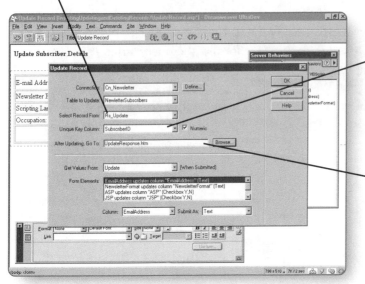

NOTE

The unique record identifier/primary key is automatically selected in the Unique Key Column drop-down list.

7. Type a file name into the After Updating, Go To field. This file will be displayed after the record has been updated. Ideally, you will want to acknowledge that the record has been updated.

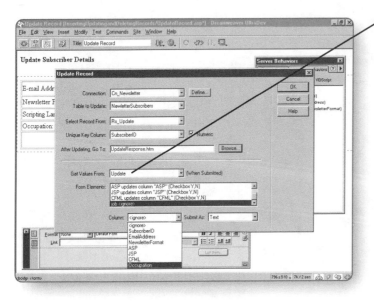

8. Select the form that will be used to update data if the form that UltraDev has selected is incorrect. This will only happen if there is more than one form on your Web page. The selection will be highlighted.

NOTE

UltraDev will automatically match form objects to the database table columns where the record will be updated, provided the form objects and the database columns have the same names. This is why you should always label your form objects accordingly. If UltraDev fails to match a form object to any column in the database table, <ignore> will be placed beside the field name. In this event, you will have to match the form objects to table columns manually.

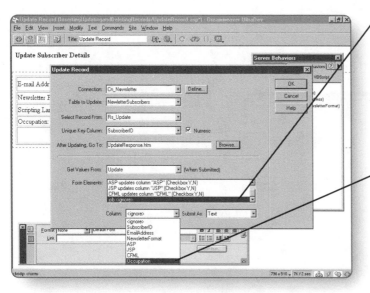

9. Select the column name where the data in the currently selected form object will update. The selection will be highlighted. You are really just matching the form objects to database columns/fields.

10. Click on the name of the form elements that must be matched to a table column. The form object will be selected.

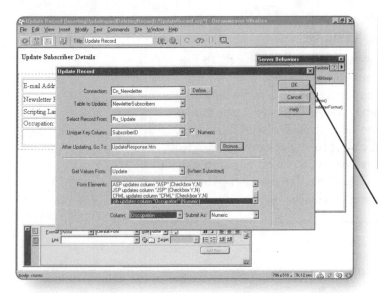

NOTE
After a table column has been selected, the type of data that the column stores is detected. This could be either a text or numeric value.

11. Click on OK. The Update Record dialog box will close.

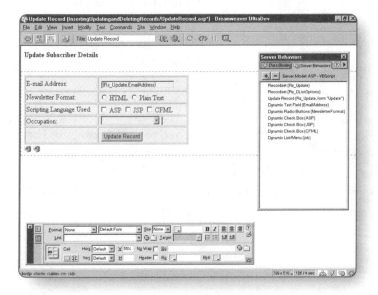

12. Press Ctrl+s. The Web page containing the update form will be saved.

Testing the Update Record Server Behavior

You can only test the Update Record Server Behavior from a Web browser. The Live Data window does not currently support this function.

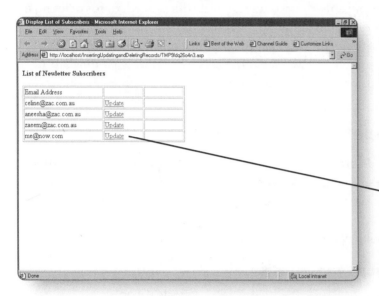

1. Preview search results in the Web page that contain the update link in a Web browser. The Web page will be displayed in the Web browser. If you are not familiar with saving or previewing a page, please refer to Chapter 1.

2. Click on the update link that corresponds to a record that you wish to update. The Web page that contains the update form will be displayed. The form objects will display the data that has been retrieved from the database.

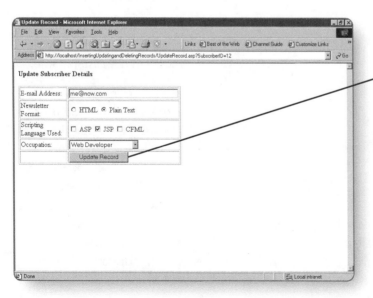

3. Edit the data in the form objects.

4. Click on Update Record. The record will be updated and the page that you specified in the After Updating, Go To field in the Update Server Behavior dialog box will be displayed.

Deleting Records

The last database maintenance feature that you need to provide for your users is the ability to delete outdated or invalid data. Removing records from a database frees up valuable space and speeds up data retrieval. The procedure for deleting a record is not much different from updating, but still deserves its own chapter. Beware that this capability can be very dangerous if placed in the wrong hands. Always make sure that you only allow access to users who know what they are doing, because no Undo command is available.

Linking to a Delete Form

Before a record can be deleted, the user must first select the record to be deleted. You will need to display a summary of records and create a detail link to the delete form. The detail link will pass the unique ID number of the record to the delete form.

1. Create a search results page that will display summary data from each record.

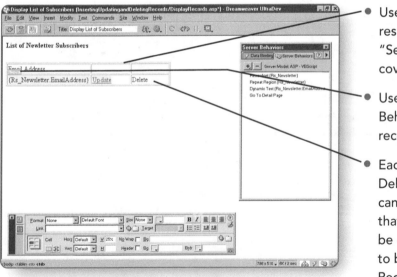

- Use a table to lay out the results. Chapter 11, "Searching a Database," covers this topic in detail.

- Use the Repeat Region Server Behavior to display multiple records in the results table.

- Each record must have a Delete link, which the user can click on to open the form that will allow the record to be deleted. The link will need to be within the Repeat Region, so that a Delete link is inserted for each record displayed. If you would like to allow your users to update records as well, also include an update link. The steps involved in creating an update link are covered in the previous section, "Updating Records."

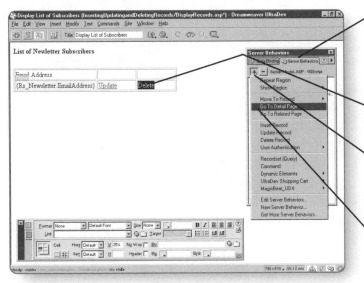

2. Click on the Server Behaviors tab, if not already selected. The Server Behaviors palette will be displayed.

3. Select the Delete link. The text will be highlighted.

4. Click on the + sign of the Server Behaviors palette. A submenu will appear.

5. Click on Go To Detail Page. The Go To Detail Page dialog box will open.

6. Type in the name of the Web page that will contain the delete form.

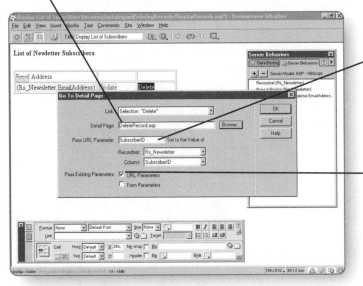

NOTE

The primary key of the table will be detected. This value will be passed to the Web page containing the delete form.

7. Click inside the URL Parameters check box. A check will be placed inside the box. The unique identifier of the current record will be passed to the delete form as a URL parameter. That means that it will be appended to the URL as a QueryString.

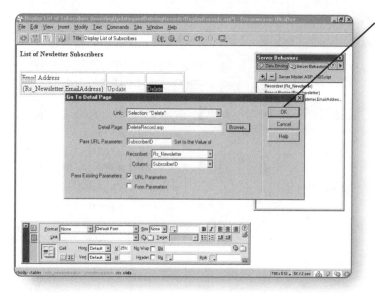

8. Click on OK. The Go To Detail Page dialog box will close and the Update link will be created.

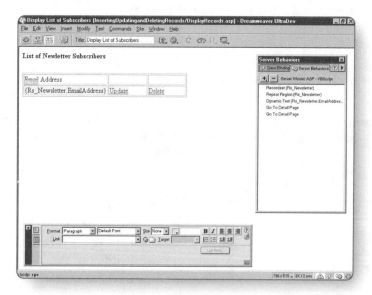

9. Press Ctrl+s. The search results Web page will be saved.

Creating a Delete Form

You don't need to display the contents of a record that is going to be deleted within form objects. There is no need for users to edit fields when the record is going to be deleted. You should, however, display the entire record that will be

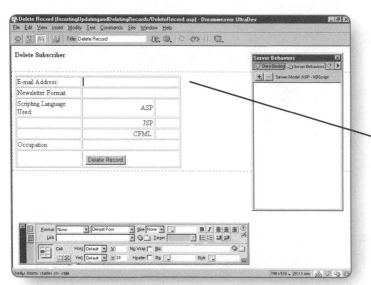

deleted. This will give your users the opportunity to preview the record before deleting it. Remember, once a record has been deleted, there is no way to restore it.

1. Create an HTML Form. The delete form should not contain form objects. There is no need for a user to update data that will be deleted. You only need to display the entire record that will be deleted.

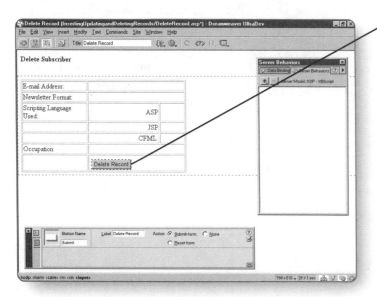

2. Create a Submit button. The form must have a submit button that indicates the purpose of the form, which in this case is to delete a record in the database. It is very important that the Delete button be appropriately labeled. This will prevent users from clicking on it accidentally.

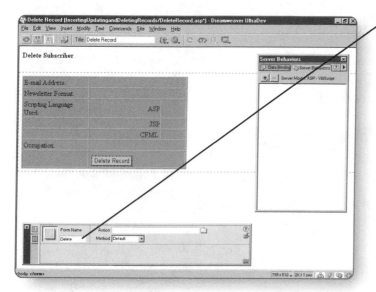

3. Type a name for the form that indicates its purpose.

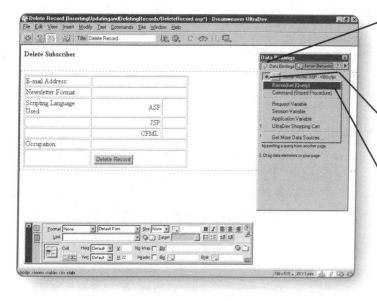

4. Click on the Data Bindings tab, if not already selected. The Data Bindings palette will be displayed.

5. Click on the + sign. A submenu will appear.

6. Click on Recordset(Query). The Recordset dialog box will open.

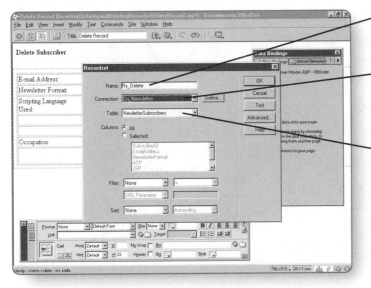

7. Type in a name for the recordset.

8. Select a database connection. The option will be selected.

9. Select the table that contains the record that you need to delete. The option will be selected.

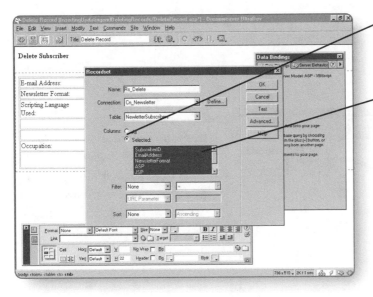

10. Click on the Selected option box. The option will be selected.

11. Select the fields that must be returned by the query. Only select the fields that the user should view before they decide that the record must be deleted. These fields will be bound to the Web page as dynamic text.

12. Select the field that corresponds to the value being passed to the delete form via the QueryString. In this case, it must be the unique ID field also known as the primary key. The field will be highlighted.

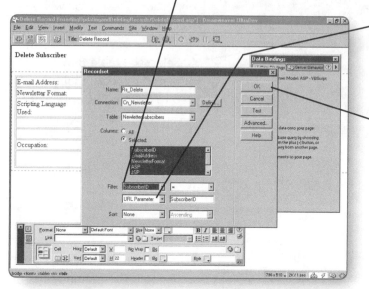

13. Select URL Parameter, because the ID number must be retrieved from the QueryString. The option will be highlighted.

14. Click on OK. The Recordset dialog box will close.

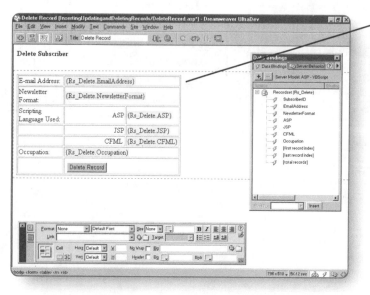

15. Bind the fields retrieved from the database to the Web page. Chapter 8, "Retrieving Data from a Database," covers this topic comprehensively. This will allow the user to view the record before deciding to delete it.

Using the Delete Record Server Behavior

Using the Delete Record server behavior is slightly more involved than using the Insert Record server behavior. In addition to specifying the database connection and the table where the record should be deleted and matching form objects to table columns, you also need to specify the unique ID number of the record to be deleted. This value is passed to the delete form in the Querystring.

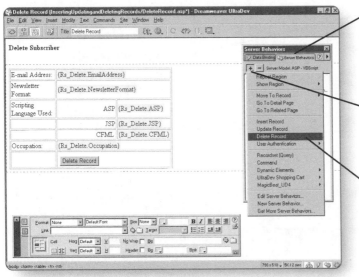

1. Click on the Server Behaviors tab. The Server Behaviors palette will be displayed.

2. Click on the + sign in the Server Behaviors palette. A submenu will appear.

3. Click on Delete Record. The Delete Record dialog box will open.

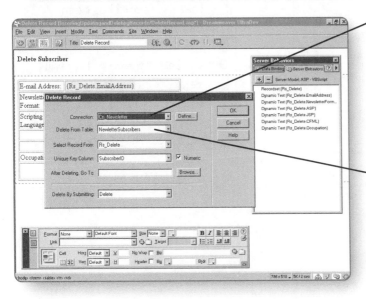

4. Select the connection for the database that needs a Web-based interface to delete data. Creating a connection is covered in Chapter 8, "Retrieving Data from a Database."

5. Select the table that will contain the record to be deleted. The table name will be selected.

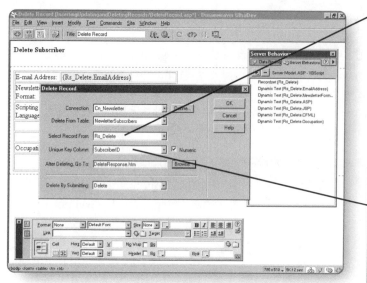

6. Select the recordset that is bound to the delete form if the recordset that UltraDev has selected is incorrect. This will only happen if there is more than one recordset bound to the Web page.

NOTE

The unique record identifier/primary key is automatically selected in the Unique Key Column drop-down list.

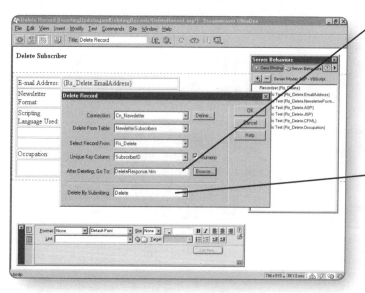

7. Type a file name into the After Deleting, Go To field. This file will be displayed after the record has been deleted. Ideally you will want to acknowledge that the record has been deleted.

8. Select the form that will delete the record when submitted, if the form that UltraDev has selected is incorrect. This will only happen if there is more than one form on your Web page.

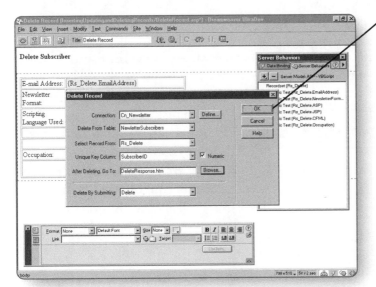

9. Click on OK. The Delete Record dialog box will close.

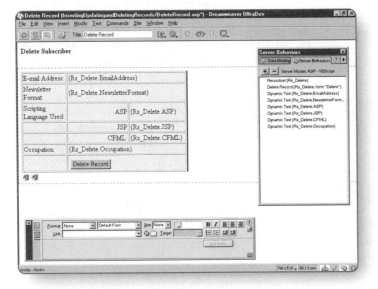

10. Press Ctrl+s. The Web page containing the delete form will be saved.

Testing the Delete Record Server Behavior

You can only test the Delete Record server behavior from a Web browser. Live Data View does not currently support this function.

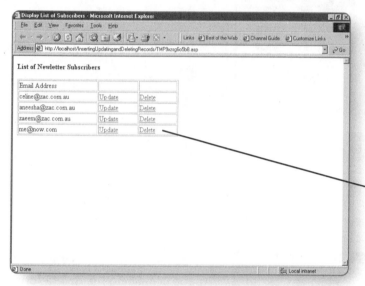

1. Press F12 to preview the search results in the Web page that contains the delete link. The Web page will be displayed in the Web browser. If you are not familiar with saving or previewing a page, please refer to Chapter 1.

2. Click on the delete link that corresponds to a record you wish to delete. The Web page that contains the delete form will be displayed. The contents of the record that is about to be deleted will be displayed.

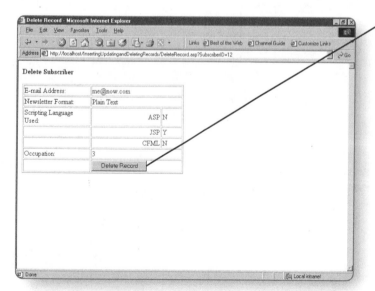

3. Click on the Delete Record button. The record will be deleted and the page that you specified in the After Deleting, Go To field in the Delete Record dialog box will be displayed.

14

Password-Protecting Your Web Site

You have thus far developed Web pages that can be viewed by all visitors to your Web site. There are many situations when you will need to password-protect certain areas of your site. Perhaps you would like to collect information for marketing purposes from your visitors or simply allow users that have paid a subscription fee access to your Web site. You also need to password-protect the areas that have been built solely for administration purposes. This chapter will help you implement a database-driven password-protection system with the Authentication server behaviors. In this chapter, you'll learn to:

- Design a database to store membership information
- Create a Login page
- Validate users against a database
- Display an Invalid Login error message
- Allow new users to register
- Password-protect individual pages in your site
- Log a user out

Designing the Authentication Database

The authentication database contains a list of all users that have access to the restricted areas. The database in the first instance only needs to contain a single table which stores a unique ID for each user, his username, and password. You could also store other information such as a user's name, address, e-mail address, and phone number. We will keep our table simple and only store an e-mail address.

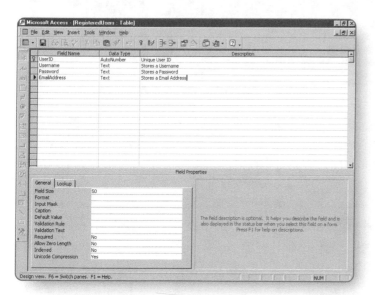

Creating a Login Page

The Login page contains a form that requires the user to enter her username and password. The Log In User server behavior must be applied to this page. It inserts code to check whether the user exists in the database and that the password is correct.

1. Create the Login form. You may use tables to help lay out the form.

2. Insert a Text field for the username.

3. Insert a Password field for the user to enter her password.

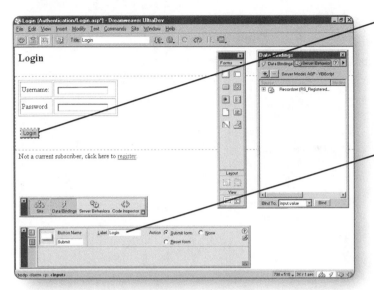

4. Insert a Submit button. The user will click on the button to send the login details to the server for processing.

NOTE

The label must indicate the purpose of the button.

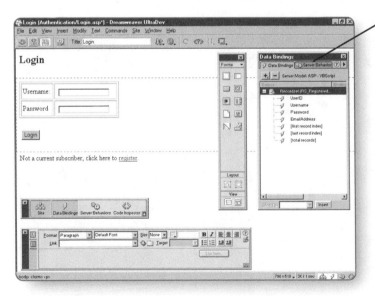

5. Click on the Server Behaviors tab. The Server Behaviors palette will be displayed.

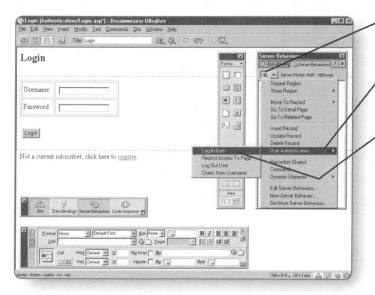

6. Click on the + sign. A submenu will appear.

7. Click on User Authentication. A submenu will appear.

8. Click on Log In User. The Log In User dialog box will open.

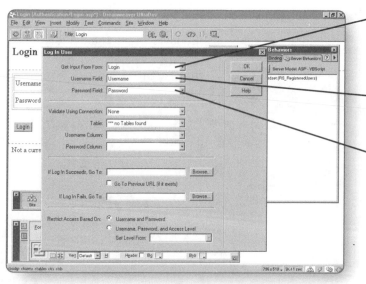

9. Select the form that contains the Username and Password fields.

10. Select the name assigned to the Username field.

11. Select the name assigned to the Password field.

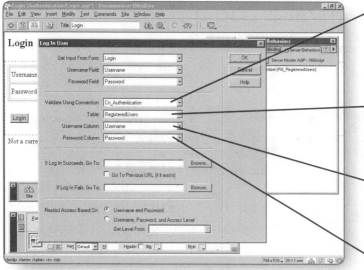

12. Select the database connection. The database must contain a list of registered users and their passwords.

13. Select the table where the details of registered users are stored.

14. Select the database column/field where the username is stored.

15. Select the database column/field where the password is stored.

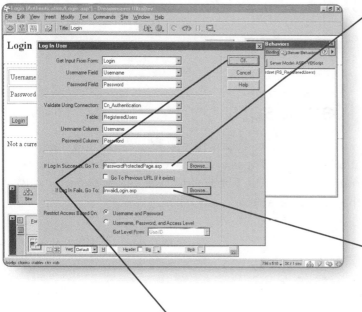

16. Type in the name of the Web page that must be displayed after the user has successfully logged in to the site.

> ### NOTE
> This will usually be a password-protected Web page.

17. Type in the name of the Web page that must be displayed if the login is unsuccessful.

18. Click on OK. The Log In User dialog box will close.

Creating the Invalid Login Page

The invalid login error message will be displayed if the user has accidentally entered the incorrect login details or simply does not exist in the database of valid users.

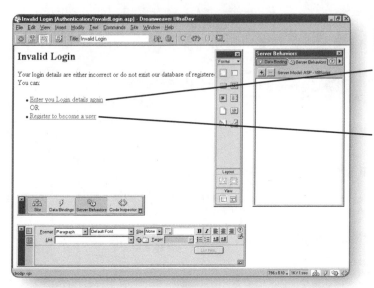

1. The Invalid Login page must link to the:

- Login page so that users can have another attempt at entering their login details.

- Registration page so that new visitors wishing to access restricted areas can enter their details to register.

Registering New Users

You could also allow new users wishing to access restricted areas to add their details to the authentication database. The user will have to enter the information you require and a preferred username. The Check New User server behavior must be used to ensure that the username is not already taken.

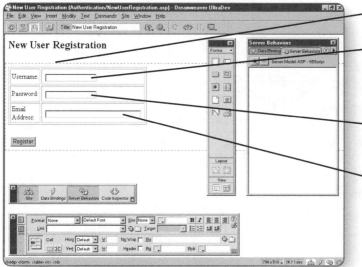

1. Create the Registration form.

2. Insert a Text field for the user to enter his preferred username.

3. Insert a Password field for the user to enter his password.

4. Insert any other fields that you require before a user can be registered. Sample fields include the user's First name, Surname, Address, and E-mail address.

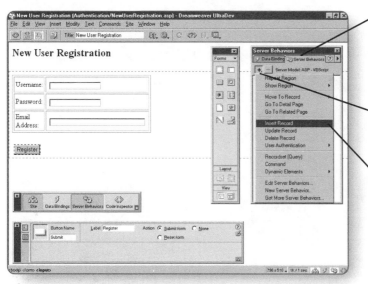

5. Click on the Server Behaviors tab, if it is not already selected. The palette will be displayed.

6. Click on the + sign. A submenu will appear.

7. Click on Insert Record. The Insert Record dialog box will open.

8. Select the database connection.

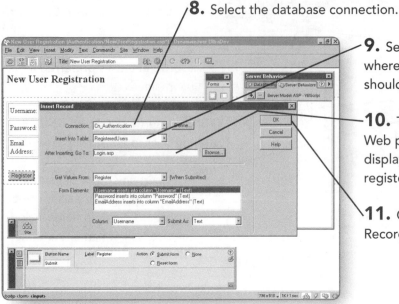

9. Select the database table where the registration details should be inserted.

10. Type in the name of the Web page that must be displayed after the user has registered.

11. Click on OK. The Insert Record dialog box will close.

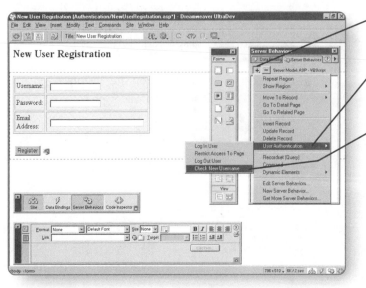

12. Click on the + sign. A submenu will appear.

13. Click on User Authentication. A submenu will appear.

14. Click on Check New Username. The Check New Username dialog box will open.

NOTE

The Check New Username server behavior will ensure that another user is not already using the username.

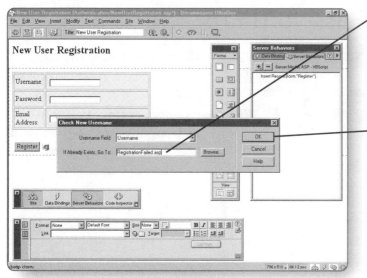

15. Type in the name of the Web page that will be displayed if the username is already in use. This page should display a failed registration error message.

16. Click on OK. The Check New Username dialog box will close.

Creating the Failed Registration Page

The failed registration page will only be displayed if a user's preferred username is already in use.

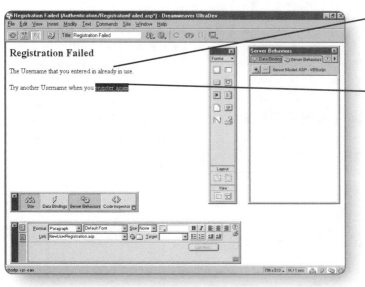

1. Inform the user that another user is already using the username.

2. Insert a link back to the Registration page. This will allow the user to register again.

Creating a Password-Protected Page

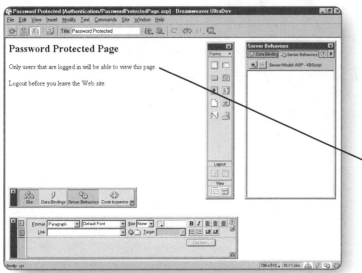

The Restrict Access to Page server behavior must be applied to all pages that require password-protection. These Web pages will not be displayed until the user has entered a valid username and password.

1. Open a Web page that you only want registered users to view.

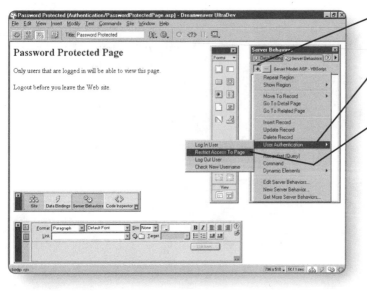

2. Click on the + sign. A submenu will appear.

3. Click on User Authentication. A submenu will appear.

4. Click on Restrict Access to Page. The Restrict Access to Page dialog box will open.

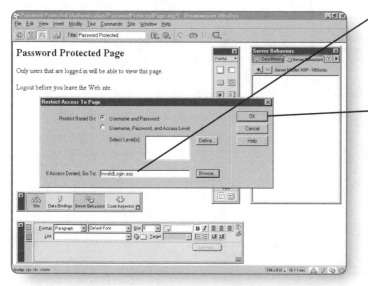

5. Type in the name of the Web page that must be displayed if the user has not logged in to the site.

6. Click on OK. The Restrict Access to Page dialog box will close.

Creating a Logout Link

On each password-protected page, you should allow the user to log out of the Web site. This not only frees up valuable server resources but also provides additional security. This ensures that no other person can access the Web site while the browser is still open.

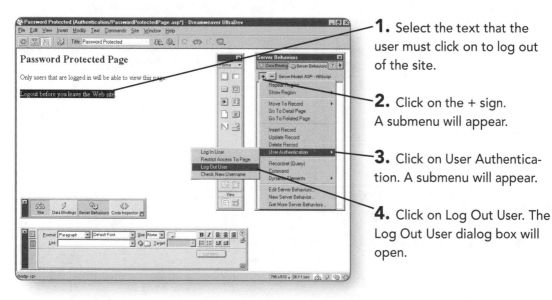

1. Select the text that the user must click on to log out of the site.

2. Click on the + sign. A submenu will appear.

3. Click on User Authentication. A submenu will appear.

4. Click on Log Out User. The Log Out User dialog box will open.

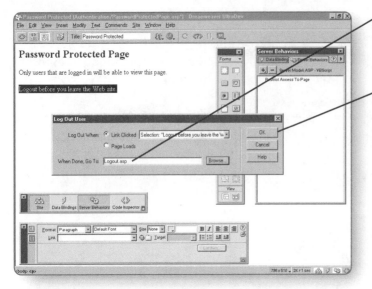

5. Type in the name of the page to display after the user has been logged out.

6. Click on OK. The Log Out User dialog box will close.

Creating the Logged Out Page

The Logged Out Web page simply displays any message you would like to display after the user has no access to restricted areas of the site.

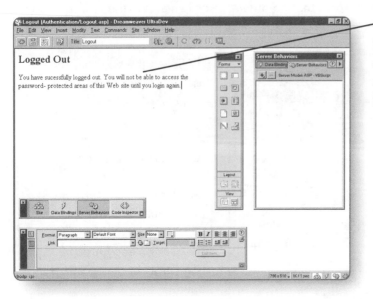

1. Inform the user that he has been successfully logged out and will not be able to access restricted areas of the site until he logs in again.

Using Access Levels

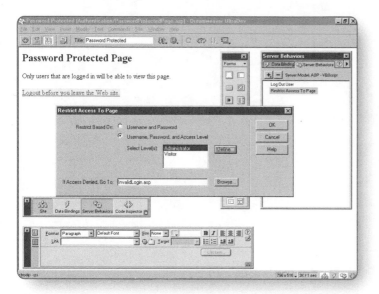

We have only utilized a username and password to authenticate a user and allow access to restricted areas. This means that all users with a valid username and password can access your entire site. You may not want all your users to enjoy the same privileges. The User Authentication behaviors allow you to restrict access based upon levels. The authentication database needs an additional field to store the access level of each user.

15

Writing Your Own ASP Code

Server behaviors are extremely powerful, but you can't use them for every situation. There will come a time when you will need to customize the code generated by UltraDev. This is where a basic knowledge of a server-side scripting language such as ASP (Active Server Pages) will come in handy.

Although UltraDev supports three languages, this book only covers ASP. It is the easiest of the three to learn, even if you don't have a programming background. Don't be fooled by its simplicity, however-you can still achieve powerful results. In this chapter, you'll learn to:

- Insert code in a Web page
- Comment your code
- Use operators, variables, and functions
- Use loops and conditional statements
- Create functions and subroutines

Inserting ASP Code into a Web Page

The biggest advantage of using ASP is that server-side scripts are embedded in HTML. This template-based approach is much easier than using CGI (Common Gateway Interface) languages such as Perl, in which the entire HTML file has to be printed line by line to the Web browser. ASP is embedded in a Web page using the <% and %> script delimiters. Anything within these delimiters is processed as server-side script.

TIP

You'll find a brief introduction to UltraDev's other compatible languages, JSP and ColdFusion, in Appendix C.

Thus far you have only used UltraDev as a visual tool to create dynamic database-driven Web sites, but UltraDev is also equipped with a capable script editor. Unlike other visual Web page creation tools, UltraDev does not interfere with the code you write.

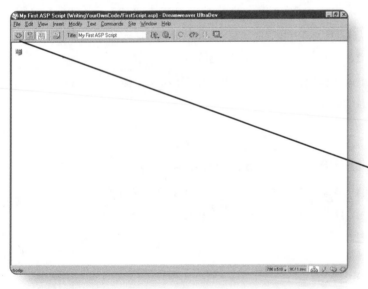

1. Create a new Web page with an .asp extension. The ASP code placed in a file with an .htm extension will be displayed as text in a Web browser. The ASP engine only interprets files that contain the .asp extension.

2. Click on the Show Code View icon. The source code of the Web page will be displayed.

> **NOTE**
> You will see the HTML tags that define a Web page. These include the opening and closing:
>
> - HTML tags
> - Head tags
> - Title tags
> - Body tags

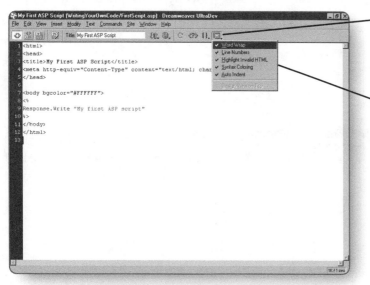

3. Click on the Code View options icon. A submenu will appear.

You can configure the code editor by enabling:

- **Word Wrap.** This will wrap the code in the HTML Source window and free you from scrolling to read lengthy lines of HTML and ASP code.

- **Line Numbers.** Each line of code on the Web page will be numbered. This will help you when you need to debug your script. Error messages always display the line number on which the error occurred.

- **Highlight Invalid HTML.** Invalid HTML will be detected and highlighted in yellow.

- **Syntax Coloring.** Allows you to easily differentiate HTML, JavaScript, and Server-Side ASP, JSP, or CFML code. This feature makes editing and debugging much easier.

- **Auto Indent.** This will automatically indent certain tags. Indentation is a handy way to make your code more readable.

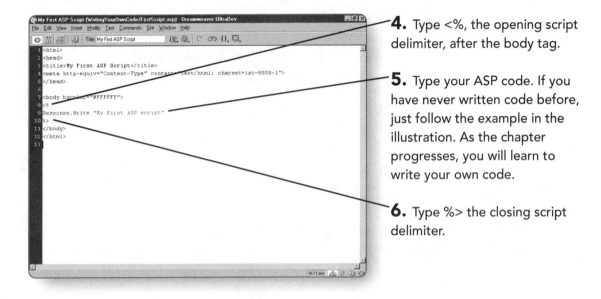

4. Type <%, the opening script delimiter, after the body tag.

5. Type your ASP code. If you have never written code before, just follow the example in the illustration. As the chapter progresses, you will learn to write your own code.

6. Type %> the closing script delimiter.

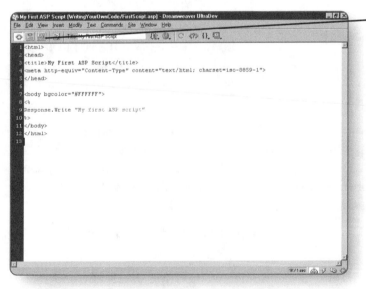

7. Click on the Show Design View icon. The Web page will be displayed.

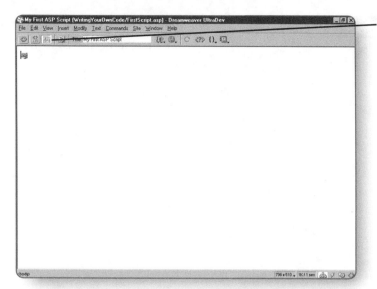

8. Click on the Live Data View icon. The result of the ASP script will be displayed.

NOTE

You can preview the results of your scripts in Live Data view. This saves you from having to launch a Web browser each time you need to test your code. There are times, however, when you will have to preview your page in a Web browser because Live Data Mode does not support the functionality you are testing. You will be advised in the relevant section if this is the case.

9. Click on Live Data View icon. You will be returned to Design view.

Displaying the ASP Reference

UltraDev comes with references for CSS (Cascading Style Sheets), HTML, and JavaScript. You can also download references for ASP and JSP from the UltraDev Exchange at **http://www.macromedia.com/exchange/ultradev**.

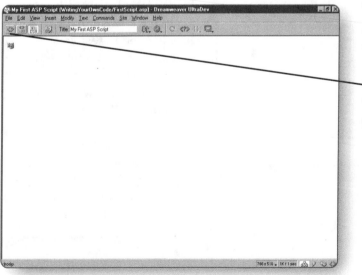

The ASP reference is very comprehensive and will help you with ASP syntax.

1. Click on the Show Code View icon. The source code of the Web page will be displayed.

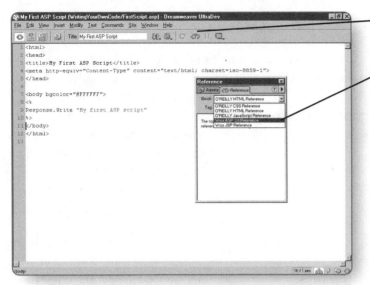

2. Click on the Reference icon. The Reference palette will open.

3. Select the Reference you would like to view. The tag drop-down box will be populated accordingly.

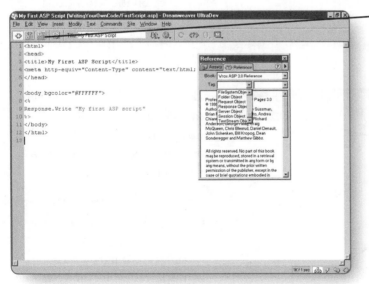

4. Click on the Show Design View icon. The Web page will be displayed.

Commenting Your Code

Comments are used as a form of communication between yourself and other programmers who will maintain your code at a later time. As a general rule, comments should explain what may not be obvious in your code. A comment must be placed within the script delimiters and preceded by an apostrophe ('). An apostrophe can only be used to create a single comment line.

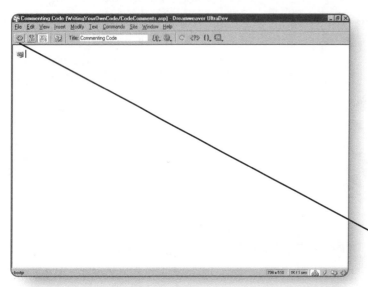

1. Create a new Web page with an .asp extension. The script will not be executed if the page has another extension.

2. Click on the Show Code View icon. The source code of the Web page will be displayed.

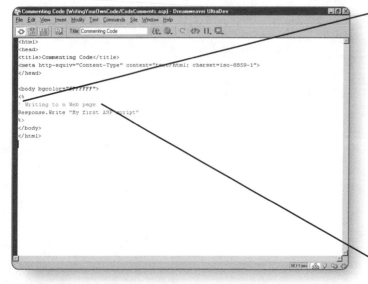

3. Type an apostrophe within the <% and %> script delimiters. The text you enter after the apostrophe will be a comment.

CAUTION

Text included outside the script delimiters will be displayed when the Web page is viewed.

---

4. Type in the comment after the apostrophe.

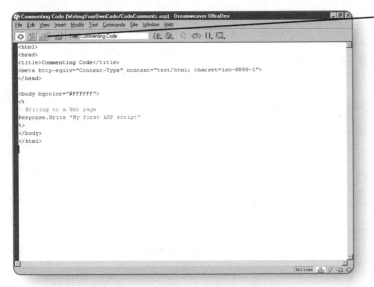

5. Click on the Show Design View icon. The Web page will be displayed.

Declaring Variables

Variables are used to store data so that it can be processed and updated at a later stage. You should always give your variables meaningful names. The variable name should define the type of information that is being stored. This will make your code more readable.

1. Create a new Web page with an .asp extension. The script will not be executed if the page has another extension.

2. Click on the Show Code View icon. The source code of the Web page will be displayed.

3. Use the Dim keyword to declare variables.

4. Type in the variable name after the Dim keyword.

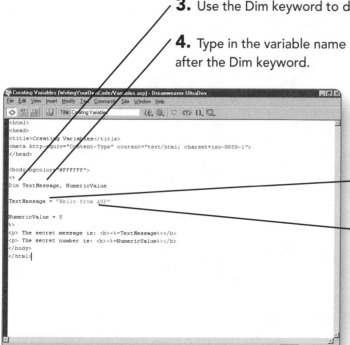

5. Use the = sign to set the value of a variable.

6. Type the value of the variable after the = sign.

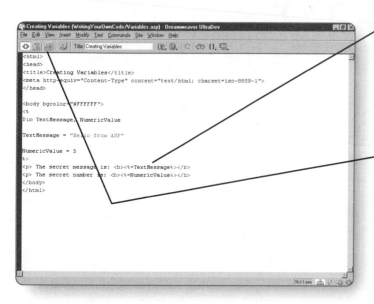

7. Type the name of a variable within the <%= and %> delimiters. The value stored in the variable will be printed to the Web page when the script is executed.

8. Click on the Show Design View icon. The Web page will be displayed.

Using Mathematical Operators

Mathematical operators allow you to perform addition, subtraction, multiplication, and division.

Mathematical Operator	Description
+	Adds two numbers
-	Subtracts one number from another
*	Multiplies two numbers
/	Divides one number by another
Mod	Returns the remainder after dividing two numbers

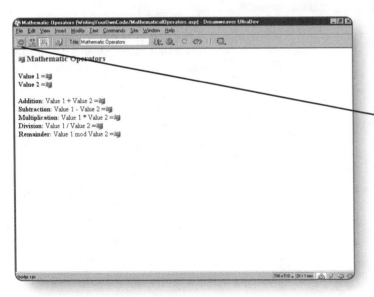

1. Create a new Web page with an .asp extension. The script will not be executed if the page has another extension.

2. Click on the Show Code View icon. The source code of the Web page will be displayed.

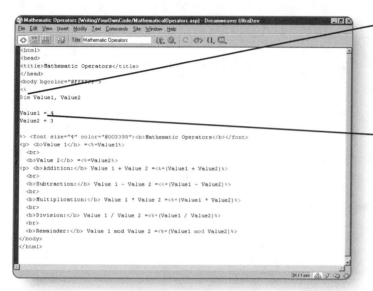

3. Use the Dim keyword to declare variables. These variables will be used to perform simple mathematic operations.

4. Use the = sign to assign values to the variables.

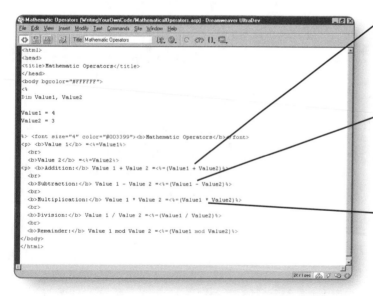

5. Type + between the variables that you want to add. The result will be displayed when the Web page is previewed.

6. Type - between the variables that you want to subtract. The result will be displayed when the Web page is previewed.

7. Type * between the variables that you want to multiply. The result will be displayed when the Web page is previewed.

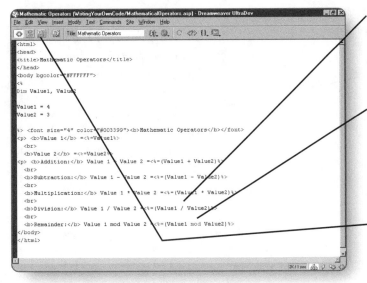

8. Type / between the variables that you want to divide. The result will be displayed when the Web page is previewed.

9. Type Mod between the variables that you want to divide and only return the remainder. The result will be displayed when the Web page is previewed.

10. Click on the Show Design View icon. The Web page will be displayed.

Using Comparison Operators

A comparison operator compares the value in one element with the value of another. Comparison operators can be used to compare both strings and numeric data. You can test whether values are equal, not equal, greater or less than each other.

Comparison Operator	Name	Description
=	equal	Returns TRUE if the variables are equal.
<>	not equal	Returns TRUE if the variables are not equal.
>	greater than	Returns TRUE if the variable on the left is greater than the value on the right.
>=	greater than or equal to	Returns TRUE if the variable on the left is greater than or equal to the value on the right.
<	less than	Returns TRUE if the variable on the left is less than the value on the right.
<=	less than or equal to	Returns TRUE if the variable on the left is less than or equal to the value on the right.

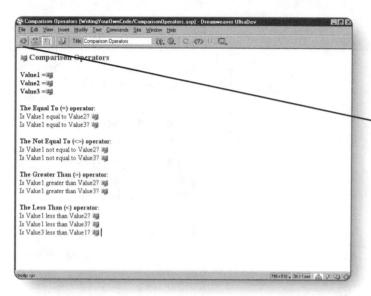

1. Create a new Web page with an .asp extension. The script will not be executed if the page has another extension.

2. Click on the Show Code View icon. The source code of the Web page will be displayed.

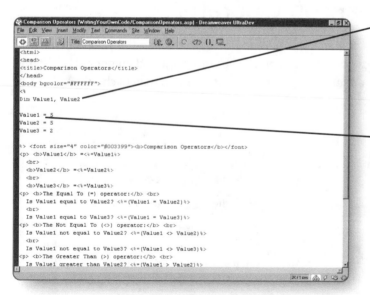

3. Use the Dim keyword to declare variables. These variables will be used to illustrate the use of comparison operators.

4. Use the = sign to assign values to the variables.

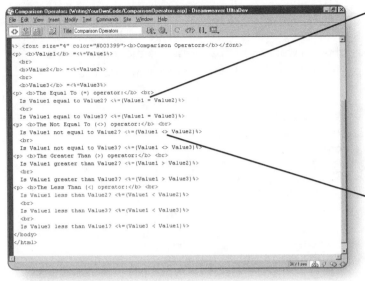

5. Type = between the variables that you want to compare. This will test whether the variables contain numeric data that is equal. The result will be displayed when the Web page is previewed. If both variables are equal, the expression will return TRUE.

6. Type <> between the variables that you want to compare. This will test whether the variables contain numeric data that is not equal. The result will be displayed when the Web page is previewed. If the variables are not equal to each other, the expression will return TRUE.

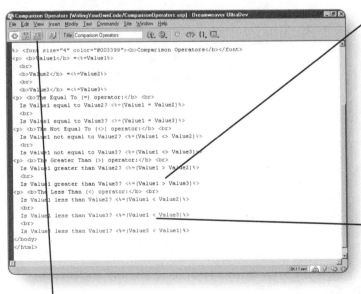

7. Type > between the variables that you want to compare. This will test whether the variable on the left is greater than the variable on the right. The result will be displayed when the Web page is previewed. If the variable on the left is greater than the variable on the right, the expression will return TRUE.

8. Type < between the variables that you want to compare. This will test whether the variable on the left is less than the variable on the right. The result will be displayed when the Web page is previewed. If the variable on the left is less than the variable on the right, the expression will return TRUE.

9. Click on the Show Design View icon. The Web page will be displayed.

Using Logical Operators

Logical operators are useful when working with expressions that need to return logical values. These expressions mainly use Comparison operators.

Logical Operator	Description
AND	Returns TRUE when both expressions are TRUE.
OR	Returns TRUE if either expression is TRUE.

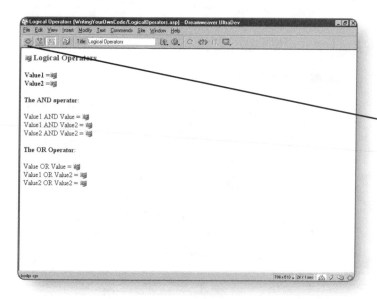

1. Create a new Web page with an .asp extension. The script will not be executed if the page has another extension.

2. Click on the Show Code View icon. The source code of the Web page will be displayed.

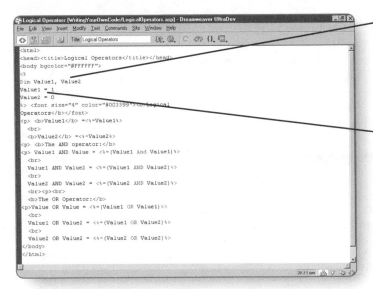

3. Use the Dim keyword to declare variables. These variables will be used to illustrate the use of logical operators.

4. Use the = sign to assign values to the variables. Logical operators can only be performed on Boolean data such as 1/0 and True/False.

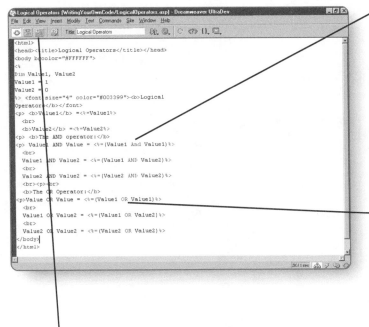

5. Type AND between the variables. If both variables contain a True value (i.e., a value equal to 1), the expression will return TRUE. If either variable contains a False value (i.e., a value equal to 0), the expression will return FALSE. The result will be displayed when the Web page is previewed.

6. Type OR between the variables. As long as one variable contains a True value (i.e., a value equal to 1), the expression will return FALSE. The result will be displayed when the Web page is previewed.

7. Click on the Show Design View icon. The Web page will be displayed.

Using Conditional Statements

Conditional statements are used to execute code that should only be run if certain conditions are met. They allow you to make decisions.

Using the If...Then...Else Statement

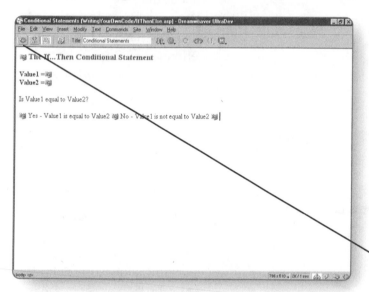

The code within the If...Then block will only be executed if the logical expression returns a True value. Include an Else clause if you want to execute code when a logical expression returns a False value.

1. Create a new Web page with an .asp extension. The script will not be executed if the page has another extension.

2. Click on the Show Code View icon. The source code of the Web page will be displayed.

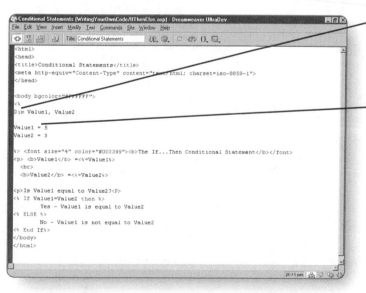

3. Use the Dim keyword to declare variables. These variables will be compared within an expression.

4. Use the = sign to assign values to the variables.

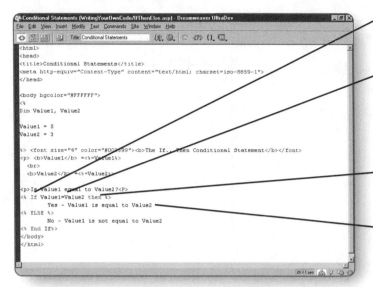

5. Type If within the <% and %> script delimiters.

6. Type the expression that must return a True value for the content within the If statement to be displayed.

7. Type Then after the expression.

8. Type the content you want to display if the expression returns a True value.

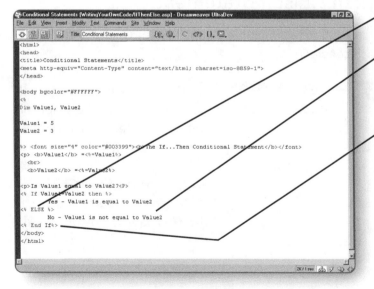

9. Type Else after the content.

10. Type the content you would like to display if the expression returns a False value.

11. Type End If to end the If statement.

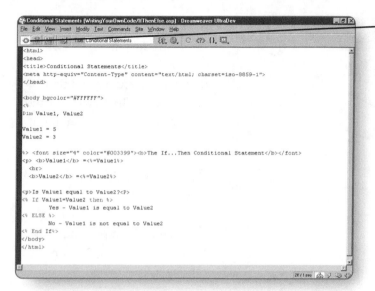

12. Click on the Show Design View icon. The Web page will be displayed.

Using the If...Then...ElseIf Statement

The ElseIf statement allows you to test multiple expressions and execute the appropriate code for each condition.

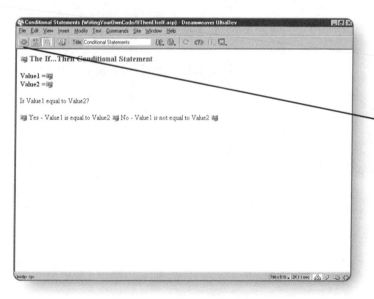

1. Create a new Web page with an .asp extension. The script will not be executed if the page has another extension.

2. Click on the Show Code View icon. The source code of the Web page will be displayed.

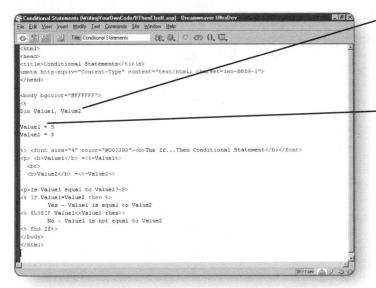

3. Use the Dim keyword to declare variables. These variables will be compared within an expression.

4. Use the = sign to assign values to the variables.

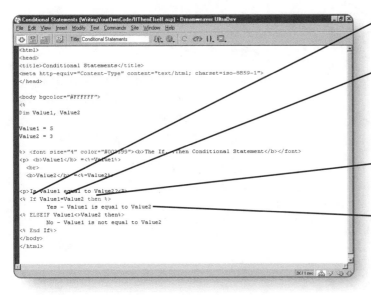

5. Type If within the <% and %> script delimiters.

6. Type the expression that must return a True value for the content within the If statement to be displayed.

7. Type Then after the expression.

8. Type the content you want to display if the expression returns a True value.

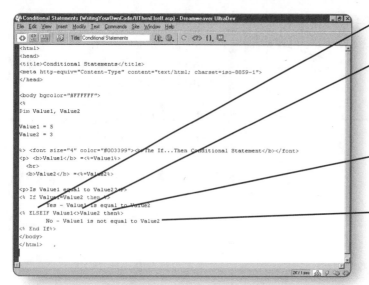

9. Type ElseIf after the content.

10. Type the expression that must return a True value for the content within the ElseIf statement to be displayed.

11. Type Then after the expression.

12. Type the content you want to display if the expression in the ElseIf statement returns a True value.

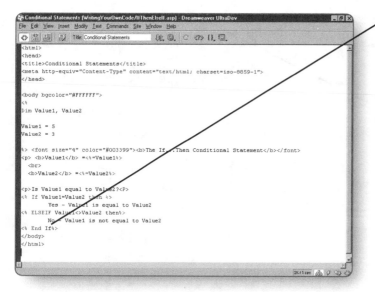

13. Type End If to end the If statement.

14. Click on the Show Design View icon. The Web page will be displayed.

Using Loops

Each line of code that you write will only be executed once. Loops come in handy when you need to repeat a few lines of code until a condition is met. The For loop is very flexible and simple to use.

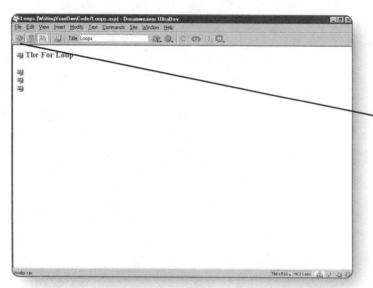

1. Create a new Web page with an .asp extension. The script will not be executed if the page has another extension.

2. Click on the Show Code View icon. The source code of the Web page will be displayed.

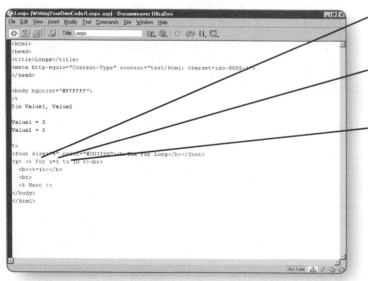

3. Type For within the <% and %> script delimiters.

4. Set the initial value of the counter variable.

5. Type To after setting the counter variable.

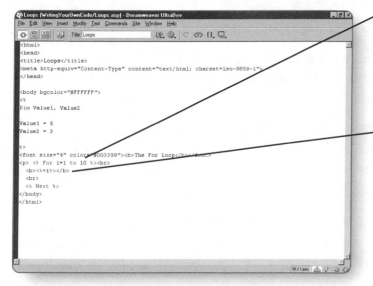

6. Type the amount of times you would like to repeat the loop. This sets the value the counter can reach before the loop finishes.

7. Type the HTML or ASP code that must be executed.

NOTE

While you're learning to use a loop, why not print the counter variable to the Web page. Each time the code within the loop is executed the counter will be incremented.

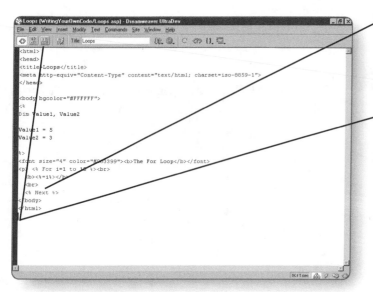

8. Type Next after the code that needs to be repeated. Any code after Next will not be included in the loop.

9. Click on the Show Design View icon. The Web page will be displayed.

Using String Functions

String functions provide a means for you to manipulate data retrieved from a form or database. You can concatenate, search, replace, and compare strings. The table below contains a brief summary of the String functions available.

String Function	Description
Concatenation	
&	Joins strings together.
Removing Leading and Trailing Spaces	
LTrim(string)	Removes spaces at the beginning of the string.
RTrim(string)	Removes spaces at the end of the string.
Trim(string)	Removes both leading and trailing spaces.
Changing the String Case	
UCase(string)	Converts the string to uppercase.
LCase(string)	Converts the string to lowercase.
Search Strings	
InStr(stringA,stringB)	You can search for stringB within stringA.
Replace Text in a String	
Replace(stringA, stringB,stringC)	If stringB is found in stringA, replace it with stringC.

Creating Subroutines

A subroutine illuminates the need to retype code that you often use in a Web page. Once you create a subroutine all you need to do is call the subroutine and the code will be executed.

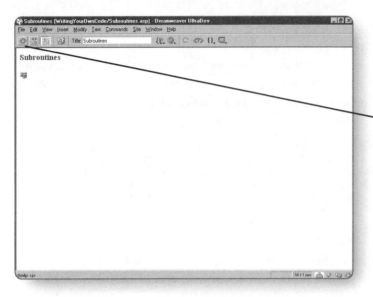

1. Create a new Web page with an .asp extension. The script will not be executed if the page has another extension.

2. Click on the Show Code View icon. The source code of the Web page will be displayed.

NOTE

A subroutine must be created before it can be called. The ideal place to insert a subroutine is just before the opening HTML tag.

---

3. Type SUB within the <% and %> script delimiters. The SUB keyword is used to create a subroutine.

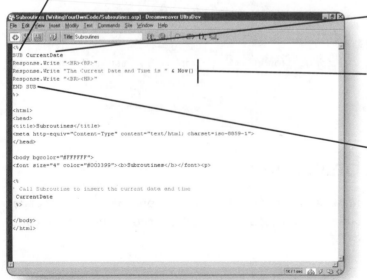

4. Type the name of the subroutine after the SUB keyword.

5. Type the ASP code that must be executed when the subroutine is called.

6. Type END SUB after the ASP code.

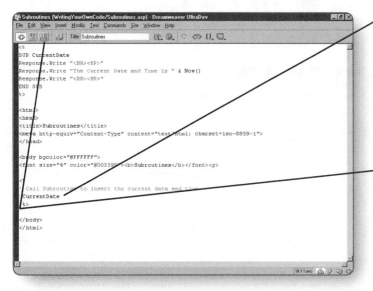

7. Type the name of the subroutine you want to call within the <% and %> script delimiters. The code in the subroutine will be executed and the result will be displayed when you preview the Web page.

8. Click on the Show Design View icon. The Web page will be displayed.

Passing Values to a Subroutine

You can also pass parameters to a subroutine. The parameters are stored in variables and can be processed.

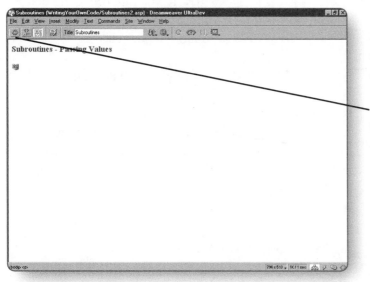

1. Create a new Web page with an .asp extension. The script will not be executed if the page has another extension.

2. Click on the Show Code View icon. The source code of the Web page will be displayed.

3. Type SUB within the <% and %> script delimiters. The SUB keyword is used to create a subroutine.

4. Type the name of the subroutine after the SUB keyword.

5. Type variable names for the attributes that can be passed to the subroutine. The attributes must be placed in braces.

NOTE

You can define more than one attribute. Use a comma to separate the parameter names.

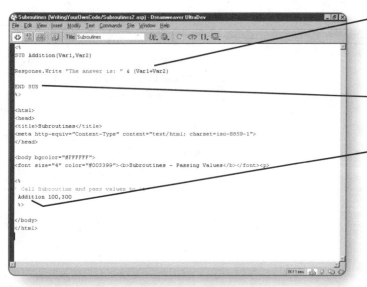

6. Type in the ASP code that must be executed when the subroutine is called.

7. Type END SUB after the ASP code.

8. Type the name of the subroutine you want to call.

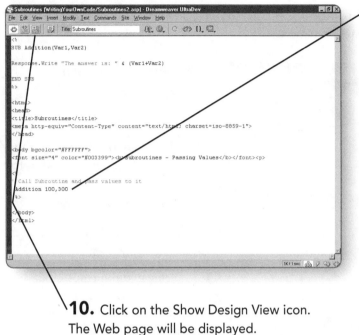

9. Type the values you want to pass to the subroutine after the name of the subroutine you are calling. The code in the subroutine will be executed and the result will be displayed when you preview the Web page.

NOTE

If more than one value is passed to the subroutine, a comma must separate each value. Make sure that the values are passed in the correct order.

---

10. Click on the Show Design View icon. The Web page will be displayed.

Creating Functions

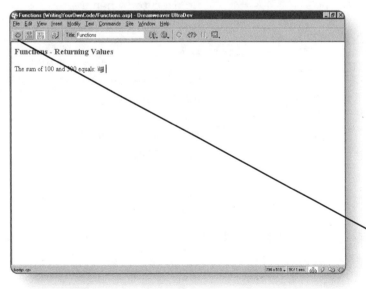

Functions are similar to subroutines but can return results. You can call a function anywhere within a Web page as long as the call is made from within the script delimiters.

1. Create a new Web page with an .asp extension. The script will not be executed if the page has another extension.

2. Click on the Show Code View icon. The source code of the Web page will be displayed.

3. Type FUNCTION within the <% and %> script delimiters. The FUNCTION keyword is used to create a function.

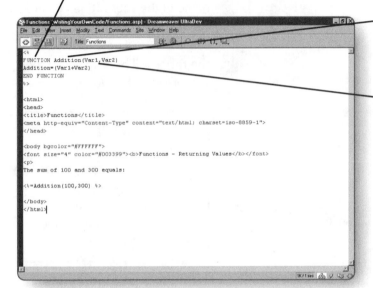

4. Type the name of the function after the FUNCTION keyword.

5. Type variable names for the attributes that can be passed to the function. The attributes must be placed in braces.

NOTE

You can define more than one attribute. Use a comma to separate the parameter names.

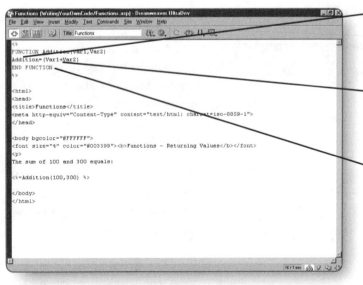

6. Type the ASP code that must be executed when the function is called.

7. Assign the value that the function must return to the function name.

8. Type END FUNCTION after the ASP code.

9. Type the name of the function. This will print out the value returned.

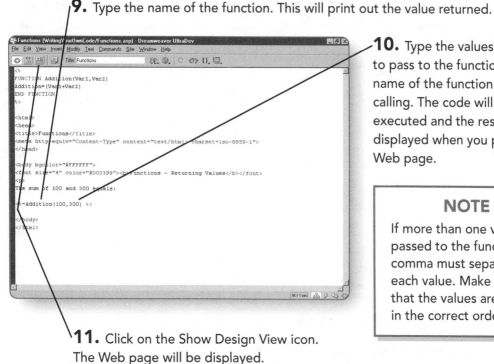

10. Type the values you want to pass to the function after the name of the function you are calling. The code will be executed and the result will be displayed when you preview the Web page.

NOTE

If more than one value is passed to the function, a comma must separate each value. Make sure that the values are passed in the correct order.

---

11. Click on the Show Design View icon. The Web page will be displayed.

Using Built-in ASP Objects

ASP includes a number of objects that aid Web development. These objects include the Response, Request, and Session objects. In simple terms, an object is made up of numerous methods and properties. A method defines a specific function that the object can perform. Object properties can either be set or read from a script.

Using the Response Object

The Response object is used to send output to a Web browser. The Response object is used to write text, HTML code and variables to a Web page.

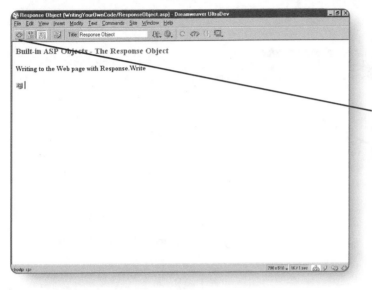

1. Create a new Web page with an .asp extension. The script will not be executed if the page has another extension.

2. Click on the Show Code View icon. The source code of the Web page will be displayed.

3. Type Response.Write within the <% and %> script delimiters.

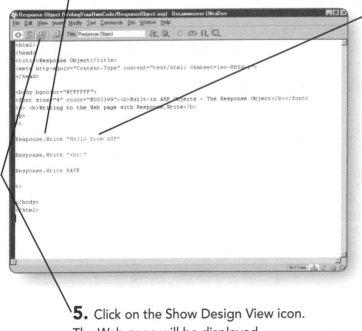

4. Pass the string that needs to be printed to the Response.Write method. A string needs to be enclosed in quotation marks. The string will be printed to the Web page when it is previewed.

NOTE

You can also use the Response.Write method to print:

- HTML code that can be rendered by a Web browser
- The result of a function or subroutine

5. Click on the Show Design View icon. The Web page will be displayed.

Using the Request Object

The Request object is used to retrieve all the data that the browser has sent to the Web server. This includes information sent using either the Get or Post method of a form. The Request object is also used to retrieve Server/Environmental Variables. In Chapter 6, "Validating and Retrieving Form Data," you learned how to use the Request Variables Data Source from the Data Bindings palette. The Request Variable data source allowed you to retrieve this information and bind it to a Web page. You will now learn the ASP code.

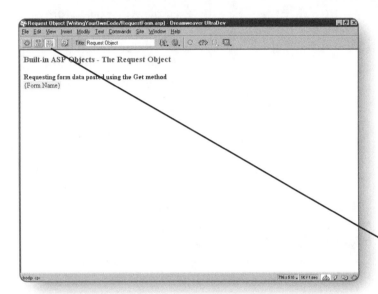

1. Create a new Web page with an .asp extension. The script will not be executed if the page has another extension.

2. Click on the Show Code View icon. The source code of the Web page will be displayed.

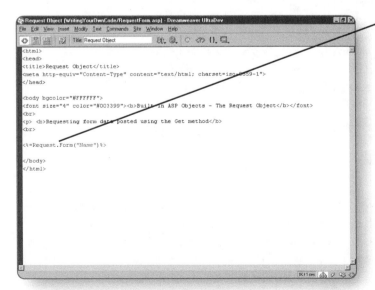

3. Type Request.Form() within the <%= and %> script delimiters. This will print the value retrieved from the form to the Web page. The Request.Form() method is used to retrieve data sent using the Post method.

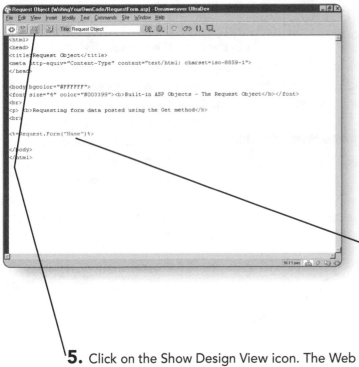

NOTE

You can also assign the value retrieved from the Request.Form method to a variable, which you then could process. For example, you could store the contents of a form to a text file, send it as an email message, or insert it into a database.

4. Pass the name of the form object to the Request.Form method. The name of the form object must be placed in quotation marks.

5. Click on the Show Design View icon. The Web page will be displayed.

NOTE

- You can retrieve data sent using the Get method by passing the form object name to the Request.QueryString method.
- You can retrieve Server/Environment variables using the Request.ServerVariables method. For a list of Server variables, please refer to Chapter 6, "Validating and Retrieving Form Data."

Using the Session Object

The Session object allows data to be stored in variables that can be accessed by other pages in your Web site. These variables are only stored while a user is visiting your Web site and will expire when he leaves. Sessions provide an easy solution to maintaining state across your Web site. I have dedicated a chapter to using cookies and sessions in ASP. Please refer to Chapter 18, "Maintaining State."

16

Creating Interactive Web Pages

Not all Web pages need to be linked to a database to be dynamic. You can use ASP to generate dynamic content. If used effectively, you can provide your site visitors with an interesting and interactive experience. In this chapter, you'll learn to:

- Insert the current date and time into a Web page
- Generate a greeting based upon the time
- Randomize the content on a Web page
- Redirect a user to another Web page
- Use SSI (Server-Side Includes)

Inserting the Current Date and Time

ASP can be used to insert the current date and time according to your Web server. You can also use the FormatDateTime function to display the date and time in a number of user-friendly formats.

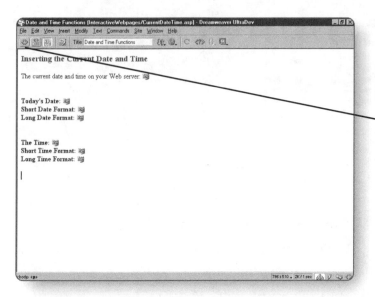

1. Create a new Web page with an .asp extension. The script will not be executed if the page has another extension.

2. Click on the Show Code View icon. The source code of the Web page will be displayed.

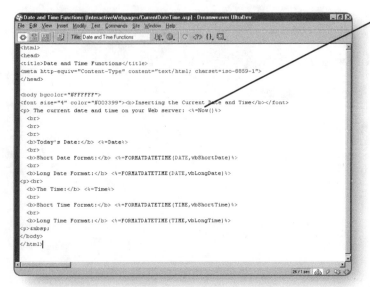

3. Type the Now function between the <%= and the %> delimiters. Inserting the Now function between these delimiters will write the current date and time to the Web page.

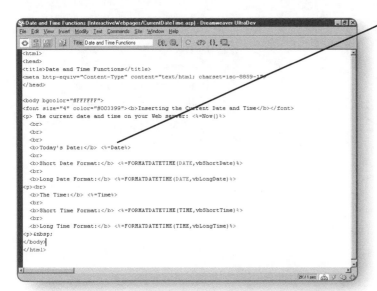

4. Type the Date function between the <%= and the %> delimiters. Inserting the Date function between these delimiters will only write the current date to the Web page.

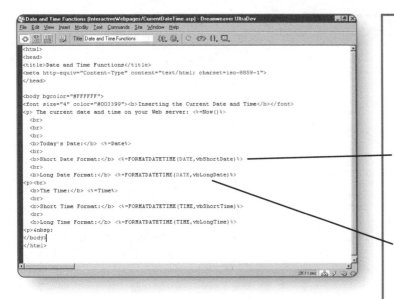

NOTE

The FormatDateTime function can be used to convert the current date to a more user-friendly format.

- A short date can be displayed by passing the vbShortDate constant to the FormatDateTime function.

- A long date can be displayed by passing the vbLongDate constant to the FormatDateTime function.

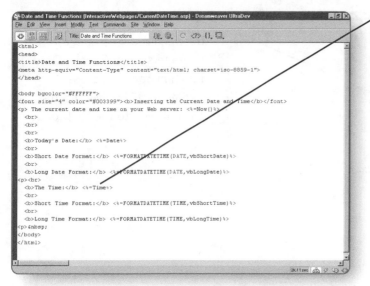

5. Type the Time function between the <%= and the %> delimiters. Inserting the Now function between these delimiters will only write the current time to the Web page.

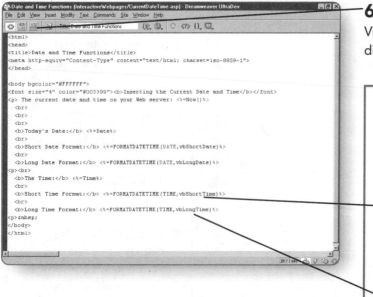

6. Click on the Show Design View icon. The Web page will be displayed.

NOTE

The FormatDateTime function can be used to convert the current time to a more user-friendly format.

- A short time can be displayed by passing the vbShortTime constant to the FormatDateTime function.

- A long time can be displayed by passing the vbLongTime constant to the FormatDateTime function.

Generating a Time-based Greeting

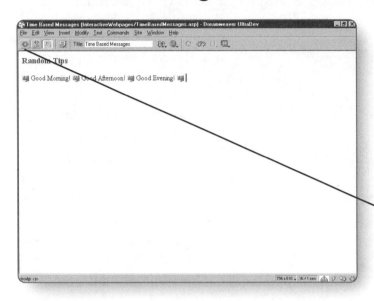

You can display a customised greeting for each individual user based on the time that they entered your Web site.

1. Create a new Web page with an .asp extension. The script will not be executed if the page has another extension.

2. Click on the Show Code View icon. The source code of the Web page will be displayed.

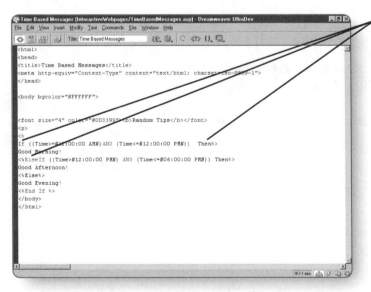

3. Use an If....Then...ElseIf statement to determine which message should be displayed.

4. Within the If and ElseIf statements, you will need to define the time range that matches the message to be displayed. To do this, you will need to evaluate which time range the current time matches. Programmatically, you can achieve this by:

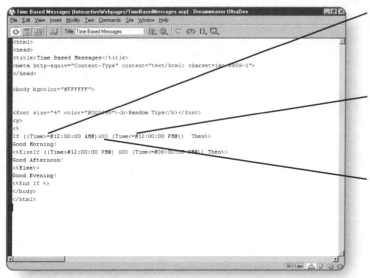

- Using a comparison operator to test whether the current time is equal to or after the start of the time range.

- Using a comparison operator to test whether the current time is before or equal to the end of the time range.

- Using the AND logical operator to ensure that both criteria are met before the message gets displayed.

5. Click on the Show Design View icon. The Web page will be displayed.

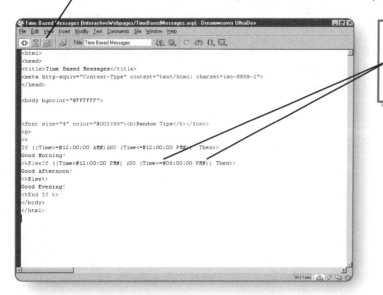

NOTE

A hard-coded time value must be within # delimiters.

Creating Countdown

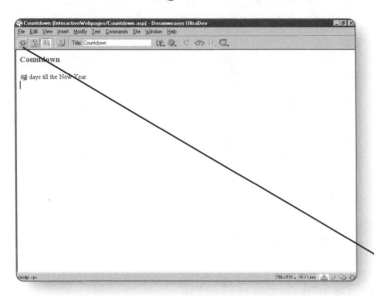

Ever wanted to countdown to an important event such as the release of a new product or a New Year? You'll be amazed at how easy it is to countdown to an event using the DateDiff function.

1. Create a new Web page with an .asp extension. The script will not be executed if the page has another extension.

2. Click on the Show Code View icon. The source code of the Web page will be displayed.

3. Type the DateDiff function between the <%= and the %> delimiters. Inserting the DateDiff function between these delimiters will write the result returned by the DateDiff function to the Web page.

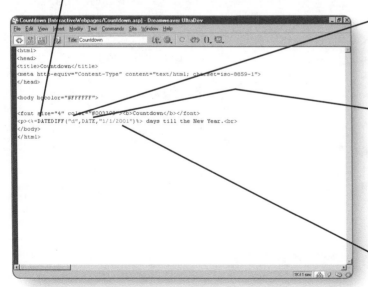

4. Type d as the first parameter passed to the DateDiff function. This will set the countdown to be calculated in days.

5. Type Date as the second parameter passed to the DateDiff function. The Date functions will return the current date, from where the countdown should be calculated.

6. Type the date that corresponds to the event that you are counting down to.

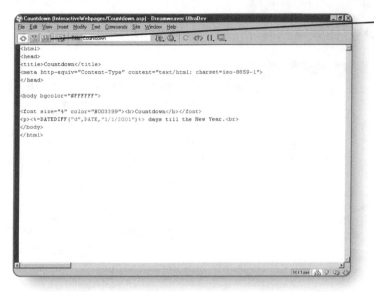

7. Click on the Show Design View icon. The Web page will be displayed.

Displaying Random Content

Randomized content can provide your Web site visitors with a unique experience each time they visit your Web site. You can display random messages or images.

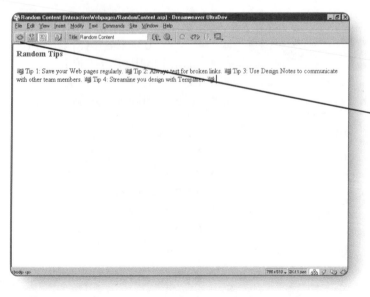

1. Create a new Web page with an .asp extension. The script will not be executed if the page has another extension.

2. Click on the Show Code View icon. The source code of the Web page will be displayed.

3. Create a variable that will be used to store the total number of items that you can randomly select.

4. Assign a numeric value to the variable that was created to store the number of random items available.

5. Call the RANDOMIZE function. This function will re-seed the random generator.

6. Multiply the variable that stores the number of items available by RND. RND is the random number returned by the ASP engine. The result should be converted to an integer using the Int function and stored in a variable.

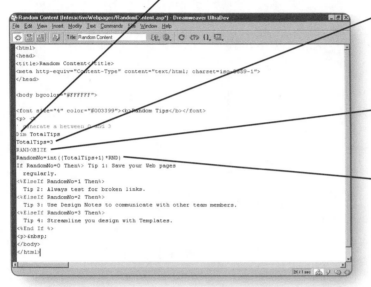

7. Use an If...Then...ElseIf statement to determine which random item should be displayed.

- Within the If and ElseIf statements, you will need to test if the random number matches the item to be displayed.

- The random content could be text or an image. You may even include both as random content.

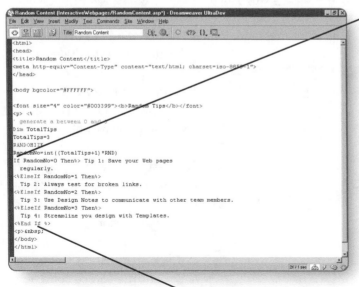

8. Close the If statement with an End If statement.

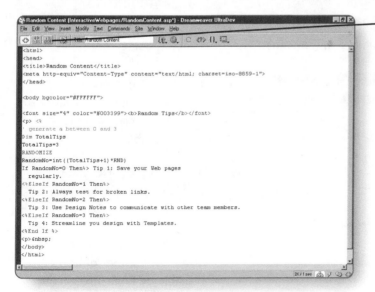

9. Click on the Show Design View icon. The Web page will be displayed.

Redirecting

The Redirect method of the Response object allows you to redirect a user to a new Web page. You're probably wondering why you may ever need to use this functionality. It is handy when you restructure your Web site and don't want users that have bookmarked a page to get an error message. Rather than deleting the old page, redirect the user to the new page. Some browsers don't handle redirecting very well, so you should always place a link to the new Web page as well.

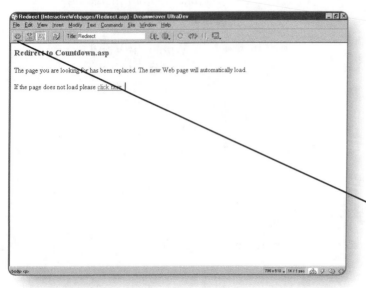

1. Create a new Web page with an .asp extension. The script will not be executed if the page has another extension.

2. Click on the Show Code View icon. The source code of the Web page will be displayed.

3. Type Response.Redirect within the <% and %> delimiters.

4. Pass the name of the redirect Web page. Users will be redirected to this page if they visit the current Web page.

5. Include a link to the redirect page because some old Web browsers don't support Server Side redirects.

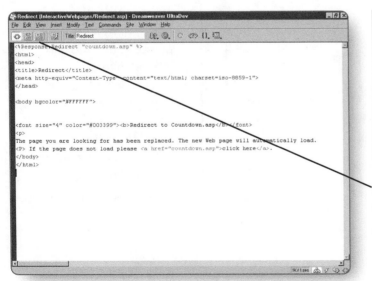

6. Click on the Show Design View icon. The Web page will be displayed.

Server-Side Includes

SSIs are code segments such as headers and footers that can be reused across your web site. The included files are stored and processed on the server. UltraDev does not have to insert the code when the Web site is uploaded to the server.

You can also include functions and subroutines in SSI files that have an .asp extension. This is great, because it allows you to store your subroutines and functions in a central location that can easily be accessed by all the pages in your Web site.

1. Create an include file with an .asp extension.

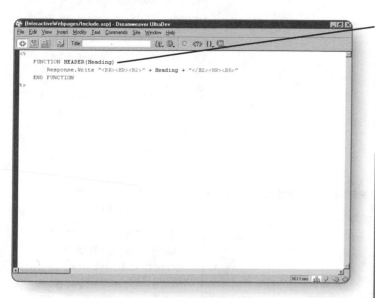

2. Create a function or subroutine. Refer to Chapter 15, "Writing Your Own ASP Code," for detailed information on creating functions and subroutines.

NOTE

- The functions/ subroutines must be placed within <% and %> delimiters.
- You can include as many functions/subroutines as you require.
- The include file should not contain opening and closing HTML tags.

Using the SSI File

The subroutine can now be called from any ASP page that that uses the include directive to import the SSI file.

1. Create a new Web page with an .asp extension. The script will not be executed if the page has another extension.

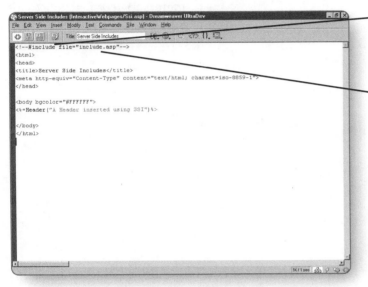

2. Insert an include directive. This is inserted within <!-- and --> delimiters.

3. Pass the file name of the file to be included to the file parameter.

NOTE

Once a file contains an include directive, you can now call any function/ subroutine contained within the include file.

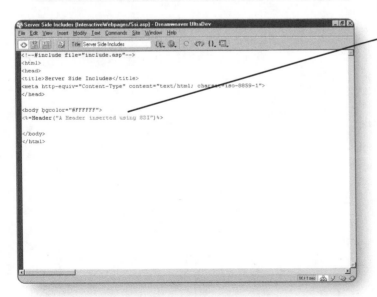

4. Type the function/subroutine name between <%= and %> delimiters. This will write the results returned to the Web page.

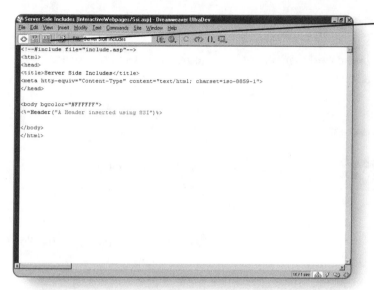

5. Click on the Show Design View icon. The Web page will be displayed.

NOTE

You can also pass parameters to your functions/ subroutines as required.

17

Sending E-mail Messages

Allowing users to provide feedback is an important feature that all Web sites should have. In the past, this has usually been achieved with a mailto link, but that requires the user to have his or her browser correctly configured to send a message. Sending messages from a server is a much more reliable solution and is not as difficult as you might think. IIS (Internet Information Server) already has all the functionality required to easily send e-mail from a Web server. You can send messages in plain or HTML format and with or without attachments. In this chapter, you'll learn to:

- Send an e-mail message using CDO
- Send carbon copies (CC) and blind carbon copies (BCC) of an e-mail
- Create an e-mail form
- Process an e-mail form
- Attach files to an e-mail message
- Send HTML formatted e-mail
- Use the Jmail component to send e-mail

Sending E-mail Messages Using CDONTS

Sending E-mail Messages using CDONTS (Collaborative Data Objects for Windows NT Server) makes sending e-mail from your server possible. The CDO.Newmail object creates a new e-mail message and the Send method posts the message.

This section provides a line-by-line explanation of the ASP code used for sending an e-mail message. Use the sample code as a template. You only need to change the address, subject, and message properties of the Newmail object.

> ## NOTE
>
> Before you can use CDONTS, your server must have the SMTP (Simple Mail Transport Protocol) service installed. You should consult your server administrator.
>
> You can't test CDONTS locally if you are running Personal Web server. It is only available with Windows NT/2000 Server.

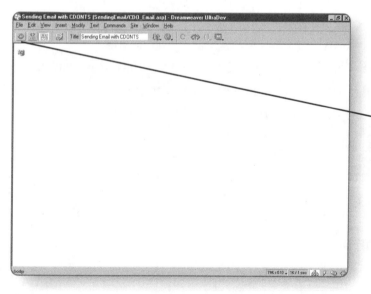

1. Create a new Web page with an .asp extension. The e-mail script will not be executed if the page has another extension.

2. Click on the Show Code View icon. The source code of the Web page will be displayed.

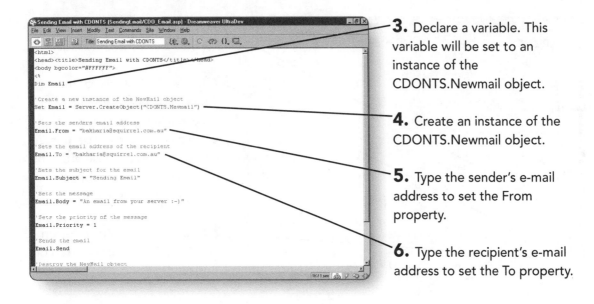

3. Declare a variable. This variable will be set to an instance of the CDONTS.Newmail object.

4. Create an instance of the CDONTS.Newmail object.

5. Type the sender's e-mail address to set the From property.

6. Type the recipient's e-mail address to set the To property.

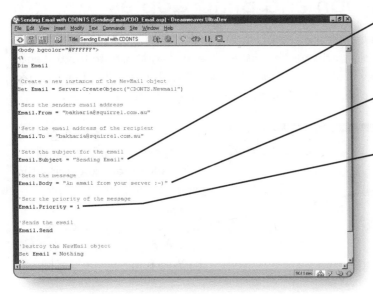

7. Type the subject of the e-mail to set the Subject property.

8. Type the e-mail message to set the Body property.

9. Type a value for the priority of the e-mail message. The priority can be set to 0 for Low Priority, 1 for Normal Priority or 2 for High Priority.

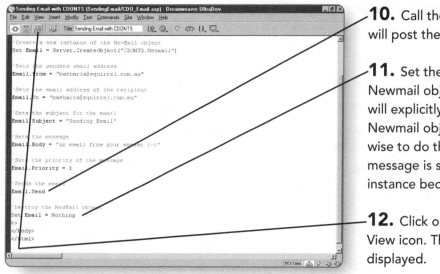

10. Call the Send method. This will post the e-mail message.

11. Set the instance of the Newmail object to nothing. This will explicitly destroy the Newmail object instance. It is wise to do this because after the message is sent, the object instance becomes invalid.

12. Click on the Show Design View icon. The Web page will be displayed.

Sending Carbon and Blind Copies

You may also need to send carbon and blind carbon copies of an e-mail to secondary recipients. This is achieved by assigning e-mail addresses to the Bcc and Cc properties of the Newmail object. A blind carbon copy is useful if you would like to send the e-mail to recipients that other recipients should not know about.

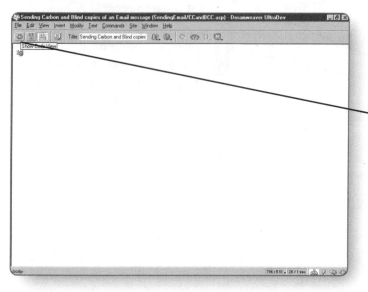

1. Create a new Web page with an .asp extension. The e-mail script will not be executed if the page has another extension.

2. Click on the Show Code View icon. The source code of the Web page will be displayed.

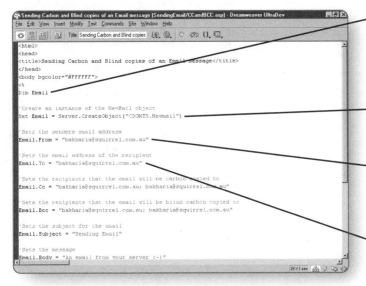

3. Declare a variable. This variable will be set to an instance of the CDONTS.Newmail object.

4. Create an instance of the CDONTS.Newmail object.

5. Type the sender's e-mail address to set the From property.

6. Type the recipient's e-mail address to set the To property.

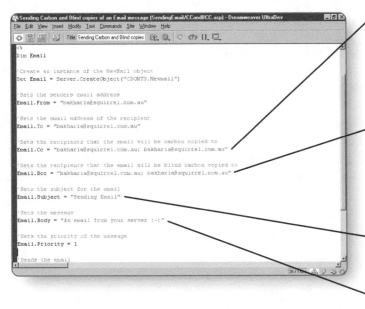

7. Type the recipients to whom the message must be carbon copied to. Many recipient e-mail addresses can be included, but a semicolon must separate them.

8. Type the recipients to whom the message must be blind carbon copied. A semi-colon must separate recipient e-mail addresses.

9. Type the subject of the e-mail to set the Subject property.

10. Type the e-mail message to set the Body property.

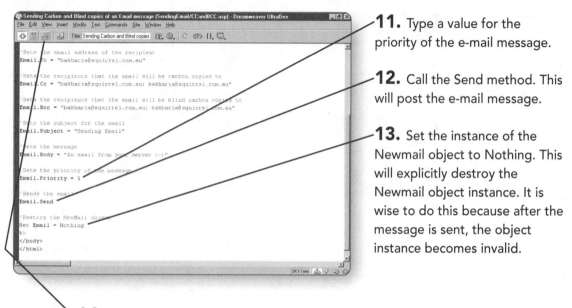

11. Type a value for the priority of the e-mail message.

12. Call the Send method. This will post the e-mail message.

13. Set the instance of the Newmail object to Nothing. This will explicitly destroy the Newmail object instance. It is wise to do this because after the message is sent, the object instance becomes invalid.

14. Click on the Show Design View icon. The Web page will be displayed.

Creating an E-mail Form

Your next step is to create a form to collect information from a Web site visitor. The form must contain a textfield that will allow visitors to enter their e-mail address and a textarea field to allow for messages that span multiple lines. You can add as many fields as you like, but these two are essential. This information will then be sent using the Post method to an ASP file that will process the information and send it via e-mail to your site's Web master.

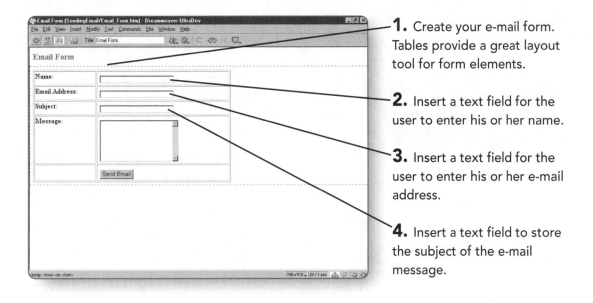

1. Create your e-mail form. Tables provide a great layout tool for form elements.

2. Insert a text field for the user to enter his or her name.

3. Insert a text field for the user to enter his or her e-mail address.

4. Insert a text field to store the subject of the e-mail message.

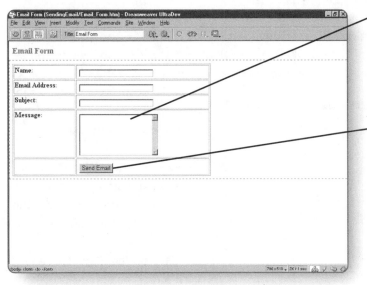

5. Insert a multiline text field for the user to enter the message. This will allow more than a single line of text to be entered.

6. Insert a Submit button. The user will click on the button to send the message to the server for processing.

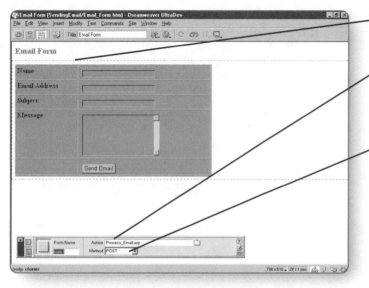

7. Select the form by clicking on the dashed red line.

8. Type the name of the file that will process the form and send the e-mail.

9. Select Post from the Method drop-down box.

Processing the Form

The contents of form fields will be retrieved using the Request.Form object and assigned to properties of the CDONTS.Newmail object. We will also include some basic form validation to ensure that the user has not left any essentials fields blank. If the To property is blank when the e-mail is sent, an error message will be produced.

1. Create a new Web page with an .asp extension. The e-mail script will not be executed if the page has another extension.

2. Click on the Show Code View icon. The source code of the Web page will be displayed.

3. Declare a variable that will be set to an instance of the CDONTS.Newmail object.

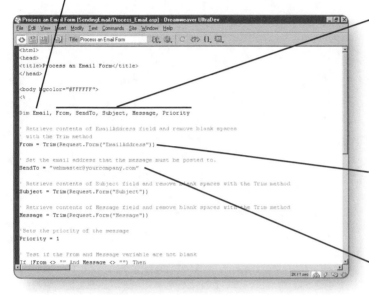

4. Declare a variable to store data for each property of the CDONTS.Newmail object. The NewMail properties will not be set directly. This will allow us to retrieve the posted form data and perform data validation.

5. Retrieve the contents of the E-mail Address field and remove blank spaces with the Trim method.

6. Type in the recipient e-mail address.

7. Retrieve the contents of the Subject field and remove blank spaces with the Trim method.

8. Retrieve the contents of the Message field and remove blank spaces with the Trim method.

9. Type in a value to set the priority of the message.

10. Test if the From and Message fields are not blank. If the From and Message fields are blank, steps 13-14 will be executed; if not steps 10-12 will be executed.

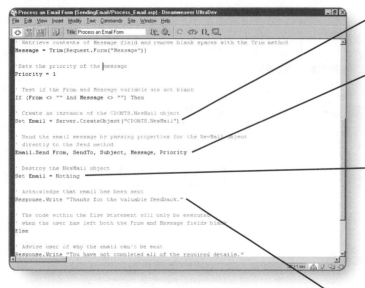

11. Create an instance of the CDONTS.NewMail object.

12. Pass the To, From, Subject, Message, and Priority variables to the Send method. This will send the e-mail message.

13. Set the instance of the Newmail object to nothing. This will explicitly destroy the Newmail object instance. It is wise to do this because after the message is sent the object instance becomes invalid.

14. Type a message to notify the user that the e-mail has been sent.

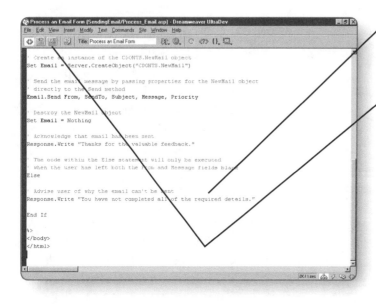

15. Type a message to be displayed if the From and To fields are left blank.

16. Click on the Show Design View icon. The Web page will be displayed.

Sending Messages with Attachments

Sometimes you may need to send e-mail and include a file attachment. This is easily achieved by passing the path and filename of the file to the AttachFile property.

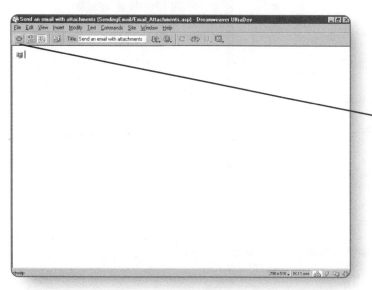

1. Create a new Web page with an .asp extension. The e-mail script will not be executed if the page has another extension.

2. Click on the Show Code View icon. The source code of the Web page will be displayed.

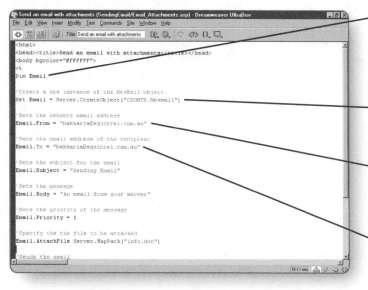

3. Declare a variable. This variable will be set to an instance of the CDONTS.Newmail object.

4. Create an instance of the CDONTS.Newmail object.

5. Type in the sender's e-mail address to set the From property.

6. Type in the recipient's e-mail address to set the To property.

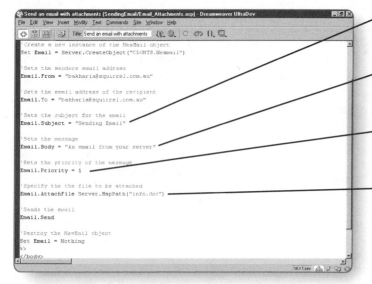

7. Type the subject of the e-mail to set the Subject property.

8. Type the e-mail message to set the Body property.

9. Type a value for the priority of the E-mail message.

10. Type the name of the file to be attached to set the AttachFile property. The Server.MapPath method is used to map a virtual path to a physical path.

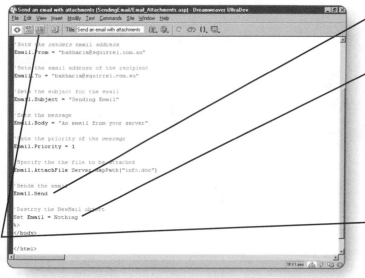

11. Call the Send method. This will post the e-mail message.

12. Set the instance of the Newmail object to Nothing. This will explicitly destroy the Newmail object instance. It is wise to do this because after the message is sent, the object instance becomes invalid.

13. Click on the Show Design View icon. The Web page will be displayed.

Sending HTML-Formatted Message

E-mail can look pretty bland sometimes because it is in plain text. If you want to apply formatting to your e-mail messages, you could send the message as HTML text. This will allow images and tables to be inserted in the message. Many e-mail clients already support HTML-formatted e-mail.

To send HTML formatted messages, the Mail and Body properties of the CDONTS.Newmail object must be changed. The default Body property value for plain text is 1. This must be changed to 0 to send an HTML message. The Mail property describes how the E-mail is composed and has a default value of 1. The Mail property must be set to 0 to send mime formatted messages.

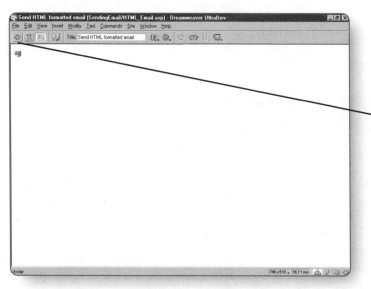

1. Create a new Web page with an .asp extension. The e-mail script will not be executed if the page has another extension.

2. Click on the Show Code View icon. The source code of the Web page will be displayed.

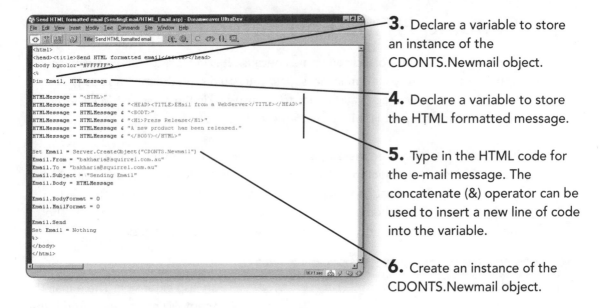

3. Declare a variable to store an instance of the CDONTS.Newmail object.

4. Declare a variable to store the HTML formatted message.

5. Type in the HTML code for the e-mail message. The concatenate (&) operator can be used to insert a new line of code into the variable.

6. Create an instance of the CDONTS.Newmail object.

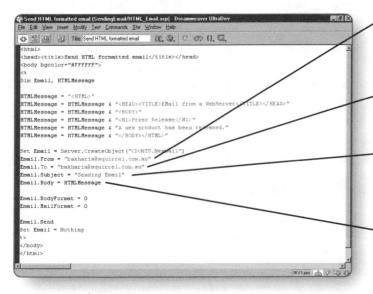

7. Type in the sender's e-mail address to set the From property.

8. Type in the recipient's e-mail address to set the To property.

9. Type in the subject of the e-mail to set the Subject property.

10. Set the Body property to the variable storing the HTML formatted message.

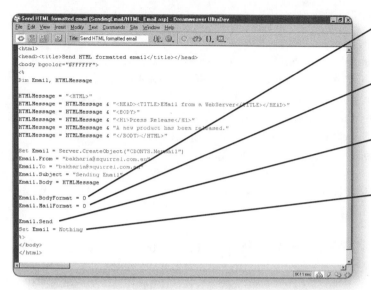

11 Set the BodyFormat property to 0.

12. Set the MailFormat property to 0.

13. Call the Send method. This will post the E-mail message.

14. Set the instance of the Newmail object to nothing. This will explicitly destroy the Newmail object instance. It is wise to do this because after the message is sent, the object instance becomes invalid.

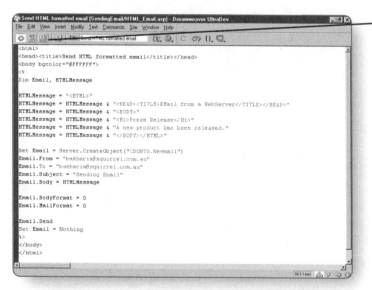

15. Click on the Show Design View icon. The Web page will be displayed.

Using Jmail

CDONTS may not be available on the Web server that you are using. This may be the case if the Web site is hosted externally by an ISP (Internet service provider). Usually another ASP component that is capable of sending e-mail will be installed. Jmail is a popular free e-mail component that matches the power and flexibility provided by CDONTS. Sending e-mail with Jmail is very similar to using CDONTS. Jmail can be downloaded from http://www.dimac.net.

The JMail.SMTPMail object is used to create a new e-mail message and the Execute method is used to post the e-mail message.

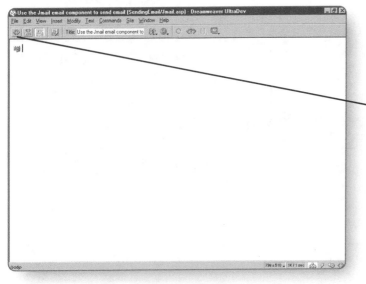

1. Create a new Web page with an .asp extension. The e-mail script will not be executed if the page has another extension.

2. Click on the Show Code View icon. The source code of the Web page will be displayed.

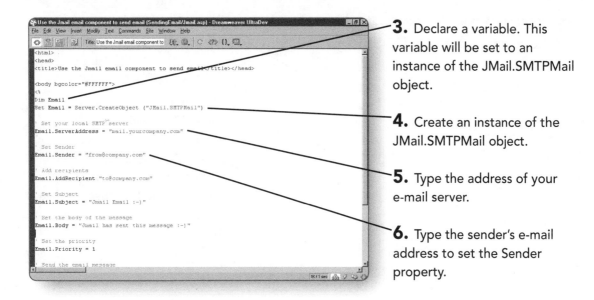

3. Declare a variable. This variable will be set to an instance of the JMail.SMTPMail object.

4. Create an instance of the JMail.SMTPMail object.

5. Type the address of your e-mail server.

6. Type the sender's e-mail address to set the Sender property.

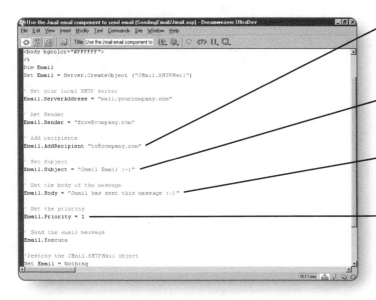

7. Type the recipient's e-mail address to set the AddRecipient property.

8. Type the subject of the e-mail to set the Subject property.

9. Type the message to set the Body property.

10. Type a value for the priority of the e-mail message.

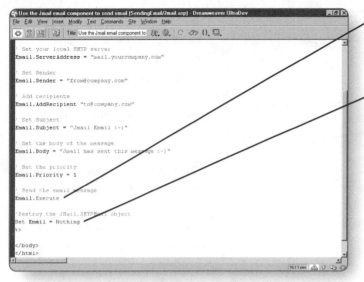

11. Call the Execute method. This will post the e-mail message.

12. Set the instance of the JMail.SMTPMail object to nothing. This will explicitly destroy the JMail.SMTPMail object instance. It is wise to do this because after the message is sent, the object instance becomes invalid.

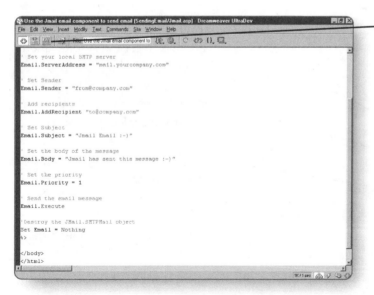

13. Click on the Show Design View icon. The Web page will be displayed.

18

Maintaining State

You need to identify users and track their activities when creating complex Web applications. Unfortunately, HTTP (Hypertext Transfer Protocol) does not store any information between page requests because it is a stateless protocol. This certainly presents a challenge because without a permanent connection between the server and browser you won't be able to create shopping carts, authenticate users, and personalize content. Sessions and cookies both provide a practical solution, each of which has its own strengths. Cookies store information on a user's computer that can be retrieved at a later date. Sessions, on the other hand, share the information entered by a user across multiple pages in your Web site. In this chapter you'll learn to:

- Create a cookie
- Read a cookie
- Store and retrieve session variables
- Use query strings and hidden form objects to maintain state

Working with Cookies

Cookies are small amounts of data stored within a Web browser on the user's computer. The information stored within a cookie can be retrieved immediately or when the user returns to the Web site depending upon the expiry date that you set. You don't need to worry about other Web sites retrieving your cookie values because only pages that reside on the same domain can access your data.

The use of cookies has always been fairly controversial. They were initially seen as a security and privacy risk because they could store sensitive data. The biggest disadvantage of using a cookie is that it is stored on the user's computer. This means that you will only be able to retrieve the data if your user is visiting your Web site from the same computer. You should also be aware that many Web browsers allow users to easily disable cookies.

Creating a Cookie

The Cookies collection of the Response object is used to create a cookie. Each cookie that you store must have a unique name and an optional expiry date. The expiry date that you set will determine whether the cookie will expire when the user leaves the site or can be retrieved at a later date. If no expiry date is set, the cookie will be deleted when the browser is closed or the session expires.

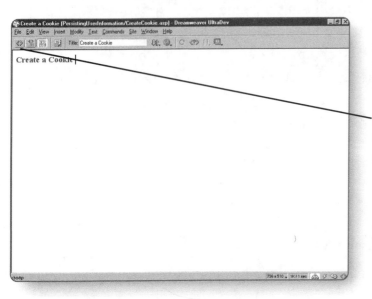

1. Create a new Web page with an .asp extension. The script will not be executed if the page has another extension.

2. Click on the Show Code View icon. The source code of the Web page will be displayed.

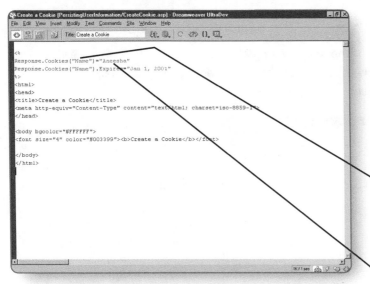

3. Pass the name of the cookie to the Response.Cookies method. This will create a cookie with the specified name.

4. Set the value of the cookie.

5. Set the Expires property of the Response.Cookies method by assigning an expiry date.

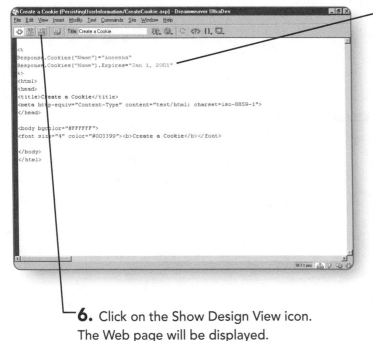

6. Click on the Show Design View icon. The Web page will be displayed.

Reading a Cookie

The Cookies collection of the Request object is used to retrieve the value stored in a cookie. You must know the name of the cookie and be within the same domain to read a cookie successfully.

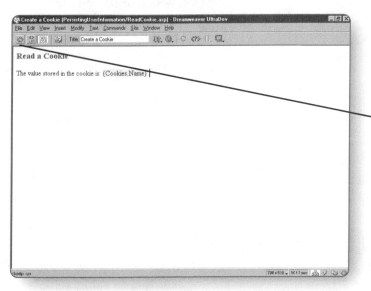

1. Create a new Web page with an .asp extension. The script will not be executed if the page has another extension.

2. Click on the Show Code View icon. The source code of the Web page will be displayed.

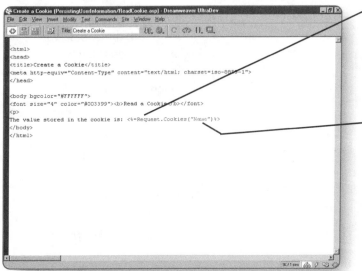

3. Type Request.Cookies between the <%= and the %> delimiters. This will write the value stored in the cookie to the Web page.

4. Pass the name of the cookie to the Request.Cookies method.

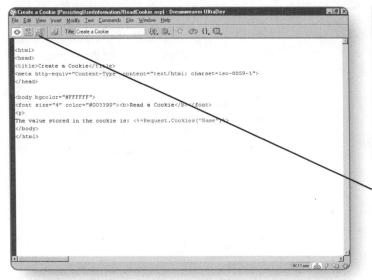

TIP

You can also use the Request Variable Data Source from the Data Bindings palette to retrieve a cookie and bind the value to a Web page.

5. Click on the Show Design View icon. The Web page will be displayed.

Working with Sessions

A session starts when a user enters your Web site and ends when a user leaves. Sessions can only be used to store information while a user is visiting your Web site. Sessions are much simpler to implement because you don't need to specify an expiry date. They rely on cookies, but this is taken care of in the background. When a session begins, a unique Session ID is generated and stored as a cookie. All session variables are actually stored on the Web server. This is very secure because no information is stored as a cookie. Session variables are specific to a particular user and can't be shared with other users.

Creating Session Variables

The Session object is used to create a new session variable and assign an initial value. Each session variable that you store must be given a unique name. When a user leaves the Web site or has not requested a page from the Web server in 20 minutes, the session will expire. When a session expires, all the session variables associated with the inactive user will be deleted.

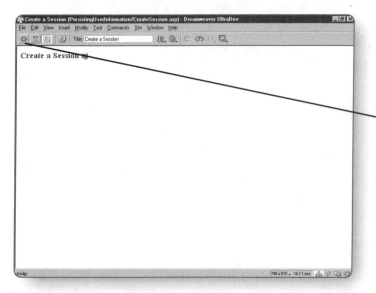

1. Create a new Web page with an .asp extension. The script will not be executed if the page has another extension.

2. Click on the Show Code View icon. The source code of the Web page will be displayed.

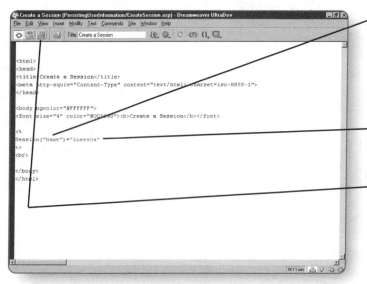

3. Pass the name of the session variable to the Session object. This will create a session variable with the specified name.

4. Set the value of the session variable.

5. Click on the Show Design View icon. The Web page will be displayed.

Reading Session Variables

The Session object is used to retrieve the value stored in a session variable. You must know the name of the session variable. You can also retrieve the unique Session ID that is stored for each user. Sessions provide a simple way for variables to be shared across multiple Web pages.

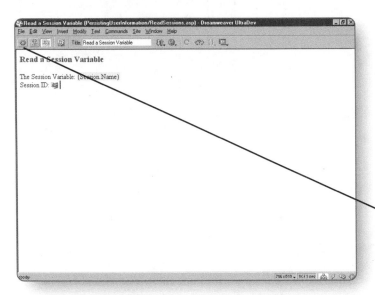

1. Create a new Web page with an .asp extension. The script will not be executed if the page has another extension.

2. Click on the Show Code View icon. The source code of the Web page will be displayed.

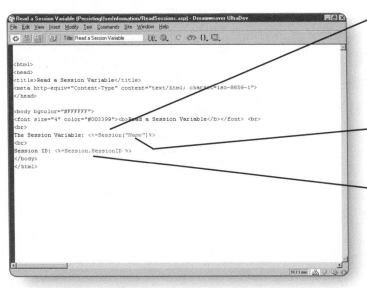

3. Type Session between the <%= and the %> delimiters. This will write the value stored in the session variable to the Web page.

4. Pass the session variable name to the Session object.

5. Type Session.SessionID between the <%= and the %> delimiters. This retrieves the unique Session ID for the current user.

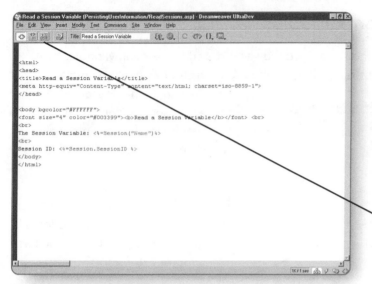

> **TIP**
>
> You can also use the Request Session Data Source from the Data Bindings palette to retrieve a session variable and bind the value to a Web page.

6. Click on the Show Design View icon. The Web page will be displayed.

Terminating a Session

A session is automatically terminated if no page requests have been made for 20 minutes. You can easily extend this period by setting the Timeout property of the Session object.

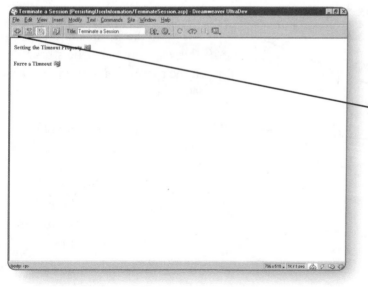

1. Create a new Web page with an .asp extension. The script will not be executed if the page has another extension.

2. Click on the Show Code View icon. The source code of the Web page will be displayed.

3. Type Session.Timeout between the <% and %> delimiters.

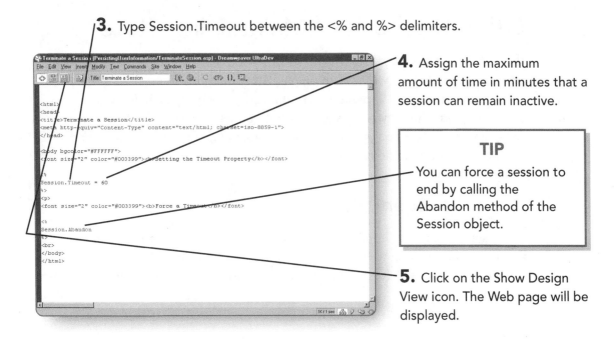

4. Assign the maximum amount of time in minutes that a session can remain inactive.

TIP

You can force a session to end by calling the Abandon method of the Session object.

5. Click on the Show Design View icon. The Web page will be displayed.

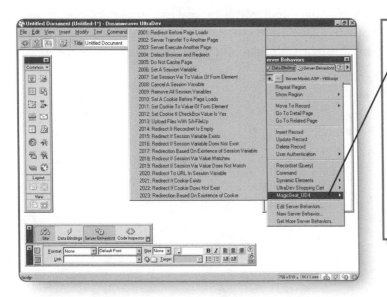

TIP

The MagicBeat Server Behavior Suite is a collection of 23 server behaviors that will help you to work with cookies and sessions in UltraDev. The server behavior can be downloaded from the MagicBeat Web site (**http://www. magicbeat.com**).

Other Methods of Maintaining State

As mentioned previously, cookies and sessions both have disadvantages. If these present a problem, you will have to employ other methods to maintain state across multiple pages. You can append data to the query string or use hidden form objects to pass data between pages, but both of these methods will have to be implemented on every page. The concepts are simple, but implementing them on every page is a very tedious task.

Using the Query String

If the user is navigating from page to page by clicking on links then you should append the information to the query string. Consult Chapter 6, "Validating and Retrieving Form Data," for more information on creating and retrieving data stored in a query string.

Using Hidden Form Objects

If the user is using a form to navigate your Web site, you can store data in hidden form fields. Consult Chapter 5, "Creating HTML Forms," and Chapter 6, "Validating and Retrieving Form Data," for more information on creating and retrieving data from a form.

19

Working with Files and Folders

Text files can sometimes be a handy replacement for databases. You should consider using text files when you only need to store a small amount of data that rarely gets updated. The FileSystemObject object will allow you to access files, folders, and drives on a Web server. In this chapter, you'll learn to:

- Read text from a file
- Write text to a file
- Determine whether a file exists
- Copy, move, and delete files
- Display the contents of a folder

Reading a File

ASP can read a text file and then display its contents in a Web page. The OpenTextFile method of the FileSystemObject makes all of this possible.

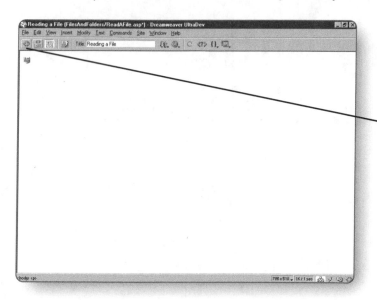

1. Create a new Web page with an .asp extension. The script will not execute if the page has any other extension.

2. Click on the Show Code View icon. The source code of the Web page will be displayed.

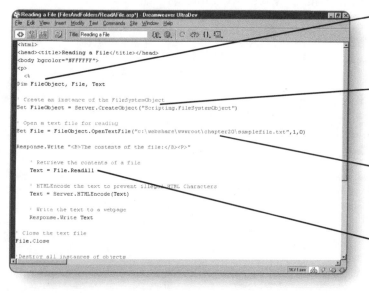

3. Declare a variable to store an instance of the FileSystemObject.

4. Create an instance of the FileSystemObject and store it in a variable.

5. Pass the file name and path to be opened for reading to the OpenTextFileObject.

6. Call the ReadAll method to retrieve the whole text file.

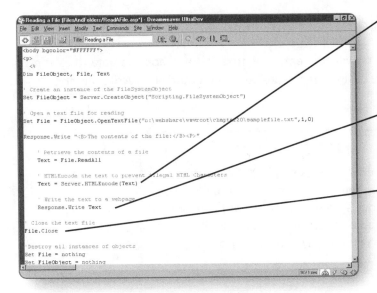

7. Use the Server.HTMLEncode method to ensure that all characters display correctly in a browser.

8. Use the Response.Write method to write contents of the file to a Web page.

9. Close the file by calling the Close method.

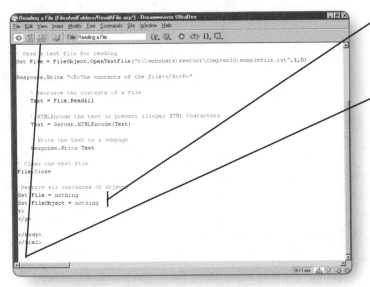

10. Set all object instances to Nothing. This will free up resources on the server.

11. Click on the Show Design View icon. The Web page will be displayed.

Writing a File

With ASP, you have the power to create new text files and append data to existing files. This is achieved by calling the CreateTextFile method. The Write method writes a string to a file.

> ## NOTE
>
> If your site is hosted on Windows NT/2000 Server, the folder that will contain the new file must have read/write access. Check with your system administrator if you are not sure. You will be able to test your scripts locally with Personal Web Server without any security concerns.

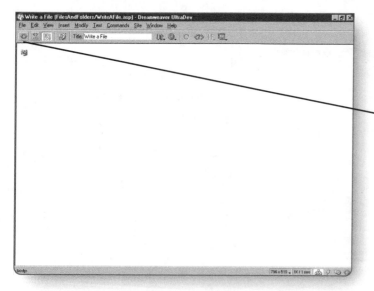

1. Create a new Web page with an .asp extension. The script will not execute if the page has any other extension.

2. Click on the Show Code View icon. The source code of the Web page will be displayed.

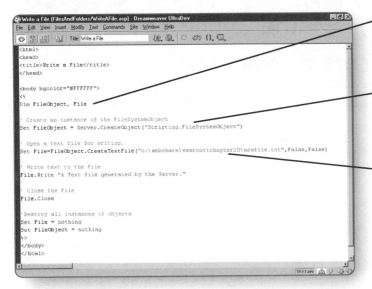

3. Declare a variable to store an instance of the FileSystemObject.

4. Create an instance of the FileSystemObject and store it in a variable.

5. Pass the file name and path to be opened for writing to CreateTextFile.

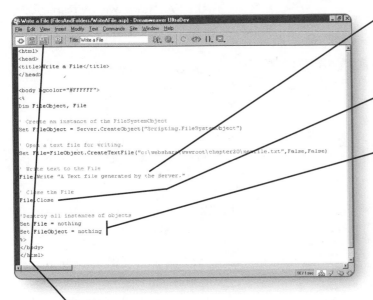

6. Call the Write method and pass the string to be written to the file.

7. Close the file by calling the Close method.

8. Set all object instances to Nothing. This will free up resources on the server.

9. Click on the Show Design View icon. The Web page will be displayed.

Determining Whether a File Exists

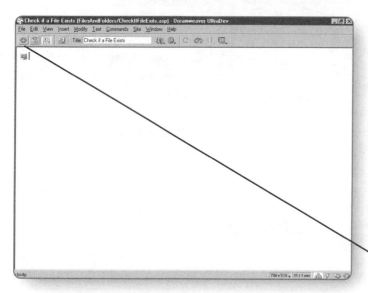

If you attempt to write to or read from a file that does not exist, you will get an error message. However, you can perform your own error checking using the FileExists property of the FileSystemObject.

1. Create a new Web page with an .asp extension. The script will not execute if the page has any other extension.

2. Click on the Show Code View icon. The source code of the Web page will be displayed.

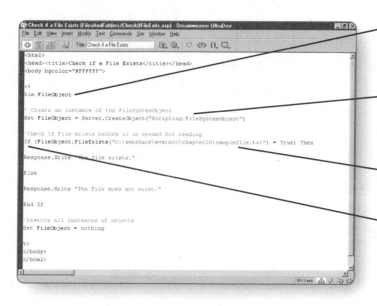

3. Declare a variable to store an instance of the FileSystemObject.

4. Create an instance of the FileSystemObject and store it in a variable.

5. Pass the file name to the FileExists method.

6. Use an If statement to determine whether the FileExists method returns TRUE.

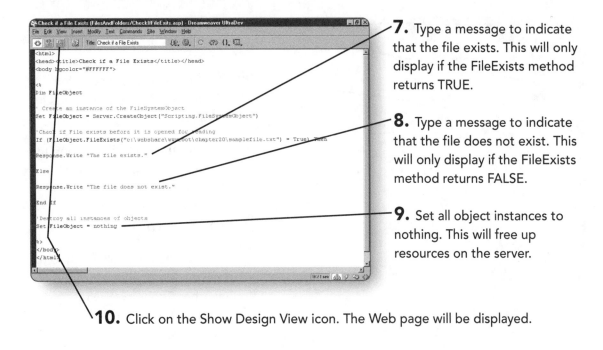

7. Type a message to indicate that the file exists. This will only display if the FileExists method returns TRUE.

8. Type a message to indicate that the file does not exist. This will only display if the FileExists method returns FALSE.

9. Set all object instances to nothing. This will free up resources on the server.

10. Click on the Show Design View icon. The Web page will be displayed.

Copying, Moving, and Deleting Files

The FileSystemObject also has methods that allow you to copy, move, and delete files. You should always test these methods on your local machine before uploading them to a live server. If there are errors, you could accidentally delete your entire Web site!

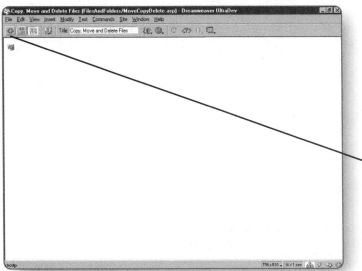

1. Create a new Web page with an .asp extension. The script will not execute if the page has any other extension.

2. Click on the Show Code View icon. The source code of the Web page will be displayed.

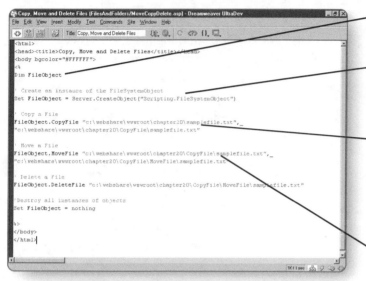

3. Declare a variable to store an instance of the FileSystemObject.

4. Create an instance of the FileSystemObject and store it in a variable.

5. Use the CopyFile method to copy a file from one location to another. The CopyFile method requires the current and destination paths.

6. Use the MoveFile method to move a file from one location to another. The MoveFile method requires the current and destination paths.

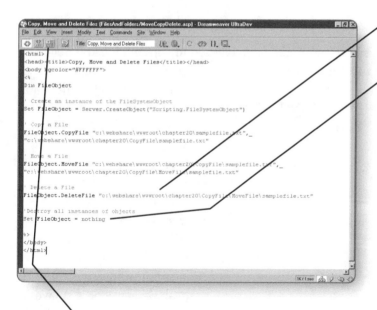

7. Use the DeleteFile method to delete a file.

8. Set the instance of the FileSystemObject to nothing. This will free up resources on the server.

9. Click on the Show Design View icon. The Web page will be displayed.

Displaying Folder Contents

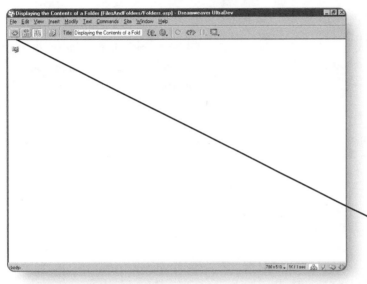

You might find it useful to display the contents of a folder. This simple script displays all the files in the specified folder in an unordered list.

1. Create a new Web page with an .asp extension. The script will not execute if the page has any other extension.

2. Click on the Show Code View icon. The source code of the Web page will be displayed.

3. Declare a variable to store an instance of the FileSystemObject.

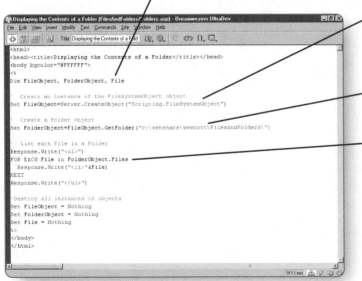

4. Create an instance of the FileSystemObject and store it in a variable.

5. Pass the folder path to the GetFolder method.

6. Loop through the Files collection. You'll notice that the loop does not have a counter. A counter can't be used because you don't know how many files there are in a particular folder. Use a For Each loop instead. The code within the loop will be executed for each file found in the folder (such as all the files returned in the Files collection).

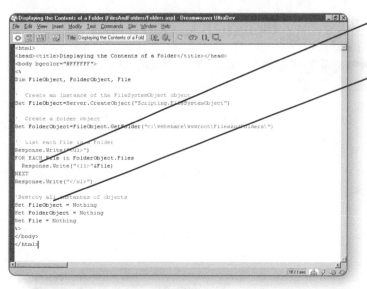

7. Use Response.Write to display the file names in a list.

8. Set the instance of the FileSystemObject to nothing. This will free up resources on the server.

9. Click on the Show Design View icon. The Web page will be displayed.

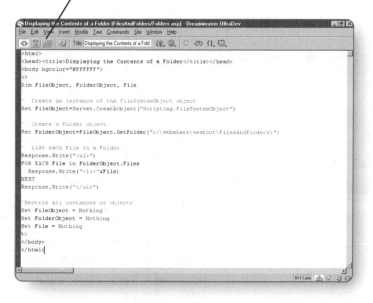

After reading this chapter, you can take control of the files and folders that reside on your Web server. You can now build a simple guestbook, store the data retrieved from a form in a file, and create custom user activity log files.

20

Customizing UltraDev

UltraDev is very versatile in terms of extensibility. The Server Behavior Builder has totally revolutionized the creation of simple, but essential, server behaviors that can easily be reused. With a basic knowledge of HTML and JavaScript, you will also be able to customize the interface and build more complex extensions (objects, commands, and behaviors). The UltraDev Exchange Web site contains many extensions that are free to download and use. These will no doubt prevent you from having to hand-code that added bit of functionality that UltraDev is missing. In this chapter, you'll learn to:

- Customize the Launcher
- Download and install extensions from UltraDev Exchange
- Use the Server Behavior Builder
- Extend UltraDev with JavaScript

Customizing the Launcher

The Launcher allows you to easily open and close various palettes, windows, and inspectors. The Launcher by default only displays items that are essential for creating dynamic database-driven Web sites. You can, however, add and remove items from the Launcher to best suit your Web development needs.

Adding an Item to the Launcher

It is very easy to add palettes, windows, and inspectors, but you should only add items that you regularly use. The size of the Launcher increases as you add items and this could infringe on valuable screen space.

1. Click on Edit. The Edit menu will appear.

2. Click on Preferences. The Preferences dialog box will open.

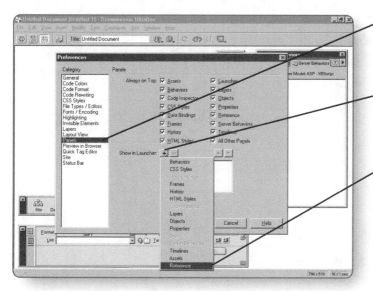

3. Click on Panels in the Category list. The associated settings will be displayed.

4. Click on the + sign. Items that can be included on the Launcher are displayed.

5. Click on the name of an item. The item will be added to the Show in Launcher list.

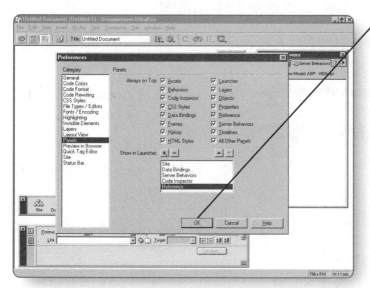

6. Click on OK. The settings will be saved and the Preferences dialog box will close.

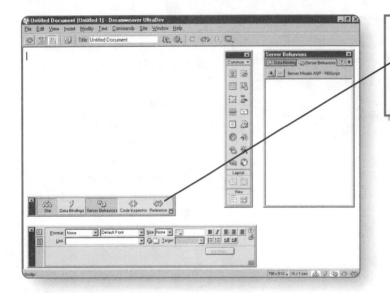

Removing an Item from the Launcher

The Launcher may contain an icon for a floating palette, window, or inspector that you rarely use. In much the same manner that items were added, they can be

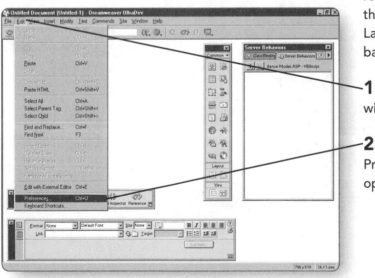

removed. This provides you with the flexibility to customize the Launcher on a project-by-project basis.

1. Click on Edit. The Edit menu will appear.

2. Click on Preferences. The Preferences dialog box will open.

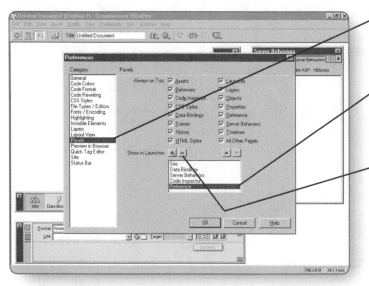

3. Click on Panels in the Category list. The associated settings will be displayed.

4. Click on the name of the item you would like to remove. The item will be highlighted.

5. Click on the - sign. The item will be removed from the Show in Launcher list.

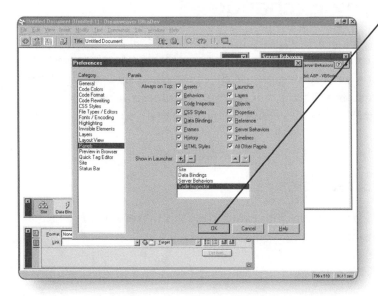

6. Click on OK. The settings will be saved and the Preferences dialog box will close.

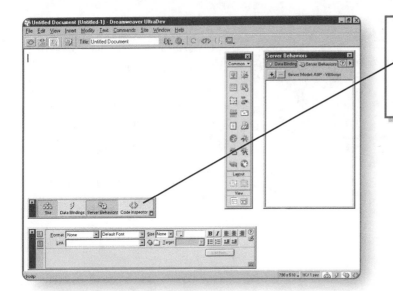

NOTE

The item will be removed from both the Launcher and Mini-Launcher.

Using UltraDev Exchange

UltraDev Exchange is a Web site maintained by Macromedia that contains objects, behaviors, and commands created by other developers. These extensions are free to download and use after you register. Always check the UltraDev Exchange Web site before you create custom solutions, because you could save valuable time by using existing extensions. You can also upload extensions that you have developed for others to use.

Downloading Extensions

UltraDev Exchange groups extensions into categories. This makes it easy to locate and download the extensions that you require.

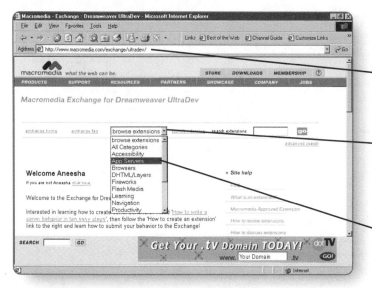

1. Open a Web browser. Your start page will be displayed.

2. Type in the URL for UltraDev Exchange and press Enter. The Web site will load.

3. Click on the down arrow of the Category drop-down list. The list of available categories is displayed.

4. Click on a category. A Web page with a list of extensions within the category will load.

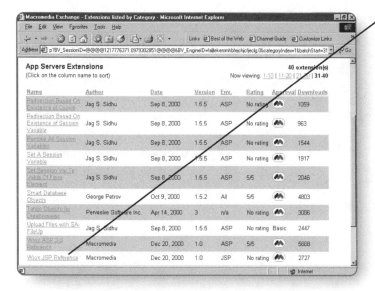

5. Click on the name of an extension. A Web page for the extension will load. It will contain a full description of the extension.

6. Click on the download button appropriate for your computer. The File Download dialog box will open.

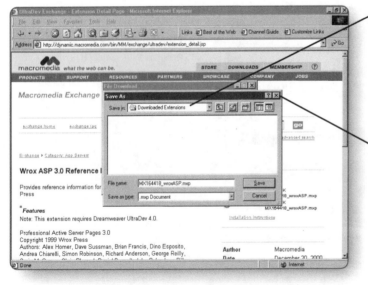

7. Save the file to the Download Extensions folder within the Dreamweaver UltraDev folder. Dreamweaver UltraDev will give the file an .mxp extension.

8. Click on the close button of the window. The Web browser will close.

Installing Extensions

The Extension Manager provides a central location from which you can view and remove existing extensions. The Extension Manager also simplifies the process of installing new extensions.

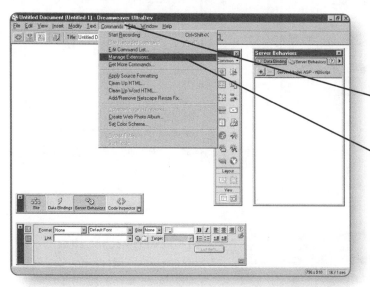

1. Open UltraDev. A blank Web page will be displayed in the Document window.

2. Click on Commands. The Commands menu will appear.

3. Click on Manage Extensions. The Extension Manager will open.

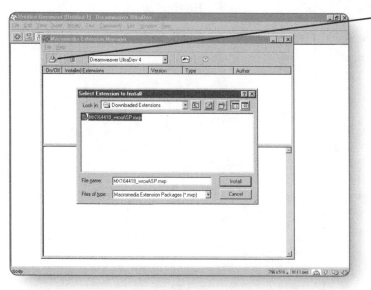

4. Click on the Install New Extensions button. The Select Extension to Install dialog box will open and display the contents of the Download Extensions folder.

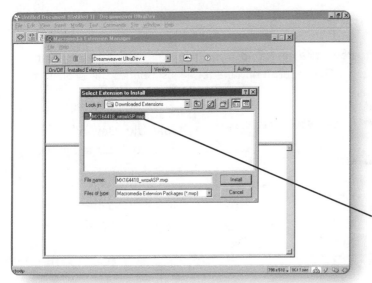

5. Double-click on the file name of the extension. A disclaimer will be displayed.

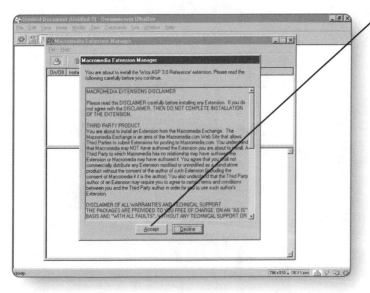

6. Click on Accept after reading the Extension Disclaimer. A message box saying that the extension has been successfully installed will be displayed.

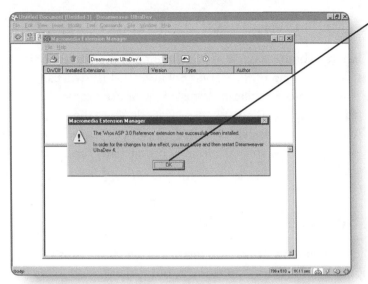

7. Click on OK. The Extension Manager window reappears.

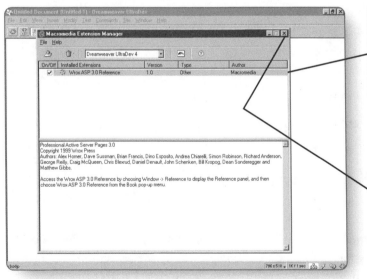

NOTE

The extension will be included in the list of installed extensions. You will need to restart UltraDev before you can utilize the extension.

8. Click on the Close button. The window will close and return to UltraDev. You can now use the extension.

Using the Server Behavior Builder

You have probably developed a library of code to implement common functionality in your Web applications. With the help of the Server Behavior Builder, you can turn your code into reusable components. Building a server behavior used to be a complex task that required an understanding of XML, JavaScript, and the Dreamweaver UltraDev API. The Server Behavior Builder allows you to concentrate your efforts on Web development while still enjoying the productivity rewards that customized behaviors bring.

Preparing Your Server-side Code

The Server Behavior Builder can be used to create server behaviors for your ASP (both VBScript and JScript), JSP, and ColdFusion scripts, but you will need to create each separately. Creating a server behavior is very easy if you follow the process outlined here.

1. Divide your code into separate blocks. A server behavior can insert code at various positions in a Web page. These include:

- Before/After the opening HTML tag
- Before/After the closing HTML tag
- Before/After the current selection
- Replacing the current selection

2. Decide where the separate code blocks should be inserted in the current document.

3. Determine the parameters that will be used to customize the script. There will usually be constants in your code that must be specifically set each time you insert the code. The Server Behavior Builder will automatically create a user-friendly interface for data entry.

Creating a Countdown Server Behavior

In Chapter 16, "Creating Interactive Web Pages," we discussed the ASP code required to count down the days remaining before an event occurs. We will now utilize the Server Behavior Builder to convert the Countdown script into a reusable and easily customizable component.

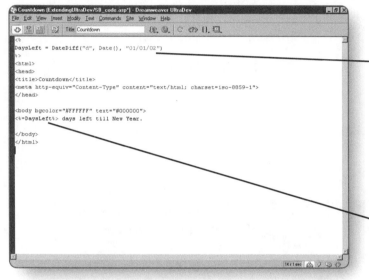

1. The code has been separated into two code blocks.

- The first code block uses the DateDiff method to calculate the number of days remaining and stores the result in the DaysLeft variable. This code block needs to be inserted before the opening HTML tag.

- The second code block simply uses the <%= and %> delimiters to print the DaysLeft variable to the Web page. This code block must replace the current selection. It could be inserted anywhere within the body of the Web page.

2. The date of the event needs to be a modifiable parameter. Each time you use the Countdown behavior you will be counting down to a different event.

We are now ready to create the Countdown server behavior.

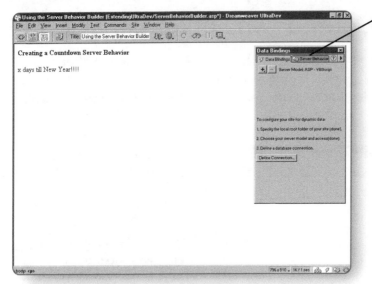

3. Click on the Server Behaviors tab. The Server Behaviors palette will be displayed.

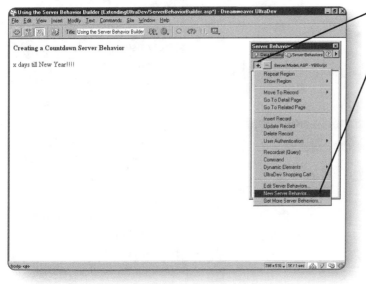

4. Click on the + sign. A submenu will appear.

5. Click on New Server Behavior. The New Server Behavior dialog box will open.

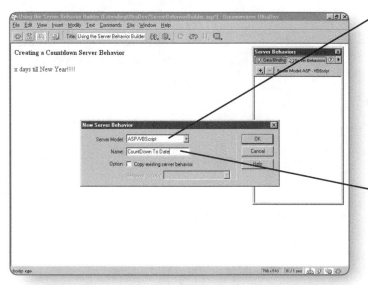

6. Select the Server Model. The code that you want to implement as a server behavior must be written in the appropriate scripting language. The Countdown server behavior that we are creating is written for ASP in VBScript.

7. Type in the name of the server behavior.

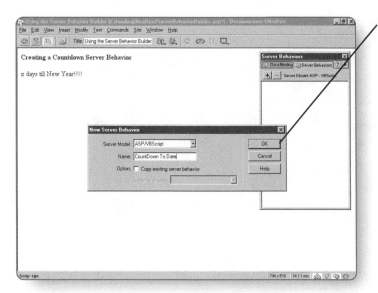

8. Click on OK. The Server Behavior Builder dialog box will open.

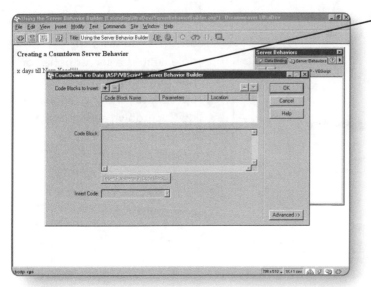

9. Click on the + sign to add the first code block. The Create a New Code Block dialog box will appear.

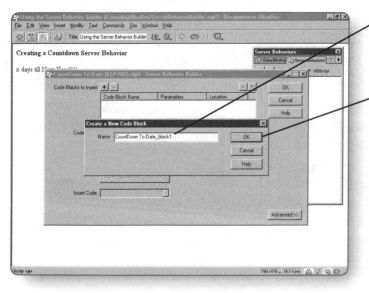

10. Type in the name of the code block. The default value is usually a safe bet.

11. Click on OK. The Create a New Code Block dialog box will open.

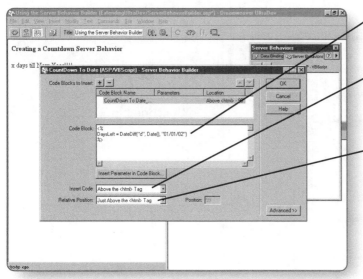

12. Paste the first code block into the Code Block field.

13. Select Above the <html> Tag from the Insert Code drop-down box.

14. Select Just Above the <html> Tag in the Relative Position drop-down box.

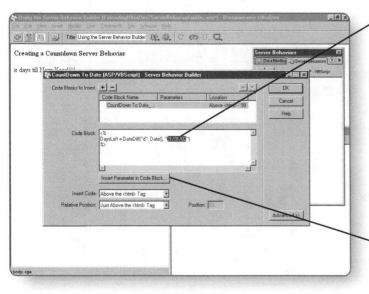

15. Select the hard-coded value that needs to be replaced by a parameter. The value will be highlighted.

CAUTION

Don't include the surrounding quotation marks in the selection.

16. Click on Insert Parameter in Code Block. The Insert Parameter in Code Block dialog box will open.

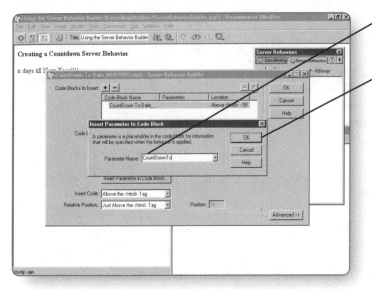

17. Type in a name for the parameter.

18. Click on OK. The parameter will be inserted in the code block.

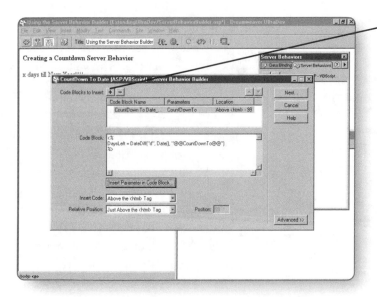

19. Click on the + sign to insert the second code block. The Create a New Code Block dialog box will open.

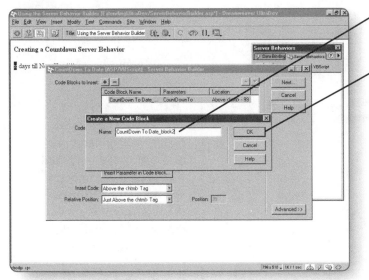

20. Type in a name for the second code block.

21. Click on OK. The Create a New Code Block dialog box will close.

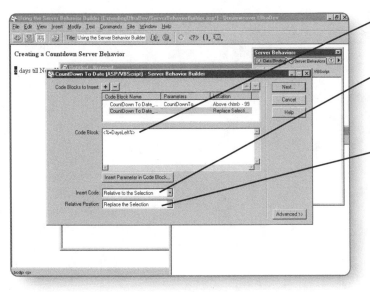

22. Paste the second code block into the Code Block field.

23. Select Relative to the Selection from the Insert Code drop-down box.

24. Select Replace the Selection in the Relative Position drop-down box.

NOTE

When creating your own server behaviors you will need to repeat steps 17–20 for each code block.

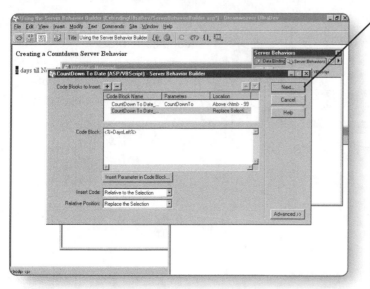

25. Click on Next. The Generate Behavior dialog box will open.

> **NOTE**
>
> The Server Behavior Builder will generate a dialog box for behaviors that accept parameters. You need to determine the type of form controls required. The default form control that gets assigned to all parameters is a text field.

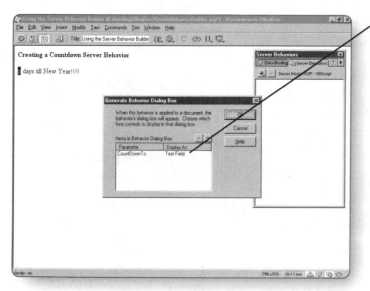

26. Click within the Display As column. A submenu will appear.

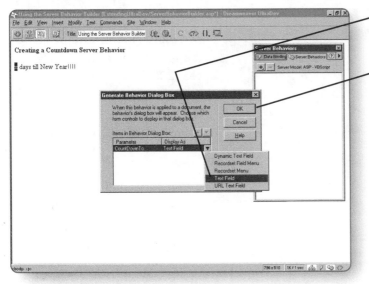

27. Select the appropriate form control.

28. Click on OK. The Generate Behavior dialog box will close.

Using the Server Behavior

Behaviors created with the Sever Behavior Builder are automatically listed in the Server Behaviors palette. The generated server behaviors function just like the standard behaviors included with UltraDev. You can easily insert, customize, and remove a server behavior from a Web page.

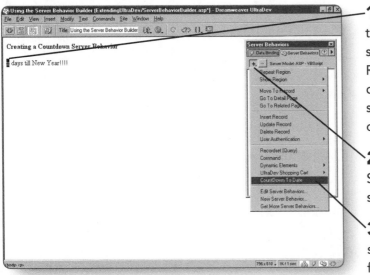

1. Select the placeholder text that must be replaced by the second Countdown code block. Remember that the second code block in the Countdown script simply prints the number of days left.

2. Click on the + sign in the Server Behaviors palette. A submenu will appear.

3. Click on the name of the server behavior. The dialog box for the behavior will open.

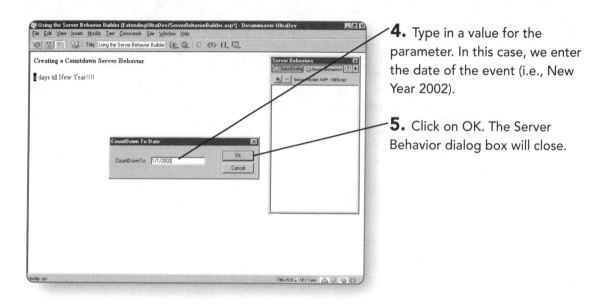

4. Type in a value for the parameter. In this case, we enter the date of the event (i.e., New Year 2002).

5. Click on OK. The Server Behavior dialog box will close.

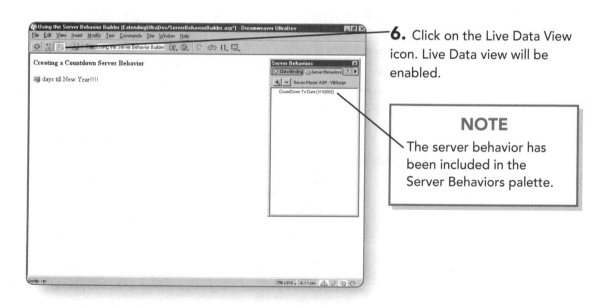

6. Click on the Live Data View icon. Live Data view will be enabled.

NOTE

The server behavior has been included in the Server Behaviors palette.

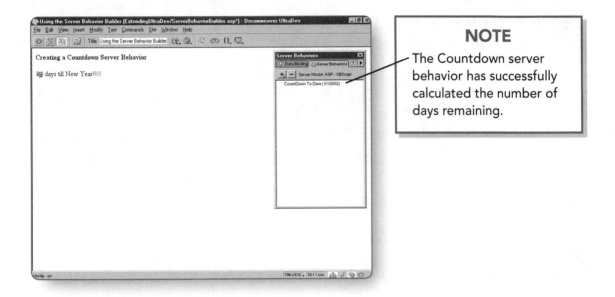

NOTE

The Countdown server behavior has successfully calculated the number of days remaining.

Creating Complex Extensions

With a working knowledge of JavaScript you will be able to create new commands, server behaviors, objects, inspectors, and floating palettes. The Dreamweaver UltraDev Document Object Model (DOM), a tree structure that describes the contents of HTML documents in terms of objects and properties, is fully programmable.

Viewing the Extending Dreamweaver Documentation

It is beyond the scope of this book to detail the UltraDev DOM and JavaScript API, but Extending Dreamweaver documentation is available.

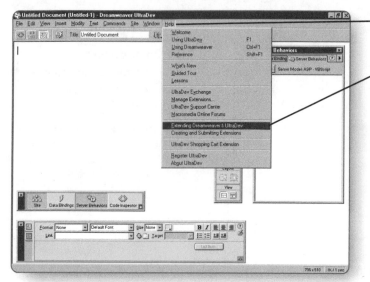

1. Click on Help. The Help menu will appear.

2. Click on Extending Dreamweaver & UltraDev. The Extending Dreamweaver UltraDev documentation will be displayed in your default browser.

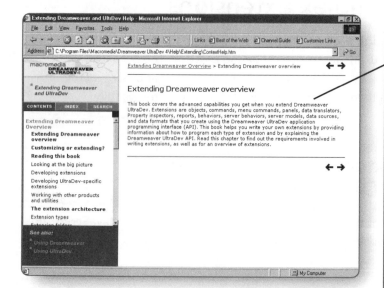

NOTE

The Extending Dreamweaver UltraDev documentation serves as an excellent resource to get you started. The documentation contains detailed information about the Document Object Model, Dreamweaver JavaScript API, Design Notes API, File I/O API, HTTP API, and the Database API. You will also find well-documented examples of objects, property inspectors, floating palettes, and behaviors.

A

Installing Dreamweaver UltraDev

You have taken the plunge and purchased Dreamweaver UltraDev. All that stands between you and creating dynamic database-driven applications is installing the software on your computer. This appendix will guide you through the process of installing UltraDev and put you in the thick of things right away. In this appendix you'll learn to:

 Explore the contents of the UltraDev CD-ROM

 Install Dreamweaver UltraDev

Exploring the Contents of the Dreamweaver UltraDev CD-ROM

The UltraDev CD-ROM contains much more than just the UltraDev installation program. You will find both free-to-use and trial versions of popular Web development software such as a ColdFusion Application Server and HomeSite, a versatile HTML editor.

1. Right-click on the Start button. A shortcut menu will appear.

2. Click on Explore. The Windows Explorer window will open and display the available drives and folders on your computer.

3. Click on the CD-ROM drive icon. The contents of the CD-ROM will be displayed.

NOTE

The UltraDev CD-ROM contains:

- **Popular Web browsers.** (Netscape and Microsoft Internet Explorer.)
- **ColdFusion Application Server.** You will need to install this if you want to build and test ColdFusion applications locally.
- **HomeSite.** An excellent HTML editor that offers more functionality than UltraDev's built-in HTML Source Editor.
- **JRun.** An application server that supports JavaServer Pages and Servlets.
- Trial versions of other popular Macromedia products such as Flash, Fireworks, Freehand, and Director.

Installing Dreamweaver UltraDev

Installing UltraDev is no different from installing any other software on your computer. The installation program has a simple wizard-driven interface. All you need to do is have your serial number handy, set the installation directory, and specify the file types that need to be associated with UltraDev.

1. Double-click on the UltraDev 4 Installer.exe file located in the root directory of the UltraDev CD-ROM. The Setup program will start.

2. Click on Next. The Software License Agreement Window will open.

3. Click on Yes after reading the License Agreement. The UltraDev Serialization window will open.

4. Type in your personal data.

5. Type in your serial number. The Next button will be enabled.

6. Click on Next. The Choose Destination Folder screen will be displayed.

7. Click on Browse to set the installation directory. The default destination folder is usually a safe bet.

8. Click on Next. The Default Editor screen will be displayed.

9. Click inside a check box if the file type should not be associated with UltraDev 4. The check will be removed.

10. Click on Next. The Select Program Folder screen will be displayed.

11. Click on Next. The default Start menu settings are usually a safe bet. The Start Copying Files screen will be displayed.

12. Click on Next to begin installing Dreamweaver UltraDev 4. Files will be copied to your hard drive.

> **NOTE**
>
> The progress bar will indicate the percentage of files that have been copied to your hard drive.

13. Click on Finish. The Installation program will end.

14. Click on the Start button. The Start menu will appear.

15. Move your mouse pointer to Programs. The Programs menu will appear.

16. Move your mouse pointer to Macromedia Dreamweaver UltraDev 4. A submenu will appear.

17. Click on Dreamweaver UltraDev 4. UltraDev 4 will open and display a blank Web page in the Document window.

> **NOTE**
>
> The Welcome palette will be displayed the first time UltraDev is opened. You can choose to:
>
> - Learn about the new features in UltraDev 4.
> - Watch an interactive multimedia tutorial on using UltraDev.
> - Follow the tutorial in the UltraDev documentation.
> - Learn the basics of building a Web page in UltraDev.

B

Installing and Using PWS
(Microsoft Personal Web Server)

PWS is a scaled-down version of Microsoft IIS (Internet Information Server). It enables you to set up a Web server on any computer running Windows 95 or 98. PWS also supports ASP, which makes it an ideal companion to UltraDev if you're building ASP-driven Web sites. You can also use PWS to test all of your Web sites locally. In this appendix, you'll learn to:

- Install PWS
- Publish your first Web page

Installing Microsoft PWS

PWS can be downloaded from the Microsoft Web site at **http://www.microsoft. com/ntserver/web/exec/feature/PWS.asp**. It is also available on the Windows 98 distribution CD-ROM in the add-ons/pws subdirectory.

> ## TIP
>
> If you are having trouble installing and using PWS on Windows ME, please visit the following Web site for a work-around solution:
>
> **http://www.billsway.com/notes_public/ PWS_WinMe.txt**

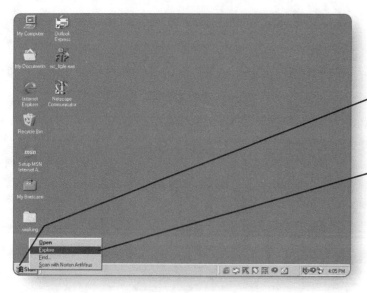

1. Insert the Windows 98 CD-ROM into the CD-ROM drive and close the tray.

2. Right-click on the Start button. A shortcut menu will appear.

3. Click on Explore. The Windows Explorer window will open and display the available drives and folders on your computer.

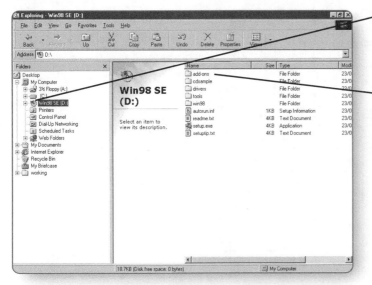

4. Click on the CD-ROM icon. The contents of the Windows 98 CD-ROM will be displayed.

5. Double-click on the Add-on folder. The contents of the folder will be displayed.

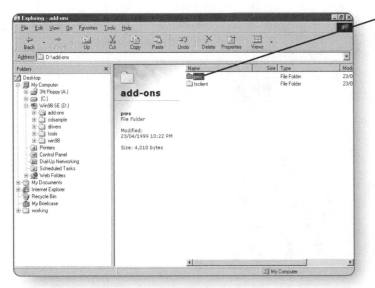

6. Double-click on the PWS folder. The contents of the folder will be displayed.

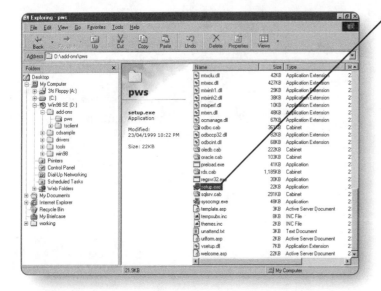

7. Double-click on the setup.exe file. The PWS setup program will start.

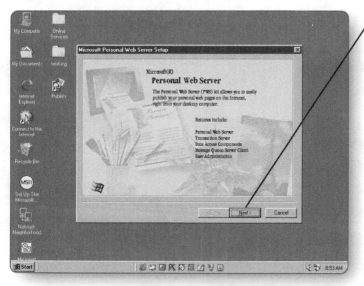

8. Click on Next. The Software License Agreement will be displayed.

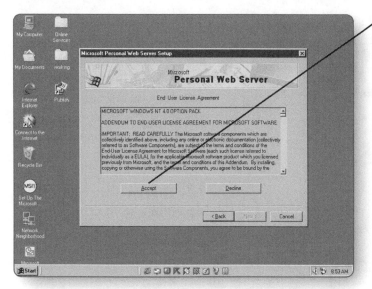

9. Click on Accept after reading the License Agreement. The types of installation available will be displayed.

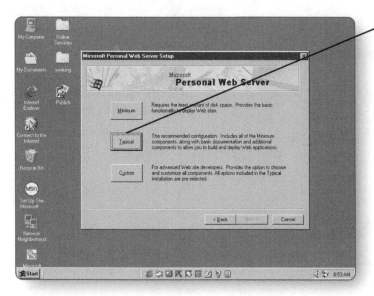

10. Click on Typical. The Web publishing directory options will be displayed.

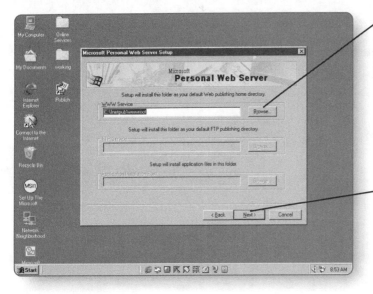

11. Click on Browse to set the Web publishing directory. The default directory is usually a safe bet. Any files placed in this folder can be accessed through a Web browser. This directory will be the home directory of your Web server.

12. Click on Next. Files will be copied to your hard drive.

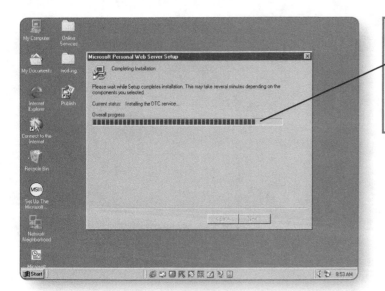

NOTE

The progress bar will indicate the percentage of files that have been copied to your hard drive.

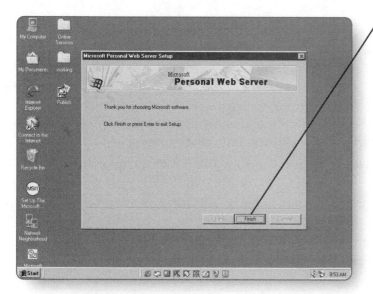

13. Click on Finish. The Installation program will end.

Publishing Your First Web Page

Publishing your first Web page is very easy. All you need to do is copy the files in your Web site to the home directory of your Web server.

1. Double-click on the PWS icon located on the Quick Launch taskbar. Personal Web Manager will open.

NOTE

Personal Web Manager will display:

- The domain name of your computer. This is the URL for your Web server. It will most likely be http://localhost, where localhost is the name of your machine. However, your domain name could be different depending on the workgroup settings on your computer.

- The path to your Web publishing directory. This is where all your Web sites must be stored.

The home directory path is mapped to the domain name so that when a browser calls the URL that matches the domain name assigned to your computer, files within the home directory are displayed.

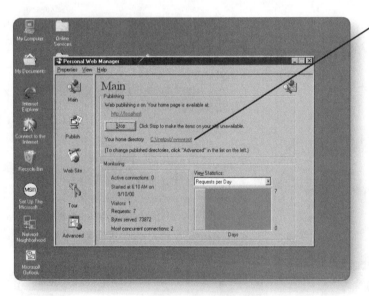

2. Click on the link to your home directory. Windows Explorer will open and display the contents of your home directory.

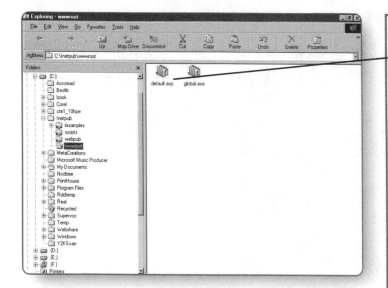

NOTE

The home directory contains a file called default.asp. This is the home page, or index file, of your Web site. Initially, this file will launch the PWS Help Web pages. You can replace the file with a new home page for your Web server. The new home page must be named either default.asp or default.htm to be recognized. All files placed within this folder can be accessed through a Web browser.

3. Click on Close. Windows Explorer will close.

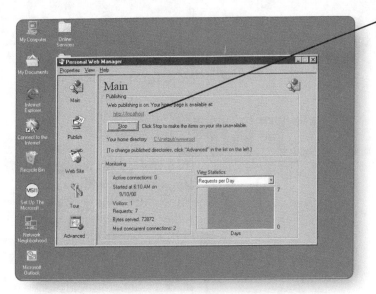

4. Click on the domain name link. Your default Web browser will open and display the home page on your Web server

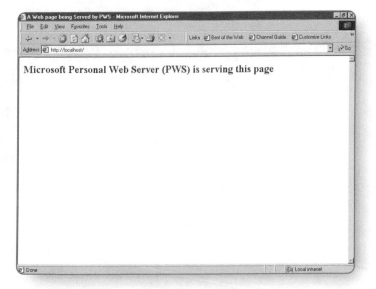

NOTE

I have replaced the original default.asp file that was created when PWS was installed with a simple Web page. Your home page can be as simple or as elaborate as you want.

C

JSP and CFML Quick Reference

JSP (JavaServer Pages) and CFML (ColdFusion Markup Language) are the other two server-side scripting languages that UltraDev generates. This book covers ASP (Active Server Pages) in detail. The purpose of this appendix is to provide you with a simple JSP and ColdFusion reference so you can instantly customize the code UltraDev generates and write your own as well. In this appendix you'll find:

- ColdFusion quick reference
- JSP quick reference

CFML Quick Reference

CFML (ColdFusion Markup Language) is made up of tags and looks very much like HTML. CFML has more than 70 tags that can be embedded in HTML. This is just a sampling of a few useful CFML tags. Please consult the CFML documentation for a detailed list of all available tags.

To Do This	Use This Tag
Define a variable	`<CFSET variablename=expression>`

Output a variable	`<CFOUTPUT>`
	And the variable is: #variablename#
	`</CFOUTPUT>`

Retrieve data from a form	`<CFOUTPUT>`
	#Form.FormObjectName#
	`</CFOUTPUT>`

Use an If statement	`<CFIF expression>`
	Displayed if the expression is true.
	`<CFELSE>`
	Displayed if the expression is false.
	`</CFIF>`

Use a Loop	`<CFLOOP` INDEX="count_variable" FROM="start_value" TO="end_value" STEP="increment">` Anything within this tag will be repeated. `</CFLOOP>`
Include a File	`<CFINCLUDE TEMPLATE="filename.htm">`

CFML Arithmetic Operators

+   Addition

-        Subtraction

*   Multiplication

/   Division

CFML Comparison Operators

EQ	Equal To
NEQ	Not Equal To
GT	Greater Than
LT	Less Than
GTE	Greater Than or Equal To
LTE	Less Than or Equal To
AND	AND Boolean operator
OR	OR Boolean operator

JSP Quick Reference

JSP is comparable to ASP but is far more powerful because it is programmed in Java. Java is a modern object-oriented language. JSP allows you to embed Java code in a Web page. The table below contains useful tasks that you could perform with very basic Java code. Please consult the JSP documentation for more information.

To Do This	Use This Tag
Define a numeric variable	`<%! int variablename=value; %>`
Define a string variable	`<%! String variablename="expression"; %>`
Output a variable	`<%=variablename %>`
Retrieve data from a form	`<%= request.getParameter("FormObjectName") %>`
Use an If statement	`<% if (expression){ %>`
Displays if the expression is true.	`<% } else { %>`
Displays if the expression is false.	`<% } %>`
Use a loop	`<% for (i=start_value; i<=end_value, i++) { %>`
Anything within this code will be repeated.	`<% } %>`
Include a file	`<%@ include file="filename.htm">`

JSP Arithmetic Operators

+	Addition
-	Subtraction
*	Multiplication
/	Division

JSP Comparison Operators

==	Equal To
!=	Not Equal To
>	Greater Than
<	Less Than
>=	Greater Than or Equal To
<=	Less Than or Equal To
&	AND Boolean operator
|	OR Boolean operator

D

Using Keyboard Shortcuts

Keyboard shortcuts are a great way to increase the speed at which you build dynamic Web sites in UltraDev. A few shortcuts are mentioned within the book, but many more are listed in this appendix. In this appendix, you'll learn shortcuts to:

- Perform common tasks in UltraDev
- Open palettes, windows, and inspectors in

Keyboard Shortcuts to Perform Common Tasks

You will need to perform a number of common tasks, such as opening and closing a file, each time you work in UltraDev. While you can use menus, keyboard shortcuts offer a much quicker alternative.

Press This Key Combination	To Do This
Ctrl+n	Create a new file
Ctrl+o	Open a file
Ctrl+s	Save a file
Ctrl+w	Close a file
Ctrl+q	Quit UltraDev
Ctrl+Shift+s	Save As
Ctrl+z	Undo your last step
Ctrl+y	Redo your last step
Ctrl+c	Copy the current selection
Ctrl+v	Paste the current selection
Ctrl+Shift+r	Enable Live Data Preview
Ctrl+Alt+i	Insert an image
Shift+F7	Check spelling
F1	Display UltraDev Help documentation
F12	Preview the current Web page in a Web browser

Keyboard Shortcuts to Open Palettes, Windows, and Inspectors

UltraDev has many, many palettes and inspectors. You can't display them all at the same time. You'll want to be able to open and close the palettes you require quickly and easily. The Launcher provides a convenient way to do this, but it can only display a limited numbers of icons. The solution is to become familiar with the keyboard shortcuts that open palettes, windows, and inspectors.

Press This Key Combination	To Open This
F8	Site window
Alt+F8	View Site Map
Ctrl+F2	Object palette
Ctrl+F3	Properties inspector
Ctrl+F10	Data Bindings palette
Ctrl+F9	Server Behaviors palette
Shift+F11	CSS Styles palette
Ctrl+F11	HTML Styles palette
Shift+F3	Behaviors palette
Shift+F10	History palette
F10	Code inspector
F11	Assets
Ctrl+Shift+F1	Reference
Ctrl+Tab	Switch views

E

Additional Resources

Developing cutting-edge Web sites that will meet your clients' needs is by no means an easy task. The Web is continually evolving and so, too, are the technologies used to deliver it. You need the ability to make educated decisions when selecting technology. This can only be achieved by researching the latest trends in Web development. There are many resources that can help you along this path. This appendix will introduce you to a few that will set you on your life-long learning journey. In this appendix, you'll find resources for:

- Dreamweaver UltraDev
- Databases (Access, SQL Server, and Oracle)
- ASP, ColdFusion, and JSP

Dreamweaver UltraDev Resources

Dreamweaver is an extremely popular Web site creation tool. There are many books and Web sites that contain information on Dreamweaver. These resources are essential if you'd like to expand on the topics covered thus far. They will also introduce you to the large Dreamweaver and Dreamweaver UltraDev community.

Books

Dreamweaver Fast & Easy Web Development
by Brenda D. Ballard
ISBN 0-7615-2905-5

This is a great book if you would like to learn more about using Dreamweaver to create Web pages. Topics covered include managing a Web site, using forms, mastering layout techniques, and using cascading style sheets.

Learn HTML In a Weekend
by Steve Callihan
ISBN 0-7615-1800-2

This book is highly recommended if you'd like to master the fundamentals of HTML. You will also learn to create frames, forms, image maps, and GIF animations. All this can certainly be achieved in one weekend.

Web Sites

Dreamweaver UltraDev
http://www.macromedia.com/software/ultradev/

Macromedia will improve UltraDev and release a new version. This could happen sooner than you think. The new version will no doubt have many more built-in features. This will only make your life easier. The Macromedia Website is the best place to check for information regarding new releases.

Dreamweaver Exchange
http://www.macromedia.com/exchange/dreamweaver

Currently, Dreamweaver Exchange contains extensions (objects, commands, and behaviors) that you can download. Extensions can greatly improve your productivity and allow you to include new functionality in your Web site effortlessly.

Dreamweaver UltraDev Exchange
http://www.macromedia.com/exchange/ultradev

UltraDev Exchange contains extensions focused on server-side scripting and Web application development. I'd recommend visiting UltraDev Exchange before you decide to hand-code any functionality that you require. You might just find an extension that does exactly what you want. You can also upload extensions that you have built for others to use.

Dreamweaver UltraDev Support Center
http://www.macromedia.com/support/ultradev/

This is a great source for technical articles on using UltraDev. The Support Center also contains tech notes, debugging tips, and the UltraDev FAQ (Frequently Asked Questions). You can also search the Knowledge Base.

Dreamweaver and UltraDev Discussion Forums
news://forums.macromedia.com/macromedia.ultradev
news://forums.macromedia.com/macromedia.dreamweaver

What would you do if you ran into a problem while using UltraDev? Posting a message to the UltraDev Discussion Forum would be a great place to start. A discussion forum is really just another phrase for newsgroup. You need a newsreader (such as Microsoft Outlook, Outlook Express, or Netscape Collabra) to subscribe to the forum. Many UltraDev experts subscribe to the newsgroup and always seem happy to help new users. Many Macromedia employees also frequent the UltraDev forum. Subscribing to the forum will allow you to keep in contact with the UltraDev community. You could end up sharing your expertise with other users!

Web Sites Dedicated to UltraDev

MagicBeat	**http://www.magicbeat.com**
UltraDeviant	**http://www.ultradeviant.co.uk**
Charon.co.uk	**http://www.charon.co.uk/Ultradev.htm**
Massimo Corner	**http://www.massimocorner.com**
UltraCulture	**http://www.ultraculture.com/Extensions.asp**
UltraCart Addons	**http://www.thechocolatestore.com/mytutorials/default.asp**
Rick's UltraDev Design Tips & Concepts	**http://www.princeton.edu/~rcurtis/ultradev**
UltraDev Workshop	**http://www.virtual-fx.net/ultradev/listtutorials.asp**
UltraDev FAQ	**http://www.ultradevfaq.com**
Extensionology	**http://www.extensionology.com**
UltraDev Extensions	**http://www.ultradevextensions.com**
UltraDev Guru	**http://www.ultradevguru.com/**
How To UltraDev	**http://www.howtoultradev.com/**

Prima Tech Web Site
http://www.prima-tech.com/ultradev

Prima Tech Publishing maintains Web pages for many of its books, and this one is no exception. You will find related titles and products that are available from Prima Publishing.

Database Resources

Databases are the backbone of any dynamic Web site. This book only provides you with an introduction to relational database theory, the Structured Query Language (SQL), and creating a simple database in Microsoft Access. The following resources will help you build upon your knowledge of database design.

Books

Access 2000 Fast & Easy
by Patrice-Anne Rutledge
ISBN 0-7615-1404-X, Prima Tech Publishing

Want to learn more about creating databases in Access? This is a great book that will help you accomplish your tasks as quickly and easily as possible.

Microsoft SQL Server 7 Administrator's Guide
by Ron Talmage
ISBN 0-7615-1389-2, Prima Tech Publishing

Your Web site might require a client/server database. SQL Server is an ideal choice. This book will help you administer SQL Server and understand relational databases.

Web Sites

SQL Zone
http://www.sql-zone.com/

SQL Zone is an easy-to-use Web site that contains articles, links, and newsgroups on SQL. If you like this site, check out ASP Zone (**http://www.asp-zone.com**).

Microsoft SQL Server Site
http://www.microsoft.com/sql

This site from Microsoft should be your first port of call if you want to upgrade your database to SQL Server. As of this writing, Microsoft is also about to introduce SQL Server 2000, which has built-in XML functionality.

Oracle Web Site
http://www.oracle.com

Oracle is the leading database vendor. Visit the Oracle Web site if you require a powerful, scalable, and well-supported database. Oracle is the leading database for developing enterprise solutions.

ASP, ColdFusion, and JSP Resources

UltraDev has revolutionized Web development software by allowing you to use the same software to develop Web sites for different application servers. This book concentrates on Active Server Pages because it is popular and easy to learn. UltraDev also supports ColdFusion and Java Server Pages. These resources will help you learn more about all of the application servers that UltraDev supports.

Books

ASP 3 Fast & Easy Web Development
by Michael Thomasson
ISBN 0-7615-2854-7

There are many more ASP features that we couldn't cover comprehensively. This book covers ASP objects, VBScript, ADO, SQL, and COM/COM+ in detail. You'll be building high-performance, scalable Web applications in no time at all.

ColdFusion Fast & Easy Web Development
by T.C. Bradley, III
ISBN 0-7615-3016-9

This is a good resource for learning the basics of the ColdFusion mark-up language. There are chapters on building dynamic queries, connecting to an FTP server, generating static Web pages, validating forms, and creating your own tags.

Java 2 Fast & Easy Web Development
by Andy Harris
ISBN 0-7615-3056-8

Java is the object-oriented programming language of the future. A basic knowledge will help you to build JSP-driven Web sites. This book provides a unique, hands-on approach to learning Java.

Web Sites

Learn ASP
http://www.learnasp.com

This Web site provides a hands-on approach to ASP. You won't find lengthy articles on ASP, just the code required to achieve a task. It's a quick and easy way to learn by example. This is where I learned ASP. If you're interested in learning more ASP and are on a tight deadline, this site is a must.

4 Guys from Rolla
http://www.4guysfromrolla.com

Articles, tutorials, and the ASP FAQ. What more could you need? The articles cover all ASP topics comprehensively. This site also has a humor section, which is worth a look.

ASP Resource Index
http://www.aspin.com

The ASP Resource Index is a one-stop shop for ASP resources. You'll find news, articles, code, and links.

ASP Components
http://www.aspin.com/home/components

Have you ever wanted to create graphics, charts, and Acrobat (.pdf) files on-the-fly? You can, and you don't have to write all the code yourself. This site has links to all the ASP components you could need.

JSP FAQ
http://www.esperanto.org.nz/jsp/jspfaq.html

This site is guaranteed to answer all of your beginner questions.

Java Server Pages (Tutorial)
http://apl.jhu.edu/~hall/java/Servlet-Tutorial/Servlet-Tutorial-JSP.html

This tutorial will introduce the basics of JSP. Visit this site if you'd like to get started with JSP immediately.

ColdFusion Advisor
http://www.cfadvisor.com

Look no further for ColdFusion news, tips, job opportunities, and tag libraries. I was very impressed with the quality of content, which is not exclusively directed toward ColdFusion users.

F

What's on the CD?

The CD-ROM that accompanies this book contains a variety of tools to help you get started using Dreamweaver UltraDev, including:

- a 30-day trial version of Macromedia Dreamweaver UltraDev 4
- a 30-day trial version of Macromedia Fireworks 4
- a 30-day trial version of Macromedia Flash 5
- a 30-day trial version of HomeSite
- a 30-day trial version of ColdFusion
- a 30-day trial version of JRun
- a 30-day trial version of Kawa
- sample code from the book
- links to useful Web resources
- additional chapters on advanced topics

Running the CD-ROM with Windows 95/98/2000/NT

The CD-ROM requires no installation, and the contents can be viewed from within a Web browser. You only need to copy files to your hard drive that you require.

To access the CD-ROM contents, follow these instructions:

1. Insert the disc into the CD-ROM drive and close the tray.

2. Open Windows Explorer and double-click on the CD-ROM drive icon. The disc contents will be displayed.

3. Double-click on the start_here.html file. Your default Web browser will open and load the Prima License Agreement.

The Prima License Agreement is the first thing that appears in the Web browser window. It also appears on the last page of this book. Before installing anything from the CD-ROM, you must read and accept the licensing agreement. Click on "I agree" to accept the license and proceed with installation. If you do not accept the licensing agreement, click on "I disagree" to cancel installation, then remove the CD-ROM from your computer.

Index

License Agreement/Notice of Limited Warranty